Marketplace Masters

"Marketplace Masters is a must read for leaders of professional service firms. One of the best-researched books ever published on the topic of marketing professional services. Packed with practical insights and in-depth examples — read this before your competition does!"

Arthur Middlebrooks, Adjunct Professor of Marketing,
University of Chicago Graduate School of Business

"*Marketplace Masters* is a must read for anyone working within the professional services arena whose firm is mired in marketing mediocrity. It affords the reader a thorough picture of the unique quantitative and qualitative marketing challenges experienced by Professional Service firms, as well as practical ideas and solutions critical to successful market-driven growth strategy. Though its in-depth research results and insightful, real-life case study example, *Marketplace Masters* provides a comprehensive blueprint to building a sustainable, premier marketing strategy for Professional Service firms."

Thomas A. Curtin Jr., Chief Marketing Officer, The Segal Company

"Marketplace Masters is rich with case studies, insights and practical advice for anyone seeking to upgrade marketing in professional service firms. While the distinctive culture of professional service firms has generally inhibited their adoption of systematic marketing techniques and processes, this book provides detailed examples of professional service firms that have recently bucked this trend and begun to improve their businesses through disciplined implementation of strategic marketing."

Paul Magill, Vice President, Marketing, IBM Global Services

"The Masters' stories are right on! I found myself having a favorite company with each story I read. Kudos for the groundwork in digging up and plowing through the "hows" of these successful examples from which we should all learn and apply."

Silvia L. Coulter, Chief Marketing and
Business Development Officer, Dorsey & Whitney LLP

"This book is a must read for all CEO's. Any professional services firm that makes the corporate commitment to embrace the practical concepts detailed in this book will leapfrog ahead of its competition by better understanding its markets and clients. The factual research and case studies eliminate the excuses for avoiding that commitment."

George C. Friedel, Senior Vice President,
Director of Strategic Sales, Parsons Brinckerhoff

"*Marketplace Masters* provides documented proof that successful marketing strategies will work in professional development firms. Her use of case studies from a number of professions lifts us out of our insular focus on our own industry and gives us direction."

Patty Grimes, Director, Client Services, Torys LLP

Marketplace Masters

How Professional Service Firms Compete to Win

Suzanne C. Lowe

Westport, Connecticut
London

Library of Congress Cataloging-in-Publication Data

Lowe, Suzanne C.
  Marketplace masters : how professional service firms compete to win /
  Suzanne C. Lowe.
    p. cm.
  Includes bibliographical references and index.
  ISBN 0-275-98119-3 (alk. paper)
    1. Professional corporations—Management.   2. Corporate reorganizations.
  3. Competition.   I. Title.
  HD62.65.L687 2004
  658.8'101—dc22   2003064765

British Library Cataloguing in Publication Data is available.

Library of Congress Catalog Card Number: 2003064765
ISBN: 0-275-98119-3

First published in 2004

Praeger Publishers, 88 Post Road West, Westport, CT 06881
An imprint of Greenwood Publishing Group, Inc.
www.praeger.com

Printed in the United States of America

The paper used in this book complies with the
Permanent Paper Standard issued by the National
Information Standards Organization (Z39.48-1984).

10 9 8 7 6 5 4 3

Contents

Case Studies

Looking Out, PART II
1. Studying a firm's clients using qualitative and quantitative research
   - Winstead Sechrest & Minick, a law firm founded in the southwestern United States
   - QRST Associates (a pseudonyn of a global professional service firm whose identity has been disguised)
2. Researching the market using economic forecasts and trend analyses
   - YaYa Media, a Los Angeles–based leader in producing games and digital entertainment as a marketing vehicle for Fortune 500 companies
3. Researching competitors by gathering competitive intelligence
   - Towers Perrin, one of the world's largest global management consulting firms, assisting organizations in managing people, performance, and risk

Digging Deeper, PART II
1. Embracing competitive differentiation
   - Malcolm Pirnie, one of the largest firms in the U.S. focused on environmental issues

Acknowledgments

Professional service marketing is a relatively new discipline; in my tenure in this field, spanning nearly twenty years, the interest of professional service firm leaders in benchmarking their strategic marketing "best practices" has grown consistently. As a result, spurred by a professional passion to begin identifying these benchmarks, I embarked on five years of formal research. This included hundreds of hours of interviews with professional service firm executives, practitioners, and academics, reams of spreadsheets, mountains of notes, and a multitude of statistics. Bit by bit, there began to emerge a picture of the competencies around which I have organized this book.

For the five annual research projects, I am indebted to the staff and members of the American Association of Healthcare Consultants, the Association for Accounting Marketing, the Associated General Contractors of America, the American Institute of Certified Public Accountants, the Professional Services Marketing Association (Canada), the Society for Marketing Professional Services, the Law Marketing listserv, the Institute of Management Consultants USA, Inc., the Association of Executive Search Consultants, the American Council of Engineering Companies, the Canadian Association of Management Consultants, AccountingWeb, the Independent Computer Consultants Association, the Information Technology Services Marketing Association, the Legal

Marketing Association, and the National Association of Legal Search Consultants. Other research participants included the subscribers of various professional service–specific publications, particularly the *CPA Marketing Report* and *Consultants News,* and many of my clients. I am also grateful for the contributions of the numerous chief marketing officers, managing or marketing partners, practice leaders, and academics who advised me on the content of the research, the structure of the research instruments, and the articulation of the findings. I am especially grateful for the professorial assistance of my husband, John, whose assistance with survey design and statistical analysis was volunteered with grace and good humor. To my nephew Brian Lowe goes my gratitude for his diligence and commitment (not to mention his designer's eye) throughout every phase of the research process for several of the studies. To George Zipf I send my thanks for his enlightened suggestions for analysis of the 2001 study.

In order to bring the research findings to life, I embarked on an extensive search for excellent examples of the competencies I wanted to profile in the book. I am sincerely grateful for the privilege of working with the following individuals whose contributions to the book's fifteen case studies were invaluable. They are Mike Baggett and Kathy Yeaton for Winstead Sechrest & Minick; Kathy Yeaton for QRST Associates; Keith Ferrazzi, Elana Weiss, and Jay Apfelberg for YaYa Media; Gary Locke, Lenore Scanlon, and Sharon Clark for Towers Perrin; Eric Dodge and John Batten for Malcolm Pirnie; Ross Mullenger, Catriona Russell, Douglas Shanks, Julian Synett, and Lisa Wilkes for Numerica Group; Bruce Keener, Quincy Watkins, Peter Tobia and Bill Shine for Kepner-Tregoe; Jim McTaggart, Domenic Dodd, Ken Favaro, and David Fondiller for Marakon Associates; Justus O'Brien, Dan Meiland, and Joslyn Todd for Egon Zehnder International; Leon Schor and Jay Wager for L.E.K. Consulting; Steve Schmidt, Art Massa, and Janet Watts for ACNielsen; Tom Dobosenski, Carol Thornton, Allison Kowalchik, Janine Rudow, and Randy Siemsen for RSM McGladrey; David Rockwell, Marc Hacker, and Allison Hecht for Rockwell Group; Marty Horn, Doug Hughes, and Jim Crimmins for DDB Worldwide; and Pam Walker and Gil Miller for Mitretek Systems. I am also thankful to Leonard Fuld of Fuld & Company for allowing me to include in its entirety his article on competitive intelligence.

In the months before the beginning of the book and during its development, I received enthusiastic encouragement from numerous friends, most notably my Squam Lake extended family, whose heartfelt support was an inspiration. I am especially thankful to Elisabeth Townsend, for her early research on competing books, and to Jeff Greene, for helping me navigate the world of publishing. I am also very lucky to have had the opportunity to work with Regina Maruca, whose editorial guidance and constructive suggestions helped bring the book to important new heights.

Above all, I am thankful to my family, whose flexibility, patience, and feedback helped sustain me through the long hours of effort. Thanks go especially to my daughter, Elaine, for her diligent work on the footnotes and her encouragement even during her hospitalization, and to my wonderful husband, John, for his loving support and unequivocal belief in my ability to accomplish this project.

Part I

Why Professional Service Firms Must Pursue Marketplace Mastery

In the first chapter of this section, I discuss the professional service sector's relatively underdeveloped approaches to strategic marketing and competition. I make the case that professional service enterprises must pursue marketplace mastery and explain how they can do so by building a market-driven infrastructure. In the remaining three chapters, I present research findings that led to my identification of the three building blocks of a market-driven infrastructure—looking out, digging deeper, and embedding innovation. These building blocks serve as the central theme throughout the book.

Competing in the Professional Service Arena

There has been a great deal written about how businesses should "know who they are," "decide which business they want to be in," and "figure out where they want to go." Seems like sound advice. But little has been written specifically for professional service firms. And when a group of consultants, or architects, or lawyers, or what-have-you, resolves to "reinvent themselves," or "refocus their businesses," or "create a unique identity in the marketplace," one of two things often happens. Either the firm begins a massive change effort without first thinking through the deep, long-term, operational implications of the action (maybe launching a branding campaign, or restructuring internally, or acquiring another firm) or it creates a high-profile task force and launches a long-term study that produces reams of data and ends up spawning more questions than existed to begin with. The outcome of either scenario can be, at the least, frustration (imagine the internal squabbling! the misdirected initiatives! the abandoned efforts!), or worse, business stagnation and derailment.

I wrote this book to help professional service firms of all shapes and sizes avoid these and similar unpalatable outcomes. I wrote it to help professional service firms *build a market-driven infrastructure*—that is, to take the small but continuous steps needed to master their competitive arena as a matter of course, so they never have to make any grand resolutions, or launch ill-researched initiatives, or create committees that produce a myriad of slide presentations (sometimes dueling against each other!) but little or no actionable, sustainable initiatives.

The practices that I explore in these pages show firms how to set up the kind of processes, policies, and initiatives that, by their very nature, improve the likelihood of achieving competitive advantage on a daily basis. Using these practices, professional service firms will never find themselves wondering "Who are we?" "What business should we be in?" or "How can we be distinctive?" By implementing a series of linked, market-driven practices, they'll already know. And armed with that knowledge, they'll be better prepared to face changes in the market. They'll be more adept at maneuvering during short-term crises. They'll be ever ready to make decisive, informed decisions about marketplace opportunities, and more capable of taking the incremental steps that will prove right over the long-term. They will be more likely to become marketplace masters.

A WAKE-UP CALL: MARKETPLACE MISERY— OR MARKETPLACE MASTERY?

Too many professional service firms (running the gamut from engineering firms to high tech and management consultants, ad agencies, accountancies, and more) compete by trying not to fail rather than by trying to win. They are engaged in a never-ending game of catch-up. They scramble to adapt (and sometimes sell!) the latest tools. They rush to enter what seem to be lucrative new arenas. They ensure that they sell what their competitor sells; that their array of offerings is at least as wide, that their palette is as interesting. They rarely allow themselves the time to try to gain an understanding of the entire marketplace context in which they compete. They shy away from truly organic "work"—that is, the kind of work that involves out-of-the-box soul searching, learning more about their clients than they already know, operationally stretching to attain new competitive advantages, measuring the results of their strategic initiatives (and making the required adjustments), or actively aligning their go-to-market strategies with their culture. They avoid real innovation, sticking instead to the seemingly safer path of innovation through acquisition or small improvements on existing products and services. In fact, they too rarely have the discipline to engage in such study, deep organizational commitment, or creativity. These things take time; time is money; short-term demands almost always win.

Putting the short term first has served many firms well in the past two decades or so. I won't argue there. We have seen some stellar success stories. Some stunning returns. But we've also seen more than a few debacles—some very high profile—which, I would wager, could have been avoided. Witness Arthur D. Little, the world's oldest management consultancy, which declared bankruptcy in early 2002, the result of taking a "too much, too fast" path.[1] The Washington Group, one of the world's largest engineering and construction firms, declared bankruptcy in 2001, less than a year after its last acquisition, for many of the same reasons.[2] That firm fell in love with growth through acquisition (and weren't the numbers stunning!) but some would argue it did not do enough pre-acquisition risk assessment along the way, and also failed to slow its pace even when signs of an economic slowdown were hard to miss.

Almost any of the large firms in the executive search sector could be cited as examples, too. In the 1990s, "talent wars" drove their double-digit revenue growth. Keen for an ever-increasing share of their clients' largesse, many of the top-tier executive search firms launched a flurry of initiatives: diversifying into technology, consulting, or assessment services; going public; and acquiring other firms. Theirs were heady choices, made with the expectation that the economy would always be "up."[3] But since 2000, many of these firms suffered steep financial losses, management defections, and workforce reductions.

Within the accounting sector, the case of Arthur Andersen is telling because of the way the firm was lured by the short-term dazzle of blended audit and consulting services. Instead, Andersen (and its Big Five brethren, which had also blurred the edges between their audit and consulting offerings and ultimately had to spin off these service lines) should have been thinking about more innovative, more appropriate, and longer-term growth avenues.

In the legal world, the high-profile dissolutions of two law firms on opposite coasts of the United States come to mind as particularly painful illustrations of these phenomena. In December 2002, Boston-based law firm Hill & Barlow, founded in 1895, decided to dissolve when its real estate group suddenly announced its en masse departure. Shorn of one-third of its revenues and partners, Hill & Barlow became the latest victim of a common business disease that an "up" economy often masks: an unbalanced service portfolio.[4] A little more than one month later, Brobeck, Phleger & Harrison, called by the *Wall Street Journal* "one of the most powerful law firms in the San Francisco area," died from the same disease. Overly dependent on declining revenues from its technology sector clients, it waited too long to build up other practices that could provide a revenue balance should the technology sector dry up. Brobeck then had to dissolve after its failed attempt to merge with a larger firm.[5]

Each of the firms I've just cited reached a decision point (or several) and went ahead without the benefit of an infrastructure that could foster a real understanding of the marketplace, guide them to make

strategically effective internal efforts to compete, and serve as a framework for systemic innovation. Each moved forward without the benefit
of constant self-assessment and market assessment built into its modus
operandi. Each underperformed (and in some cases, that is a vast
understatement) its marketplace potential.

But even beyond the bad news about specific firms, entire professional sectors took a beating in the international press for their sinking
fortunes and myopic marketplace responses. For examples, recall "The
Incredible Shrunken Headhunters" (*Business Week*, March 2002); "Like
Herding Cats: How To Get Prima Donnas to Perform" (*Economist*, April
2002); "The Incredible Shrinking Consultant" (*Fortune*, May 2003); and
"Another Slow Year Will Bring Turmoil to IT Service Market" (Kennedy
Information's *Global IT Services Report*, December 2002). The malaise
was global; no professional service business is immune.

THE CLIENT AS COMPETITOR

One of the root causes of these marketplace misfortunes is that
professional service firms, by and large, have difficulty understanding
(and adapting to) the changing roles of their clients. "Customers," in
the professional service sector, are not merely consumers. They are also
competitors of a sort and need to be studied and treated accordingly.
Why? Because clients' knowledge of the service and their needs for the
service literally change as they "consume" the service. And those
changes are significant. For example, consider a community hospital
that purchases the design of a new wing from an architecture firm. Even
as it consumes the service it has purchased, it moves to a different level
in terms of understanding, capability, and need. The people of the
hospital incrementally gain knowledge of how to envision the shape
and functionality of operating rooms, intensive care units, and clinical
offices. It doesn't happen suddenly, but eventually, this architecture
client learns about aspects of architecture and, at the same time, the
hospital's managers realize how important their own expertise is in the
design process. Maybe the architectural firm has special expertise in
hospital design. Nonetheless, the client's own experience and understanding of the circumstances under which it works give it critical
perspectives. Soon, the hospital's managers will begin buying these
once-mystical services for "convenience," or they might even build an
in-house design team that will provide them with their own architectural services. Their needs for the full-scale service the firm once provided for them will decrease, and thus they will begin to "compete"
with their service provider.

What happens when the hospital needs facility planning that em-
braces management strategy? Will the architectural firm be ready to

provide that level of service offering? Or will it be left behind entirely? An information technology services giant, EDS, offers a specific example of this scenario. An October 2002 *Wall Street Journal* article recounted EDS's woes about its clients' shifting loyalties.

Some customers are balking at the cost of EDS's consulting services, which carry higher margins than some of its other services. In some cases, customers are choosing to take certain services back in-house to save money—a switch from the conventional notion that outsourcing is cheaper. Customers still save money by letting EDS do tasks such as running computers and staffing help desks. But high-margin consulting work is increasingly being postponed or canceled, according to several companies and industry consultants.

"Five years ago, companies didn't understand the Internet so they outsourced it," says Julie Giera of Giga Information Group. "Now those things are better understood and being brought back in house."[6]

Part of the reason why EDS's clients posed a competitive threat to the firm is that they were suffering from a syndrome I call "service fatigue." Time and again, whether by EDS or any other firm, clients' expectations get raised beyond what is possible to deliver. Clients are skeptical, even wary, of any firm offering a "service." How can they be sure they are getting the best? What assurances do they have? It's hard to compare the delivery of one service with the potential delivery of the same service from a competitor. How can any firm truly get past that instinctive mistrust?

Professional service firms already know that their clients' industries are affected by economic conditions and that these conditions ultimately inform the way clients purchase their services. However, knowing this will not be enough. If a professional service firm thinks of clients as potential competitors, the deep strategic issues (identity, range of services, quality assurance, and more) naturally appear in a new light and are shaped by a broad question: "How should we compete?" Being able to answer that question readies a firm to address these and other marketplace issues more astutely than many currently can. The question, "How should we compete?" thus becomes a foundation for the fundamental preparation that firms will undergo to face *any* marketplace opportunity or challenge. For example, the architectural firm I mentioned earlier might benefit from a careful assessment of its clients and their evolving needs and, as a result, decide to develop an expertise in facility planning.

A HISTORICAL RETICENCE TO COMPETE

Another root cause of the missteps so many professional service firms have taken in recent years is their historical reluctance to engage in "competition." In all too many professional service firms, asking the

question "How will we compete?" borders on the heretical. A brief
history of professional services, offered in a fascinating 1998 article by
U.K. academics Susan Hart and Gillian Hogg, offers an explanation for
this claim. Hart and Hogg describe how the original professions of law,
church, and the military provided young aristocrats with a socially
acceptable way of making a living. These were high-status individuals;
the term *professional* was synonymous with *upper class*. In time, a newer
set of occupational professions developed, such as medicine, pharmacy,
and accountancy. In response, according to Hart and Hogg, the original
professions fought to defend their status by encouraging principles that
have come to define all other professions. These principles include a
disdain for competition, self-promotion, advertising, and bald pro-
fiteering; a belief in the principle of payment for work—rather than
working for pay; and a belief in the superiority of the motive of service.[7]

Today's professionals still uphold these principles, a fact repeatedly
made clear throughout my years of research about how firms address
and overcome their marketing challenges. For example, in my 2001
study of more than 500 professional service firms, "using new approaches to compete against rivals" was one of the *least frequently used*
of seven common methods to get closer to their clients. Some of the
study respondents' comments revealed this discomfort in stark terms:
an accounting firm respondent reported that "focusing on external
competition has never been a key part of our marketing strategy,"[8] and
an engineering firm participant said it was "not profitable" to gather
intelligence on competitors.[9] Both remarks are simply astonishing;
what's more, they could have originated within any number of other
professional sectors. Regardless of the basis of their reasoning, these
firms are inadvertently setting themselves up to be beaten by their more
market-driven rivals. The professional service sector as a whole is
maturing, and in order to survive and prosper, professional service
firms must learn to compete. Ignoring the realities of the marketplace
rarely, if ever, makes them go away.

THE ROOTS OF LONG-TERM SUCCESS IN A
MATURE PROFESSIONAL SERVICE MARKET

"Why are we losing proposals to competitors?" One of my clients, a
senior executive at a highly respected United States–based professional
service firm, asked me this question not long ago. "Sure, we've premium priced our services. But we think we serve our clients better than
anybody else." What did I tell him? His clients' expectations had simply
evolved to a point where attributes like customization, responsiveness,
and accuracy were "givens." His firm—like so many others—had, with-

out realizing it, always taken the "mile-wide, inch-deep" approach to understanding itself vis-à-vis its market. He had come away reading too much into some information and not enough into the rest, and then trying to make decisions on range of services, competitive distinctions, and innovation from that lightweight stance. Starting right then, we began to work together to help his firm master its marketplace.

"*Master* a marketplace? Are you telling me that my firm can manage the movements of its market—that we can dictate our future achievement of competitive success? Impossible!" some may say. Yes, the marketplace is "bigger" than any one business entity that exists within it, but professional service firms can move beyond their understandable marketplace nearsightedness. They can enact more deeply strategic initiatives to influence their business arena and their own competitive trajectory within it. They can move beyond their all-too-random acts of marketing to deliberately work on mastering their marketplace.

In fact, professional service marketplace mastery is already happening. It is underway in firms large and small, old and young, in a broad cross section of professions, and around the globe. I learned this after conducting five years of practitioner-oriented research about the way thousands of professional service firms were using and self-assessing the effectiveness of their marketing programs.[10] (See Table 1.1.)

THE THREE BUILDING BLOCKS OF A MARKET-DRIVEN INFRASTRUCTURE

When I conducted a side-by-side review of the five annual study findings together, I observed a distinct picture of eleven competencies that respondents were using (sometimes intentionally and sometimes not) that garnered them positive marketplace results. It was impossible not to notice that these eleven competencies fell into three groups, which I have labeled "Looking Out," "Digging Deeper," and "Embedding Innovation." Together, they form a compelling market-driven infrastructure with which professional service firms can compete more effectively, as marketplace masters. Here is how they are doing so:

- *Looking Out:* Essentially, *looking out* means using research on clients, competitors, and markets to look outside of professional or internal organizational confines to detect market shifts and opportunities. Put another way, looking out is the ability to pull up out of the day-to-day operating challenges and take a hard look at what is ahead. Many firms are ultra-sensitive to near-term opportunities and dangers and, as a result, respond *too* quickly—without due consideration—to take advantage of something that looks promising or to take evasive action to avoid damage. What hap-

TABLE 1.1　Expertise Marketing's Professional Service Firm Research Topics and Methods

Date	Topic	Sample Method	Sample Size	Professional Service Firm Respondent Type
January 1997	"The Marketing Balancing Act: Planning or Promotion?" (The use of marketing strategy in professional service firms.)	Fax	123	Management Consulting, Accounting, Financial Services, Law
January 1998	"Measuring the Effectiveness of Your Promotional Vehicles." (The use of and measurement techniques for promotional vehicles in professional service firms.)	Fax	963	Health Care, Law, Accounting, Management Consulting, Information Technology
February 1999	"Technology and Marketing: A Comparison of Professional Service Firms and Industries." (Professional service firms' use of technology to support the achievement of marketing strategies.)	Fax	322	Health Care, Law, Accounting, Management Consulting, Information Technology, Architecture, Construction, Human Resources
January 2000	"Differentiation: How Are Professional Service Firms Using It to Compete?" (Professional service firms' use and self-reported effectiveness of differentiation strategies.)	Fax, e-mail	422	Health Care, Law, Accounting, Management Consulting, Information Technology, Architecture, Construction, Human Resources
January 2001	"Becoming More Market Driven: How Are Professional Service Firms Getting Closer to Their Clients?" (Professional service firms' use and self-reported effectiveness of client attraction and prevention methods.)	Fax, e-mail	516	Accounting, Law, Executive Search, Architecutre, General Contracting, Engineering, a variety of consulting disciplines (Environment and Energy, Health Care, Human Resources, Information Technology, Management)

pens? Over time, they hit a pothole they could have avoided—or they derail completely. They may have short-term victories, but they do not build up a foundation on which they can last over the long term. They are vulnerable to the vagaries of the market. What does *due consideration* mean? It means having a reliable sounding board against which to evaluate new opportunities or threats. It means having a reliable body of research about the market on which to base judgment. It means having an early look at client, competitor, and marketplace shifts. A disappointingly low percentage of professional service firms even have a formal market research budget, yet firms that conduct formal market research reported that they were significantly more effective in attracting and retaining clients. Market research must play a more prominent role in professional firms' marketing programs than it has to date; firms that embrace this notion will enjoy the rewards of a loyal and growing client base. Later in this book I will discuss research findings and case study examples of the three practices within the looking-out building block. They are (1) studying clients using outside qualitative and quantitative research; (2) researching the market using economic forecasts and trend analyses; and (3) researching competitors by gathering competitive intelligence.

- *Digging Deeper:* I believe that the professional service sector, whose very foundation is based on intellectual capital, has yet to apply its collective brainpower to truly dig into its marketplace. Put simply, digging deeper means doing the *targeted* organizational and analytical work it takes to compete more effectively. My research findings show that, despite the availability (and increasing affordability) of powerful software applications, few firms conduct formal data mining to discover the unmet needs of clients and prospects. Digging deeper means capturing, organizing, and mining valuable client data to the point that one can discern past and potential client and marketplace patterns. There is also evidence that most professional service firms take the easy way out on efforts to differentiate themselves, avoiding the more successful—but harder—initiatives. Digging deeper means going beyond image-based positioning and branding campaigns to *become* truly different from competitors. My research also suggests that there is a discernible lack of sophistication among professional service firms about the notion of aligning competitive strategies with a firm's culture (a phenomenon that sometimes results in the scenarios I described at the start of the chapter). Digging deeper means managing a culture to achieve a strategic, market-focused goal. In addition, there is evidence that most professional firms have yet to adopt the internal management structures that support their efforts to effectively drive toward a competitive goal: account planning and formal postimplementation measurement of marketing, selling, and relationship management initiatives. Digging deeper means using account planning and measurement to increase a firm's ability to fine-tune its business focus and its marketing, business development, and service delivery strategies. Tomorrow's effective competitors will dig deeper to gain a preemptive marketplace advantage.

Later I discuss my in-depth research and cases studies on the five competencies within the digging-deeper building block: (1) embracing competitive differentiation; (2) mining client data; (3)

using account planning and relationship management programs;
(4) aligning marketing strategies with culture; and (5) using measurement to increase strategic focus and competitive advantage.

*   *Embedding Innovation:* This involves deliberately incorporating
    support of innovation into a firm's practices and policies. As a
    whole, the professional service sector relies too heavily on technol-
    ogy-based "knowledge management" and promotion-based
    "thought leadership" as platforms on which to develop new ser-
    vices. My findings uncovered little evidence of, support for, or
    implementation of other formal innovation initiatives. I believe
    innovation must be institutionalized as a critical element in every
    professional firm's strategy. In discussing the building block called
    "Embedding Innovation," I present research findings and case
    studies on three competencies. First is building a research and
    development (R&D) process, which means recognizing those ser-
    vices that are rapidly becoming commodities, and then program-
    matically steering internal efforts to build new services. A second
    competency is how firms use technology, not to enable a new
    service to be conceived, but as a basis for a new service. A third
    competency is how firms use incentives or rewards to stimulate
    professionals to innovate in alignment with the firm's strategy.

Some firms already excel at one or more of these competencies; those
are the firms around which I wrote case studies that explore what they
do and how they do it. No firm, to my knowledge, excels at all three,
but it is possible, and at any rate, it is a goal worth striving for. Even
moderate improvements in all competencies will result in a more robust
competitive position and future success.

A MARKET-DRIVEN INFRASTRUCTURE MEANS
SMALL CHANGES AND GREAT GAINS

None of these eleven practices is new. Moreover, although they require a focused, organized effort, none is particularly hard to do. So
what is the "disconnect?" Why aren't more professional service firms
much better at looking out, digging deeper, and embedding innovation? Why isn't a market-driven infrastructure a requisite for doing
business?

The answer is twofold. One, most maturing professional firms have
long since established a pace that is linked to whatever opportunities
or challenges the market is currently serving up. In their founding days,
they failed to create an explicit market-driven infrastructure (they
didn't have to). What's more, they're not at all sure it will help their

situation; consequently, investing the time and resources necessary seems too dangerous. Two, any new change effort—be it an organizational or cultural overhaul or a simple improvement in research practices—can seem daunting. Firms fear the paralysis that comes from biting off more than they can chew. (Picture a python that has just swallowed its dinner whole: that snake isn't going to move for weeks.) At the starting point, any initiative looks big and potentially menacing.

The fact is that all firms can learn to look out, dig deeper, and embed innovation—and without too much pain. What's more, if they tackle and succeed at only one of the three competencies, the other two will follow more naturally. There is no need to swallow this initiative whole. Taking baby steps—albeit deliberate ones—is appropriate, though the ultimate positive result (competitive gains) will be felt firm-wide and on a large scale over the long term.

A firm's leadership can say "Let's focus on improving our measurement of marketing and business development programs." This initiative is quite defined and, although not insignificant, quite doable. And the rewards will be profound. Not only will the firm improve in the selected area, but also the step will create a ripple effect that can catalyze other market-driven reforms within the firm. Once a professional service firm chooses to compete with one of these practices, the interface between that and other practices can become more seamless. For another example, say a firm decides to compete more strategically by improving how it looks out. One of the things it decides is to do more research on clients. After developing an infrastructure to do this, it would follow that the firm might next be able to do data mining more effectively. ("We've captured so much information on clients, we now want to organize it and use it.") Next might follow account planning. ("Now that we can easily manipulate our externally focused client data, we can build a road map for growing our services with those clients that are our best strategic assets.") Another example is a firm that decides it will dig deeper to be different from competitors. To do so, it decides to build an infrastructure that supports the creation of certain technological capabilities. This is, of course, also embedding innovation.

And so on. Firms can integrate their efforts in all three areas, so that the progress made in one area is felt and can be used by the others. If firms simply tackle and succeed at only one of the three building blocks of marketplace mastery, the other two will follow more naturally.

When a market-driven infrastructure is built in, small changes can equal great gains. And for professional service firms, this notion can, and should, look very compelling, especially considering the alternatives.

2

Looking Out

There are three building blocks of a professional service firm's market-driven infrastructure: looking out, digging deeper, and embedding innovation. Each building block, which is comprised of a number of firm-wide competencies or natural aptitudes, embodies a looking out, digging deeper, or embedding innovation way of doing business. This chapter explores the looking-out building block in depth. The following two chapters cover digging deeper and embedding innovation, in turn.

The building block called looking out features three practices or methods that allow professional service firms to get an early look at client, competitor, and marketplace shifts: (1) studying a firm's clients using outside qualitative and quantitative research; (2) researching the market using economic forecasts and trend analyses; and (3) researching competitors by gathering competitive intelligence. Each of these looking out techniques serves to give a professional service firm a reliable sounding board on which to evaluate new opportunities or threats. Collectively, they help a professional service firm to develop concrete grounding for future business decisions and new strategies.

STUDYING A FIRM'S CLIENTS USING
QUALITATIVE AND QUANTITATIVE RESEARCH

In five years of study on the perceptions about practices and performance of professional service firm marketing programs, my research team uncovered three findings that speak volumes about the way professional service firms research their current or potential clients: such research is underutilized; underfunded, even though it offers a significant return-on-investment (ROI); and, in some cases, compromised in its effectiveness.

Market Research Is Underutilized

In our 2001 study on client attraction and retention, more than five hundred professional service firm respondents revealed how they were trying to become more sensitive to their marketplace (in order to attract or retain clients). One of the least frequently used client attraction and retention methods was implementing market research: the qualitative and quantitative investigations of a client's unmet needs, desires and perceptions, or potential marketplace opportunities.[1] The largest respondent group, 59 percent, reported using primary research (conducting research directly with individual clients or other original source materials). Their research fell largely into two groups. The first was client evaluation at the conclusion of assignments or at specified times during the year. The other type was more focused on a client's perception of the profession's market. Primary research vehicles included qualitative written evaluations, one-on-one meetings, and group feedback sessions. Respondents reported conducting this research both in-house and through third parties. Of this 59 percent, only a very few firms reported that they were implementing "needs assessment" via primary research interviews to understand the client's business and identify new areas of assistance. The use of secondary research was even lower. Only 43 percent of respondents employed secondary research (information or data that someone else has collected, mostly through literature, publications, broadcast media, and other nonhuman sources). Respondents said that both industry and prospect- or client-specific research was being done. They relied heavily on nonbillable marketing staff or billable practice groups to gather secondary information, which mostly was used to prepare for initial prospect meetings or for early stages of a new client assignment. We were surprised to see so few professional service firms conducting secondary research, especially as there are so many electronic vehicles available with which to do so.[2] (See Figure 2.1.) Moreover, although I applaud those professional service firms that conduct formal market research of any kind, these percentages are paltry, leaving many marketplace insights unrevealed. The prevailing attitude about formal market research was re-

As a method for firms to become more sensitive to clients' desires and unmet needs, market research is used infrequently.

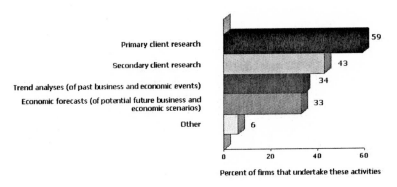

Figure 2.1 Professional Service Firms' Use of Market Research

flected in this comment by one of the study's accounting firm respondents: "We say we do this, and keep planning to do it, but we hardly ever do actually do it."[3] This remark reveals—painfully—the short-term time horizons of many professional service firms. It also illustrates professional service firms' myopic approach to funding market research.

Research Offers a High ROI Yet Is Woefully Underfunded

Out of more than five hundred study respondents in our 2001 study, only 25 percent even had a formal market research budget. This does not mean necessarily that the majority of our professional service firm study respondents conduct no market research at all; rather, they do not intentionally set aside a portion of their expenses to do so. Firms that *did have* a dedicated market research budget were two to five times more likely to report they were effective in implementing a number of client attraction and retention methods (specifically, delivering services, managing a change in their professionals' behavior, using innovation, and employing competitive practices as methods to get closer to their clients). (See Figure 2.2.)[4]

In Some Cases Market Research Is Conducted in a Way That Can Compromise Its Effectiveness

In our 1997 study of how professional service firms measured the effectiveness of their promotional vehicles, more than nine hundred

Firms that *do not* have a market research budget say they are *less effective* in getting closer to their clients.

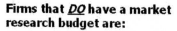

Firms that _DO_ have a market research budget are:

Nearly two to five times more likely to report they are effective in:

- delivering services . . .
- managing a change in their professionals' behavior . . .
- using innovation . . .
- employing competitive practices

. . . as a method to get closer to their clients.

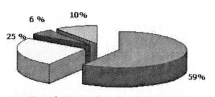

▨ Firms that DO NOT have a market research budget
▢ Firms that DO have a market research budget
▨ No response
▢ Don't know

Figure 2.2   ROI on Professional Service Firm Market Research

respondents reported on the way they assessed the results of their efforts to build awareness about their firms. We learned that a large majority of firms undertook no such post-promotion research at all. However, the minority of firms that did formally attempt to determine the effectiveness of their promotional vehicles through a qualitative survey or evaluation did so largely within the context of a client satisfaction research initiative.[5] This "blended" research approach (that is, filtering the effectiveness of a promotion effort through existing clients instead of going straight to the market, or potential clients, for a response) could, in fact, compromise a true assessment of either the promotional vehicle or a client's fundamental satisfaction. For example, how could a discontented client easily switch gears from commenting on the unsatisfactory aspects of a provider's service delivery to offering objective perspectives on that same firm's branding message, which may promise the utmost in performance and results? This finding sheds light on a larger story: most professional service firms think that "market" research means "client satisfaction" research and that client satisfaction research is adequate as a method to maintain or capture a leadership position in the marketplace. However, they have yet to envision the broader possibilities that market research offers.

The notion of a dedicated, funded market research program carries with it much significance: an interest in and an ongoing commitment to explore the marketplace, to look forward, and to solve tomorrow's vexing client challenges. Perhaps, until recent times, in a less competitive business environment, professional service firms didn't require this kind of corporate curiosity. Perhaps professional service firms didn't have the internal capability to coordinate this kind of iterative exploration. Or perhaps firms relied on their professionals to capture client-satisfaction feedback, assuming that this would be enough of a formal commitment to examine their marketplace. I could assign any number of sensible and historical reasons to why the professional service arena of yesteryear didn't wholeheartedly embrace formal market research. But the fact remains that even today, too many firms approach market research as a special activity that is undertaken only when problems arise, executive management changes hands, or a new practice leader comes on board. Moreover, too many firms still conduct research projects separately, never integrating them between practices or time periods or with their corporate strategies. This situation is not just pertinent to the smaller or less profitable professional service firms; it applies as well to some of the world's largest and most respected professional service firms, many of which have yet to commit to a formal, dedicated, ongoing, and senior management–driven market research program.

RESEARCHING THE MARKET USING FORECASTING AND TREND ANALYSES

Many of us are familiar with forecasts and trend analyses of social, economic, or technological developments. Governments produce statistical forecasts on everything from gross domestic products to wages and interest rates and beyond. Futurists and think tanks produce reports, articles, and books on their projections about upcoming developments. For marketing purposes, forecasting and trend analyses are used in numerous business sectors (retail, consumer products, food and beverage, health care, and many more) to help make sense of the past and envision the future. These businesses have made it a regular practice to analyze their external environment for the express purpose of supporting their marketplace decision making and strategy development. But the professional service sector has yet to heartily embrace forecasting or trend analysis. In our 2001 study, only 34 percent of respondents reported that they conduct trend analyses of past business and economic events.[6] (See Figure 2.1.) Of this percentage, however, many responding firms told us they were mostly using trend analysis on their own internal performance; they used it less often to detect trends in the economy or their clients' business environment. Their reviews included past billings by client project, profitability for projects, referral sources, and the like. Those professional service firms that reported they were analyzing external sources of information did so to discern how shifts in their clients' industries might affect their own businesses in the future. For example, one architecture firm respondent remarked, "[We conduct a] quarterly assessment of economic conditions and market analysis to ensure we are tracking the right opportunities." A management consulting firm commented that trend analysis "gives us a sense of where things are headed and facilitates our postulating on the critical elements needed to service the growth areas."[7] Some professional service firms conduct trends analyses on a billable basis for clients but have yet to consider that they could apply trend analyses to help their own pursuit of marketplace leadership.

The same low-level examination of external conditions exists with forecasting. A mere 33 percent of respondents reported that they undertake economic forecasts of potential future economic and business scenarios.[8] The use of forecasting tools is not widespread among any of the professions we studied, and it varied markedly from firm to firm. Like their analysis of past business and economic trends, many firms chronicled their use of forecasts for internal direction, for example, by looking at cash flow and "revenues-in-the-pipeline" reports. A health care consulting firm respondent commented, "[We] prepare quarterly and weekly cash flow and collections analysis as well as prospect pipeline reports."[9] Others looked at forecasts of external business and economic scenarios, with an emphasis on current and potential client sectors. Still, forecasting is viewed as an activity that a firm would only undertake if it were contemplating a significant cash or resource outlay. This sentiment was articulated by one of the study's law firm respondents: "This [is] done if we are pursuing a costly venture or a new business."[10] Moreover, most of the forecasting focus appears to be related to the professionals' purchase of general reports produced by industry watchdog groups or their attendance at general forecasting and trend related seminars. These forecasting sources are especially available in the architecture, engineering, and construction sectors, but are not so prevalent in others. Internally developed forecasts appear to be even less utilized.

Why do so few professional service firms conduct their own trend analyses and business forecasting initiatives? Historically there hasn't been a justifiable need and they haven't wanted to spend the money or time to undertake an initiative that was deemed to have a low ROI. The economy was good, competition was fragmented, and relationship management was an unknown concept. Investing in forecasting and trends work was simply not necessary. For most professional service firms, until recently, their annual budgeting and internal analyses of business development performance were all that they needed.

Times are changing, though. Professional service firms are waking up to their own shifting marketplace, which is nowadays comprised of increasingly sophisticated clients and competitors. The firms that are keen to become market leaders (or simply to maintain their position) are commencing more vigorous strategic planning efforts than in the past. They are initiating ever more sophisticated marketing strategies that go beyond a simple one-note perspective of trying to attract and retain a narrowly defined set of clients. Forecasting and trend analyses offer professional service firms the ability to see broader perspectives, to understand the forces that have shaped, and will shape, their clients' and their own business environment.

The good news is that forecasting and trend analysis assistance are easier and more cost effective to access than even in the recent past. There are multiple forecasting technology platforms and trend analysis services now available. These looking-out sources offer professional service firms clearly defined research assistance to answer such questions as: "What kind of strategy should we enact in order to capture market share?" "How can we accelerate the financial opportunity for our services?" "Can we validate our marketing strategies before we begin?" and "How can we prove the viability of this new service idea?"

RESEARCHING COMPETITORS BY GATHERING COMPETITIVE INTELLIGENCE

Along with client research and marketplace forecasts and trend analyses, professional service firms employ competitive intelligence all too sparingly. Of the "get closer to clients" approaches that were tested in our 2001 study of more than five hundred professional service firm respondents, "using new approaches to compete against our rivals" was one of the least frequently used. Only 39 percent of the respondents reported that they were increasing their use of intelligence gathering as a way to become more market driven.[11]

Whether consciously or not, every single professional service firm already gathers competitive intelligence. Typically, it happens serendipitously and passively, perhaps during an unexpected conversation at a business meeting or a surprise encounter with a former client who switched to a rival firm. Intelligence gathering also happens when new hires are recruited. It happens when one firm goes up against another in a proposal shoot-out. It happens when attendees gather at conferences.

There is no shortage of competitor intelligence-gathering opportunities that present themselves to professional service firms. And there is no shortage of information. Indeed, with the increased fragmentation of professional service industries, blurring between the lines of traditional services, and geographic and technological diversity of professional service providers, some firms might say that keeping up with all this information and opportunity is quite a challenge.

But there's more to this challenge than at first meets the eye. If we review the historic foundations of professionalism, we are reminded that professionals disdained the perceived crassness of overly merchant-like behavior. Philosophically, they rejected the fray of competition, holding themselves above the brutish behavior of those who "wanted" an engagement too much. With this mindset, a professional could reject even having any knowledge of a competitor, as if knowing what the competitor was doing would lower the professional into inadvertently copying from this rival. Clients, too, embraced this mindset, with a tendency to reject a professional who appeared too eager to get the assignment or too blatantly critical of a competitor's suggested approach. For the client and the practitioner, then, overt competition was unseemly; the "right" kind of competition was courtly, restrained, and passive—it was "professional." The "best" experts were above competition.

Competitive intelligence is also probably misunderstood. In his article, "What Competitive Intelligence Is and Is Not," Leonard Fuld, president of Fuld & Company and author of *The New Competitor Intelligence*,[12] offered the following ten descriptions of what intelligence is and does for a corporation, along with ten common misconceptions that he would like to dispel:

1. *Competitive Intelligence IS information* that has been analyzed to the point where you can make a decision. **Competitive Intelligence IS NOT spying.** Spying implies illegal or unethical activities. While spying does take place, it is a rare activity. Think about it; corporations do not want to find themselves in court, nor do they want to upset shareholders. For the most part, you will find spies in espionage novels, not in the executive suite.

2. *Competitive Intelligence IS a tool* to alert management to early warning of both threats and opportunities. **Competitive Intelligence IS NOT a crystal ball.** There is no such thing as a true forecasting tool. Intelligence does give corporations good approximations of reality, near- and long-term. It does not predict the future.

3. *Competitive Intelligence IS a means to deliver reasonable assessments.* Competitive intelligence offers approximations and best views of the market and the competition. It is not a peek at the rival's financial books. Reasonable assessments are what modern entrepreneurs such as Richard Branson, Bill Gates, and Michael Dell need, want, and use on a regular basis. They don't

expect every detail, just the best assessment at the time. **Competitive Intelligence IS NOT a database search.** Databases offer just that—data. Of course it is wonderful to have these remarkable tools. Nevertheless, databases do not massage or analyze the data. They certainly do not replace human beings who need to make decisions by examining the data and applying their common sense, experience, analytical tools, and intuition.

4. *Competitive Intelligence comes in many flavors.* Competitive intelligence can mean many things to many people. A research scientist sees it as a heads-up on a competitor's new R&D initiatives. A salesperson considers it insight on how his or her company should bid against another firm in order to win a contract. A senior manager believes intelligence to be a long-term view on a marketplace and its rivals. See our Strategic Intelligence Organizer tool on fuld.com for examples of the many flavors of competitive intelligence and tips on how to develop it. **Competitive Intelligence IS NOT the Internet or rumor chasing.** The Net is primarily a communications vehicle, not a deliverer of intelligence. You can find hints at competitive strategy, but you will also uncover rumors disguised as fact, or speculation dressed up as reality. Be wary of how you use or misuse the Net. Its reach is great, but you need to sift, sort, and be selective on its content.

5. *Competitive Intelligence [CI] is a way for companies to improve their bottom line.* Companies, such as NutraSweet, have attributed many millions of dollars in earned revenue to their intelligence usage. See our CI Success Stories on fuld.com for over 100 excerpts telling how companies have used CI successfully. **Competitive Intelligence IS NOT paper.** Paper is the death of good intelligence. Think face-to-face discussion or a quick phone call if you can, rather than paper delivery. Never equate paper with competitive intelligence. Yes, you must have a way to convey critical intelligence. Unfortunately, many managers think that by spending countless hours on computer-generated slides, charts and graphs, and footnoted reports, they have delivered intelligence. All they have managed to do is to slow down the delivery of critical intelligence. In the process, they have likely hidden the intelligence by over-analyzing it. Remember: Paper cannot argue a point—you can.

6. *Competitive Intelligence is a way of life, a process.* If a company uses CI correctly, it becomes a way of life for everyone in the corporation—not just the strategic planning or marketing staff. It is a process by which critical information is available for anyone who needs it. That process might be helped by comput-

erization, but its success rests upon the people and their ability to use it. **Competitive Intelligence IS NOT a job for one, smart person.** A CEO might appoint one individual to oversee the CI process, but that one person cannot do it all. At best, the CI Ringmaster, the coordinator of the program, keeps management informed and ensures that others in the organization become trained in ways to apply this tool within each of their SBUs [strategic business units].

7. *Competitive Intelligence is part of all best-in-class companies.* In my 20 years of consulting in this arena, I have witnessed that high-quality, best-in-class corporations apply competitive intelligence consistently. The Malcolm Baldridge (sic) Quality Award, the most prestigious total quality award for American corporations, includes the gathering and use of external market information (a.k.a. CI) as one of its winning qualifications. **Competitive Intelligence IS NOT an invention of the 20th century.** CI has been around as long as business itself. It may have operated under a different name, or under no name at all, but it was always present. Just review the story surrounding 19th century British financier Nathan Rothschild, who managed to corner the market on British government securities by receiving early warning of Napoleon's defeat at Waterloo. He used carrier pigeons, the E-mail of his day. He knew the information to watch and how to make sense of it; in the end, he used this intelligence to make a killing in the market.

8. *Competitive Intelligence is directed from the executive suite.* The best-in-class intelligence efforts receive their direction and impetus from the CEO. While the CEO may not run the program, he dedicates budget and personnel; most important, he promotes its use. **Competitive Intelligence IS NOT software.** Software does not in and of itself yield intelligence. The CI market is hot, and numerous software houses are producing products for the intelligence marketplace. Many more are repositioning existing software—in particular, data warehousing and data mining packages—for use in intelligence. Software has become an important weapon in the CI arsenal, but it does not truly analyze. It collects, contrasts, and compares. True analysis is a process of people reviewing and making sense of the information.

9. *Competitive Intelligence is seeing outside yourself.* Companies that successfully apply competitive intelligence gain an ability to see outside themselves. CI pushes the not-invented-here syndrome out the window. **Competitive Intelligence IS NOT a news story.** Newspaper or television reports are very broad and are not timely enough for managers concerned with specific

competitors and competitive issues. If a manager first learns of an industry event from a newspaper or magazine report, chances are others in the industry already learned of the news through other channels. While media reports may yield interesting sources for the CI analyst to interview, they are not always the most timely, or specific enough for critical business decisions.

10. *Competitive Intelligence is both short- and long-term.* A company can use intelligence for many immediate decisions, such as how to price a product or place an advertisement. At the same time, you can use the same set of data to decide on long-term product development or market positioning. **Competitive Intelligence IS NOT a spreadsheet.** "If it's not a number, it's not intelligence." This is an unspoken, but often thought of, refrain among managers. "If you can't multiply it, then it is not valid." Intelligence comes in many forms, only one of which is a spreadsheet or some quantifiable result. My firm has completed numerous strategic assessments, where the numbers only address one aspect of the problem. Management thinking, marketing strategy, and ability to innovate are only three among a host of issues that rely on a wide range of subjective, non-numeric intelligence.[13]

Given these historic and cultural underpinnings, it may not be surprising to realize how many of today's professional firms still miss the chance to take appropriate advantage of competitive intelligence-gathering opportunities. And it's perhaps not so surprising how little is done with the information that is captured. Here's an actual example of this attitude, from a study respondent: "[Gathering competitive intelligence is] not profitable. Keep your focus on the VALUE [that] your skills, acumen and knowledge can bring to specifically defined, high paying clients and leave the dregs to your competition."[14] This respondent's logic certainly seems sound, doesn't it? But consider what she could be overlooking—that her firm's competitors may be in the process of building a set of new technology-enabled services that can not only deliver them very high profit margins, but can also woo away her firm's most loyal clients. She may wish she never claimed that competitive intelligence is not profitable.

The 39 percent of our respondents who did report proactively undertaking an increasing amount of competitive intelligence offered examples of how they do so:

- Internet based client research tools. . . . "Our staff are using on-line sources to do their homework much more than ever before and are

increasingly sophisticated about business issues."—*Executive search firm*
- "Secret shopper, internet based information, annual reports."—*Information technology (IT) consulting firm*
- "Have knowledge and track all of our competitors' prices, service offerings, key personnel, customers, etc."—*Construction firm*
- "[Our] marketing [department] provides background research on prospects, clients and competitors."—*Law firm*
- "We have built an understanding of the other models in the marketplace and have developed specific competitive responses to those models."—*Management consulting firm*[15]

These intelligence-gathering techniques are relatively easy to do, and they have a clear payback. For example, during client perception interviews, a section about perceptions of competitors could be added. Marketing departments could adopt ongoing secondary research about competitors' brand messages. The outplacement department of graduate schools could be tapped to determine current outgoing students' attitudes about competing firms within a particular professional sector. Nevertheless, especially with the application of technology, the practice of intelligence gathering is itself becoming more sophisticated and powerful in its ability to deliver effective results. Those who undertake this activity are today even more likely to uncover data, analyze it, and arrive at significant marketplace insights. These are the firms that will achieve new levels of marketplace mastery.

Until recently, and quite understandably, professional service firms were able to rely on an informal, passive, and largely internal exchange of information about their clients, their market, and their competitors. Rigor was not required; it was simply enough to celebrate when and if they undertook a significant research effort. As our research has shown, professional service firms have significant strides to take before they can proudly proclaim to understand their marketplace very well. In the future—especially as the service economy continues to mature—client, market, and competitor research *will* play more prominent and ongoing roles in professional firms' marketing programs. The firms that embrace this notion are well on the way to becoming tomorrow's marketplace masters.

Digging Deeper

This building block of a market-driven infrastructure is all about process, process, process. It is the area where professional service firms truly learn how to create and sustain a market-driven infrastructure. Essentially, digging-deeper initiatives can deliver competitive advantage as much because of *how they are implemented* as because of the initiatives themselves. The effort may be significant, but the result is a firm whose practices cannot be copied and are thus undeniably competitively advantaged because of their distinctive organizational nature.

The five initiatives that make up the digging-deeper building block are: (1) embracing competitive differentiation; (2) mining client data; (3) aligning marketing strategies with culture; (4) using account planning and relationship management programs; and (5) using measurement to increase strategic focus and competitive advantage. Each of these techniques requires a strategic focus. Each represents a deliberate and genuinely systemic organizational effort that a firm would initiate in an attempt to increase its competitive advantage. Each requires internal consensus building, each demands cooperation and collaboration among staff members, and each must be supported by internal communication efforts to ensure a common pursuit of the goal.

EMBRACING COMPETITIVE DIFFERENTIATION

Professional service firms are being increasingly—and often intensely—driven to improve their competitive stances in the marketplace. Eager to latch onto any concept that could make this more possible, many have embraced the concepts of branding, positioning, and differentiation as a means to break out of the pack. Our 2000 study, which explored how professional service firms implement and assess the effectiveness of a variety of differentiation strategies to compete, certainly corroborated this assertion. We found that 81 percent of more than 400 professional service firm respondents reported they have used differentiation as a marketing approach in the previous three years.[1]

Reporting that they were mainly driven to pursue differentiation by three factors (competition, commoditization, and client demand), respondents encountered significant challenges in grappling with the whole concept. First, they were unclear about exactly what differentiation is (offering multiple and widely disparate definitions).[2] Second, most respondents (79 percent) appeared to think that differentiation is mainly an exercise in image enhancement.[3] Respondents' comments make it easy to see why they thought this way. For example, an engineering firm respondent related his painful discovery of his firm's commonplace image:

> At a trade show last March, our company shared the floor with 12 engineering firms. Our exhibits were indistinguishable. The headers trumpeted the company names, as often as not an alphabet soup of initials from principals long departed. . . . Below hung pictures of . . . the occasional camel or palm tree indicating that these were international players. There was no real way to tell one from another. No differentiation. The same is generally true in advertising, PR [public relations], events and other aspects of [our firm's] integrated marketing program[s].[4]

Another respondent recalled his own excruciating reminder of his firm's undistinguished competitive stance: "We all looked alike. We were using the same processes. Because people switch firms, we even used the same people or projects in our selling efforts on occasion. Because marketing staff move around, we even use the same language to sell ourselves. I actually found a diagram I hand-drew in 1983 in another firm's marketing materials in 1993."[5] Ouch! It is little wonder that the majority of our study's respondents pursued competitive differentiation so eagerly, and continue to do so.

Here the plot thickens, however. It appears that many professional service firms are wasting their time in their current manner of differentiating. Our study explored the use of more than 25 differentiation strategies.[6] (See Table 3.1.) When we asked respondents to indicate their

TABLE 3.1   Top Ten Most-Used Differentiation Approaches

Diffferentiation Approaches	Percent of Respondents
Improved or evolved our current services.	68%
Reorganized practices or lines of business.	55%
Entered into joint ventures, alliances, or referral networks with firms that extend our services.	53%
Hired specialized individuals.	52%
Added new variables to our prices.	46%
Repackaged current services.	43%
Used new techniques and tools to "deliver" our services (i.e., printed reports now delivered via CD-ROM)	42%
Trained professionals to follow our proprietary methodologies.	40%
Developed a new positioning.	40%

Note: Out of 26 differentiation approach choices used in the past year.

most successful differentiation strategies, we got a surprise (as did our respondents): their most-used differentiation approaches were not necessarily their most successful.[7] (See Figure 3.1.)

One might rightly ask, "Why in the world would a professional service firm implement a differentiation strategy that it knows will not be as successful as another approach?" We suspected the reasons were related to the field of differentiation being so new, featuring a multitude of strategies that are so unfamiliar. For these firms, it was likely a leap of faith to pursue a differentiation initiative in the first place. The fact that one approach was more successful than another did not penetrate far enough into the firms to cause them to change their behavior.

Are professional service firms doomed to enact differentiation strategies with so little hint of the likely outcome? Is success entirely serendipitous? Our research team analyzed the findings further in order to detect the deeper underpinnings of differentiation success in the professional service arena. For each of the studied differentiation approaches, we assigned a level-of-difficulty score, according to the risk, complexity, time involved, and level of investment of resources required. Essentially, we examined each differentiation strategy for the amount and depth of its likelihood to impact a firm's *operations*. For example, we assigned a "high" level of difficulty to the differentiation method of "implementing a formal relationship management program to strengthen our bonds with current clients." In all probability, we

The most used differentiation approaches were not necessarily the most successful.

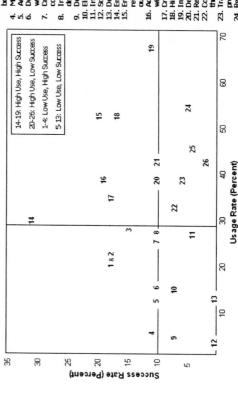

Use and Success of Differentiation Approaches in the Last Year

14-19: High Use, High Success
20-26: High Use, Low Success
1-4: Low Use, High Success
5-13: Low Use, Low Success

Usage Rate (Percent)

Success Rate (Percent)

1. Embarked on an advertising campaign.
2. Added new-to-our-firm services that blend into the services of another industry.
3. Implemented a formal relationship management program to strengthen our bonds with current clients.
4. Merged with another firm.
5. Acquired another firm.
6. Developed new risk sharing arrangement with clients.
7. Created new divisions or subsidiary companies.
8. Increased the speed of our service delivery.
9. Decreased our prices.
10. Eliminated services.
11. Increased our prices.
12. Sold parts of the firm.
13. Developed new-to-the-world services.
14. Embarked on a public relations campaign.
15. Entered into joint ventures, alliances or referral networks with firms that extend our services.
16. Added new-to-our-firm services that are within our industry.
17. Created a new visual identity.
18. Hired specialized individuals.
19. Improved or evolved our current services.
20. Developed a new positioning.
21. Repackaged current services.
22. Communicated our firm's positioning through a new motto or tag line.
23. Trained professionals to follow our proprietary methodologies.
24. Reorganized practices or lines of business.
25. Added new variables to our prices.
26. Used new techniques and tools to "deliver" our services.

Marketplace Masters

Figure 3.1 Use and Success of 26 Differentiation Approaches

surmised, a formal relationship management program requires the alignment of human resources and technology applications, a significant amount of internal leadership, training, mentoring and communication, and more. Operationally, this differentiation program requires significant coordination, focus and effort through internally-driven processes.

As another example, we assigned a "low" level of difficulty to "embarking on an advertising campaign." We estimated that an advertising campaign, even a significant one, would not have as much of an operations effect on a professional service firm as would a formal relationship management program. In all probability, the professionals of a firm could go about their day-to-day work and not have to directly participate in their firm's advertising program. It would not require the significant implementation of human resources, change management, technology, or training and development processes.

Bingo. With this analysis, we discovered that the level of difficulty of a differentiation strategy appears to be a factor affecting its choice by professional service firms. *None* of the "high-difficulty" approaches was above the median for usage rate. The "low-difficulty" approaches were generally *below the median for success rates*. And the "moderate-difficulty" approaches were often quite successful.[8] (See Figure 3.2.)

This analysis could explain why, in the early stages of their understanding about the field of differentiation, so many professional service firms embark on fundamentally image-oriented differentiation endeavors. It also suggests that, over time, when professional service firms are truly ready to differentiate themselves effectively, they will expand their use of moderate-to-difficult differentiation approaches and decrease their use of less-difficult (less-successful) approaches.

MINING CLIENT DATA

Data mining is the practice of analyzing raw data in a database to describe past trends and obtain future perspectives on strategic marketing issues such as market share, client purchasing patterns, and the like. For professional service firms, data mining is simultaneously a vexing challenge and an exciting opportunity. The findings from two of our annual studies, 1999 and 2001, illustrated fascinating shifts that are underway in its use and reported effectiveness.

In our 1999 study, a majority of more than 300 professional service firms—even the smallest ones—employed a contacts database in order to manage their clients' names, addresses, and other business information. This majority was pegged at an average of 78 percent of firms among a variety of professional service sectors.[9]

The difficulty of various differentiation approaches appears to affect their use and success.

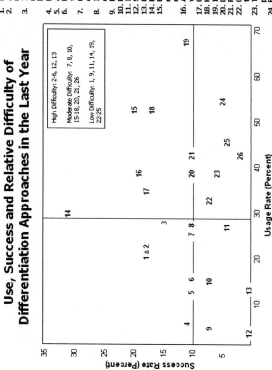

Use, Success and Relative Difficulty of Differentiation Approaches in the Last Year

1. Embarked on an advertising campaign.
2. Added new-to-our-firm services that blend into the services of another industry.
3. Implemented a formal relationship management program to strengthen our bonds with current clients.
4. Merged with another firm.
5. Acquired another firm.
6. Developed new risk sharing arrangement with clients.
7. Created new divisions or subsidiary companies.
8. Increased the speed of our service delivery.
9. Decreased our prices.
10. Eliminated services.
11. Increased our prices.
12. Sold parts of the firm.
13. Developed new-to-the-world services.
14. Embarked on a public relations campaign.
15. Entered into joint ventures, alliances or referral networks with firms that extend our services.
16. Added new-to-our-firm services that are within our industry.
17. Created a new visual identity.
18. Hired specialized individuals.
19. Improved or evolved our current services.
20. Developed a new positioning.
21. Repackaged current services.
22. Communicated our firm's positioning through a new motto or tag line.
23. Trained professionals to follow our proprietary methodologies.
24. Reorganized practices or lines of business.
25. Added new variables to our prices.
26. Used new techniques and tools to "deliver" our services.

Marketplace Masters

Fiugre 3.2 Use, Success, and Relative Difficulty of Differentiation Approaches

When we reviewed how our respondents used their contacts databases, however, it appeared that they were underutilizing them. Of the majority who use a contacts database, more than 70 percent did so only to automate traditional marketing tasks, such as computerizing their marketing mailings (82 percent), managing their day-to-day marketing interactions with clients and prospects (71 percent), or communicating marketing-oriented account information among business units (35 percent). Only 30 percent tapped their databases' strategic potential for mining and using valuable data.[10] (See Figure 3.3.)

Another example of the underutilization of contacts databases for data mining purposes was reported by the 18 percent of responding professional service firms that had been acquired or had merged with another firm within the previous year. These firms reported a 50 percent greater-than-expected use of their contacts databases for communicating simple marketing-oriented account information among business units.[11] The fundamentally important *tactical* aspects of this task are obvious (such as avoiding the embarrassment of duplicate business development efforts). It appears, nevertheless, that these newly integrated professional service brethren stopped short of undertaking the more strategic step of mining their newly merged client data for valuable marketing or business development insights.

A closer look at our 1999 findings reveals three critical tactical challenges that professional service firms face in undertaking anything related to data mining:

- *People-related challenges.* Respondents reported "data flow management" (the rather circular process of getting information from the professionals, inputting it into the firm's contacts database, and then getting that information back out again to relevant parties) was their most difficult tactical challenge. One respondent recalled the trouble of "getting information out of the heads of the rainmakers and into the database." Another respondent, a marketing manager of an international accounting firm, concurred. "They don't always see the 'what's in it for me' picture."[12]
- *Process-related challenges.* Many professional service marketers found it difficult to articulate the progression of a prospect interaction, from an inquiry to the sale of an engagement. Many were not exactly clear about when "marketing" turned into "selling."[13]
- *Database structure and protocol challenges.* Of the respondents who reported that they used their contacts database to conduct data mining, 62 percent said managing its tactical aspects was their biggest challenge. They found themselves oftentimes faced with a significant database customization task. They also cited issues involving such tasks as filtering, sorting, creating reports, merging

More than 70% who use a contacts database do so to automate traditional marketing tasks. Only 30% tap their database's strategic potential for mining and using valuable data.

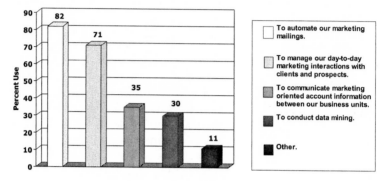

Figure 3.3 Professional Service Firms' Use of Their Contacts Databases

lists, checking spelling, and updating phone numbers. Even if they succeed at these tasks, they reported challenges of linking their contacts databases with relevant information that may be housed in another department (i.e., finance).[14]

When we looked at the use of data mining again, in our 2001 study of more than 500 professional service firms, the use of data mining hadn't changed much. Whereas 30 percent of our 1999 study respondents used data mining, only 25 percent reported they did so in our 2001 study. [15]

The practice of data mining varied widely between professions. Law firms led all the professions we studied in 2001 in implementing some kind of data mining activity from a client relationship or contact management database (see Figure 3.4).[16] (Successful data mining depends on developing a contact database that can effectively retrieve and manipulate the information that firms want to tap. We surmised that some of the variability of data-mining activities among professions may be due to the availability or acceptability of database software products in the professional service sector.)

Respondents' data-mining activities ranged from very early stages to highly sophisticated. Some of their comments included:

- "We are just starting."
- "We practice [data mining] with a set of data that seeks to ascertain our influence and awareness of business opportunities. We collect

The practice of data mining varies widely among professions.

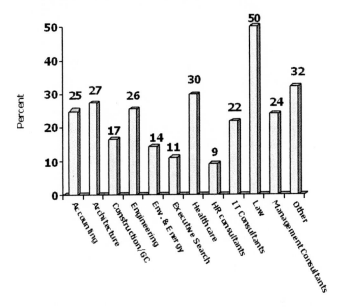

Note: IT, information technology; HR, human resources; GC, general contracting.

Figure 3.4 Data Mining Varies among Professions

the normal information about contacts, plus industry codes, nothing too fancy. We are just beginning to mine this data and it needs serious work to expand the depth and volume of our resources."

- "Our staff is held accountable for keeping our account management data system up to date. The data mining and reports are tied in to operations, backlog, probability of win, financial forecasting, and manpower loading. In other words, we don't have a separate sales/contact management database, and a separate financial forecasting database. They are linked, and we require current, accurate, realistic data gathering, analyses, and reporting—or we are sunk."

- "Who's buying what services from us and on what regularity or cyclic basis; are there particular circumstances . . . for which our clients use or don't use us; what are their selections based on—past relationship, problem solving, fees, etc. Who do they use if they don't use us? Why? We try to debrief when we win and when we lose. Since we put out thousands of proposals annually this is very hard to keep up with.[17]

For simple data mining, respondents reported they used commonly cited information such as their firm's revenues analyzed by client, the client's industry segment, the client's size (by revenues, staff, etc.), and the like. More sophisticated data mining was conducted on less commonly-gathered information such as response to their promotional efforts (e.g. mailings, seminars), price sensitivity thresholds, or critical changes (mergers, acquisitions, deregulation, market declines, new products, new competitors, and the like) (see Table 3.2).[18]

After reviewing the above 1999 and 2001 study findings, observers might conclude that there is little competitive advantage to be had from a computerized list of client and prospect information. After all, didn't we learn that, in 1999, a group of 322 professional service firm study respondents *underutilized* their databases, rarely conducting data mining and encountering *significant internal challenges* in using them for even mundane tasks? What possible benefit could one garner from such an enormous effort? No wonder contacts databases were underutilized! And didn't our 2001 findings illustrate the wide variability of data mining, both among professional sectors and within firms? This is

TABLE 3.2 Data Mining Activities Range from Simple to Sophisticated

Commonly cited type of client information gathered	Less commonly cited type of client information gathered
• Basic client contact information, including title and function in their firm, address, phone, etc. • Relevant personal client information, including names of their spouses, hobbies, etc. • Our firm's revenues by client • Industry segments • Size (by revenues, staff, etc.) • Years in business • Purchasing patterns • Amount of work done in a particular period of time • Project profits • Proposals won vs. lost	• Likes & dislikes • Growth outlook • Legislative issues that affect clients' industries • The relationship between our client contact (account manager or business developer) and our rate of success on proposals • Response to our promotional efforts, e.g. mailings and seminars • Service satisfaction • Association memberships • Market share versus our competitors • Price sensitivity thresholds • History, mission statements • Critical changes (mergers, acquisitions, deregulations, market declines, new products, new competitors, etc.) • Level of distress • Visits to our web site • Turn around time between initial intake and actual engagement • Personal preferences, social styles, processes, power structure, influence profiles • Lead sources

hardly a groundswell of endorsement. Indeed, in reviewing our findings, an early look at respondents' use of data mining would seem to prove the point that data mining *is more trouble than it is worth.* Could it be that data mining really isn't a practice that results in competitive gain?

Look again. Data mining does appear to deliver competitive results. The 2001 respondents that practiced data mining were nearly two to nearly three times more likely to report they are effective in implementing their client attraction and retention methods. These methods were delivering services, using innovation, using client relationship management strategies and tactics, employing competitive practices, and employing market research. Professional service firms that reported they *did not use data mining* declared they were *less effective* at implementing those same methods (see Figure 3.5).[19]

Exactly how might data mining make a professional service firm more effective at getting closer to its clients?

- *Service delivery:* By discerning a shift in their clients' purchase patterns for a particular set of methods or service offerings, professional service firms can adapt their standard methods to be more flexible or customized. By perceiving their clients' rising levels of dissatisfaction about project communication, professional

Firms that *do not* practice data mining say they are *less effective* in getting closer to their clients.

Firms that *do* practice data mining are:

Nearly two to nearly three times more likely to report they are effective in:

- delivering services . . .
- using innovation . . .
- using client relationship management strategies and tactics . . .
- employing competitive practices . . .
- employing market research . . .

     . . . as a method to get closer to their clients.

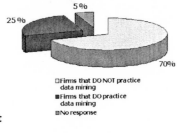

25 %   5 %

70%

☐ Firms that DO NOT practice
   data mining
▨ Firms that DO practice
   data mining
▨ No response

Figure 3.5 The Use and Effectiveness of Data Mining

service firms can adopt formal project checkpoints to enable interaction and dialogue between themselves and their client. Similarly,
by observing their clients' service fatigue for their old pattern of
doing work, professional service firms might decide to colocate
their project work and teams (e.g., deliberately changing venues to
foster new perspectives between themselves and their clients).

- *Innovation:* By noticing a decline in their profit margins on a longtime service offering, professional service firms can take steps to
create and or improve their new service development pipeline
(e.g., an internal incubator or R&D department). Similarly, they
can codevelop or pilot new services with clients.

- *Using client relationship management strategies and tactics:* By detect-
ing previously unnoticed relationship patterns between their client contacts and their own professionals, firms can create strategic
account management plans or assign appropriate account managers. By determining their relative market share vis-à-vis their competitors, firms can begin tracking and proactively working to build
their "share of customer" (e.g., cross-selling their services to a
client) or implementing other activities specifically designed to
retain their current clients. By identifying their clients' evolving
communication preferences, professional service firms can begin
to use new technologies to get closer to their clients (e.g., extranets
to allow clients online access, opt-in e-mail, pagers for their staff,
etc.).

- *Employing competitive practices:* By discovering patterns about their
clients' interactions with rivals, professional service firms can
increase their efforts and expenditures to win in final interviews
(informally known as "beauty contests" or "shoot-outs"). They can
also choose to provide free solutions in order to win an engagement, or engage in "co-opetition" (i.e., collaborating with competitors to win assignments). A glimmer of new perspectives from
their data-mining efforts could also stimulate professional service
firms to increase their intelligence gathering about competitor
activities.

- *Employing market research:* Just as with the idea of employing new
competitive practices, the revelations that firms can have from
even simple data mining can stimulate them to increase their use
of market research. With the findings from their research, they can
add new information into their databases, thus increasing its potential for richer data-mining perspectives.

Data mining is a quintessential digging deeper practice. It requires
effort, organizational focus, and a commitment to implement a distinct
process. In most cases, it necessitates an investment in a software

application that can integrate with other firm-wide business software. It requires professionals to make behavioral changes that may not feel natural at first.

As a practice grounded in intellectual capabilities, data mining is a natural fit for professional service firms. It taps their knowledge, the critical source of their unique added value for their clients. It can be deeply integrated with an organization's cultural style (The message might be "Let's data-mine for *innovation* reasons, not relationship management reasons!"). And it is a perfect launch pad from which professional service firms can begin to exceed their clients' service delivery expectations, and do so uniquely.

Moreover, data mining offers other, more broadly superior rewards. It can be an entirely reasonable platform for professional service firms to require their professionals to think less about their own personal success and more about the organization's overall success. Yes, a philosophical approach that says "take time away from your client work to give up your knowledge about that client" can appear to be antithetical within a professional service framework. Yet by doing so and by analyzing previously unnoticeable client patterns, a professional service firm will be able to formulate difficult-to-copy strategies that ultimately benefit the client—and the firm itself—in ways both parties only imagined in the past.

ALIGNING MARKETING STRATEGIES WITH CULTURE

Our own use of data mining led to some of the most unexpected findings of our 2001 study: that a professional service firm's "culture" appears to be a predictor of its success at getting closer to clients. On the data we gathered on how more than 500 professional service respondents implemented and measured a variety of methods to attract and retain clients, we applied standard mathematical algorithms (called *clustering*) to see if there were any patterns to the way they did so. We found that respondents' use of certain methods *did* fall into statistically significant mathematical clusters. These mathematical clusters appeared to have obvious "cultural" characteristics or attributes.[20] Without having a single question on our survey questionnaire about a professional service firm's culture, suddenly we found ourselves witnessing the influence of a firm's "internal personality" on its eventual success—or failure—in using certain methods to attract or retain clients.

The methods firms use to get closer to their clients fell into five different cultural groups (see Table 3.3):

TABLE 3.3 Clusters of "Cultural" Methods that Each Group Used to Become More Sensitive to the Marketplace

The "Prepared" Firm	• Implement internal training programs • Implement internal communication programs • Push responsibility for strategic planning into deeper and broader sectors of our firm • Employ career management or leadership development coaching • Implement specific client retention activities • Utilize primary client research
The "Flexible" Firm	• Utilize flexible methodologies and customized techniques to deliver services • Co-locate project work and teams (e.g., deliberately changing venues to foster new perspectives between our firm and our clients) • Require or encourage all personnel to "switch roles" occasionally, so as to interact with clients differently • Co-develop or pilot new services with clients • Engage in "co-opetition" (i.e., collaborating with competitors to win assignments) • Use trend analysis (of past business and economic events • Sell smaller or more bite-sized engagements
The "Rule-Bender" Firm	• Use warnings/disincentives • Improve service development pipeline (e.g., an internal incubator or R&D department) • Use at-risk/revenue arrangements to sell services
The "Techno-Hunter" Firm	• Use software applications (e.g., Client Relationship Management) • Work to build our "share of the customer" (e.g., cross-selling services to a client) • Using new technologies to get closer to clients (e.g., extranets, opt-in e-mail, pagers for our staff, etc.) • Increase efforts and expenditures to win in final interviews • Increase intelligence gathering about competitor activities • Utilize secondary client research • Review economic forecasts of potential future business and economic scenarios • Use non-billable salespeople
The "Accountability" Firm	• Use formal project checkpoints as a means to effectively deliver services • Use incentives to manage a change in professionals' behavior • Adapt our performance measures to evaluate our professionals' sensitivity to clients' needs • Use strategic account management plans • Sell bigger or more multifaceted engagements

- *The Prepared firm cluster:* The Prepared cluster of methods appeared quite inwardly focused, with a grouping of such internally oriented programs as training and communication plus career management or leadership development coaching for a firm's professionals.
- *The Flexible firm cluster:* The Flexible group of methods appeared very externally oriented, with a combination of such initiatives as implementing flexible methodologies and customized techniques to deliver services, requiring or encouraging all personnel to "switch roles" occasionally, and codeveloping or piloting new services with clients.
- *The Rule-Bender firm cluster:* The Rule-Bender cluster of approaches seemed quite focused on taking risks. It featured a grouping of methods such as providing free solutions in order to win an assignment, using at-risk revenue arrangements to sell services, and even using warnings or disincentives in order to manage the professionals' behavior.
- *The Techno-Hunter firm cluster:* The Techno-Hunter group of methods appeared focused on aggressive salesmanship and heavily relied on technology, such as using new technologies to get closer to clients, increased intelligence gathering about competitor activities, and the use of nonbillable salespeople.
- *The Accountability firm cluster:* The Accountable group of methods appeared oriented to preparation and performance, for instance, using incentives to manage a change in professionals' behavior, adapting performance measures to evaluate professionals' sensitivity to clients' needs, or using strategic account management plans.[21]

Next, we compared these cultural clusters with the 2001 respondents' self-rated effectiveness in their "get closer to clients" methods. We found that the firms in some of the five cultural groups *had succeeded* at using certain methods, whereas firms in a different group *had failed* at the same methods. Specifically, firms that used the methods grouped in the Prepared cluster reported that they were not effective in *any* of that cluster of methods to become more market driven. Firms in the Techno-Hunter group reported that they were only effective in using new approaches to compete against rivals (which may not be enough to help them become more sensitive to clients!). Only firms in the Rule-Bender and Accountability groups reported that they were most effective at managing client relationships.[22] (See Table 3.4)

This finding is not meant to imply that all professional service firms should abandon marketing practices that fall into the Prepared cluster of methods! On the contrary, those market-driven methods certainly do

TABLE 3.4　The Five "Cultural" Groups Are Predictors of Success at Getting Closer to Clients

Some of the five cultural groups have *succeeded* at using certain methods, while others in a different group *have failed* at the same methods.

Methods where our firm is "most effective" at becoming more market-driven	The "Prepared" Firm	The "Flexible" Firm	The "Rule-Bender" Firm	The "Techno-Hunter" Firm	The "Accountability" Firm
Delivering services		✔			✔
Managing a change in our professionals' behavior			✔		
Innovation		✔			
Client relationship management strategies or tactics			✔		✔
Using new approaches to compete against our rivals				✔	

Note: The "Prepared" firm reported that it was not effected in *any* of the methods to become more market driven. The "Techno-hunter" firm reported that it was only effective in using new approaches to compete against rivals. Only "Rule-bender" and "Accountability" firms reported that they were most effective at managing client relationships.

occupy a reasonable place in the army of management and marketing techniques that professional service firms have used and will continue to use successfully into the future. This finding is also not meant to imply that *all* firms that find themselves effective at, say, codeveloping or piloting new services with clients are, by necessity, flexible firms. This finding simply points out the fact that, for some cultures, certain methods will likely be more effective—especially if used in combination with each other—than they might be if used within a different culture.

In addition, this finding does not mean to imply that every professional service firm must force itself to fit into the five cultural groups that we discovered. Not at all—these five clusters were the manifestations of patterns from this particular set of more than five hundred professional service firm respondents in the year 2001. Depending on the processes studied, we could surmise that there would be many other types of cultural client attraction and retention methods identified and that each would have fairly unique and distinct aspects. Who would have ever thought we would be able to perceive a professional service firm's culture as looking like a techno-hunter? And yet, that is what we saw.

What was unexpected about these findings? First, the responding professional service firms' use of client attraction and retention methods naturally fell into previously unnoticed, highly differentiated cultural or personality-oriented patterns. Let's take a closer look at this finding. It makes sense, for example, that the Accountability firm would be effective at delivering its services or managing its client relationships. The whole notion of accountability speaks to an almost *personal* orientation of attending to others' needs, being mindful of the vagaries of a relationship and striving to satisfy—even exceed—clients' expectations. It also makes sense that the Techno-Hunter firm would be effective at using new approaches to compete against its rivals. A review of the methods in this cultural cluster easily evokes a picture of competitive alertness, a state of agitated hunger to win business and proactive work to *win*.

It is often believed that professional service firms leaders and marketers already understood how to market culture, but perhaps they do not. Even a casual review of a variety of firms' Web sites reveals a mind-numbing recitation of similar phrases: "our unwavering commitment to clients," "integrity," "we value diversity," "responsive," "professional excellence," "our entrepreneurial spirit," "commitment to our community," and "teamwork." But our study's findings about cultural clusters vividly demonstrate that firms actually operate at deeper, more strategically nuanced and competitively significant levels than what they typically articulate and promote to their publics.

Another unexpected aspect of our findings was even more important. We now have evidence that a firm can enhance its success at implementing market-focused methods, or at least avoid their failure, by aligning them with its cultural predilections. Does this mean, then, that a professional service firm simply has to undertake a culture identification exercise and then apply marketing strategies and business development methods that appear to fit its culture? Would that firm's marketing strategies and business development methods therefore be successful? They might, but our findings hint at a more fascinating notion: that the best way to succeed competitively is for a firm to examine the strategies and methods at which it *succeeds*, and then take a step back to see what kind of culture, or firm personality, those methods appear to spell. If more firms did this and then enacted those successful strategies—and related ones—that fit into a distinct culture or personality trait, they might be able to avoid the fate of firms in the Prepared group: vainly investing time and money implementing marketing strategies and methods that have not delivered them competitive or marketplace success.

A final perspective on this issue relates to the *intentionality* or deliberateness of a firm's choice of marketing strategies to align to its culture. As their competitive environments continue to tighten, professional service firms must assertively move beyond making fluffy swipes at identifying culture, ineffective efforts that usually end up being articulated in a plaque on their lobby walls, in their annual reports or on their web sites. In order to compete more effectively, professional service firms must wake up to the real power that lies within their walls: their people, aligned around a set of culturally preferred, personality–oriented processes. Once they determine that there indeed might be a cultural aspect to the way they select, implement, and *succeed* at market-driven processes, firms can then become more deliberate in their development. They must also become more deliberate in the way they further integrate these processes into their firm's organizational persona, so that their implementation becomes almost second nature.

USING ACCOUNT PLANNING AND RELATIONSHIP MANAGEMENT PROGRAMS

During the early years following the recent millennium, relationship management and account-planning programs dramatically grew in popularity among professional service firms. In our 2000 study on the differentiation strategies of more than four hundred professional service respondents, we learned that client relationship management was ranked in the middle of a long list of practices to achieve distinction. A mere 29 percent had "implemented a formal relationship management program to strengthen our bonds with current clients" within the past year.[23] And yet only one year later, in our 2001 study of more than five hundred respondents, new approaches to client relationships, selling, and account planning were in broad evidence:

- Client relationship management was ranked as one of the most frequently used methods to become more market driven.[24] Forty-three percent reported that their firms were creating strategic account management plans and/or assigning account managers. A health care consulting respondent commented: "Client relationship management is the responsibility of the firm principals. Relationships are maintained through face to face meetings when on [the client's] site and through phone and electronic communication on a regular basis." An information technology consulting firm remarked, "We assign both traditional [i.e., sales] account managers and technical [i.e., consulting] team leaders to all clients regardless of size to ensure that we are acting in collaboration at all times." An engineering firm respondent said, "For our larger clients we have an assigned account mgr [sic] and team who develop and implement strategies as part of business plan."[25] As part of their relationship management approaches, respondents also used client contact software applications and consciously tried to build "share of customer" (see Figure 3.6).[26]

- Forty-one percent reported that they were giving their professionals broader and deeper (general) strategic planning responsibilities as a means to encourage them to get closer to their clients.[27] For example, one architectural firm respondent said: "This is the first year (in 25 years of firm history) that key studio individuals are involved in the strategic planning and budgeting for our firm. Traditionally it's been done on the top level and not communicated to those below." An executive search firm reported, "28 people this year; 20 last year; 12 in 1998."[28]

- Even though the concept of "selling" continued to stir some level of discomfort among many professional service firms (for example, fewer than half appeared willing to vary the size of their engagements as a way to accommodate clients), respondents did relate their attempts to vary their business development approaches to clients. For example, 41 percent reported selling bigger or more multifaceted engagements; 40 percent reported selling smaller or more bite-sized engagements; and 40 percent reported using nonbillable salespeople to aid in identifying or closing new business opportunities.[29]

Despite the apparent upward trajectory of these quantitative findings from one year to the next, many of the respondents' written comments revealed the rather elementary and sometimes paradoxical ways they approached account planning and client relationship management. For example:

- Descriptions about client relationship activities fell into three categories, the first two of which are decidedly tactical. First were appreciation-oriented activities and gifts. Examples included special events such as invitational group luncheons for decision makers from target firms, special seminars, and social or community events cosponsored with clients. Second were promotion-oriented marketing activities to remind the client of the firm's presence. For example, human resource and information technology consultants reported using "regular contact through [a] monthly newsletter." An executive search firm respondent described the firm's "research reports sent to existing clients reminding them of our work." Accounting, architecture, law and financial planning firms reported using "e-mail, web pages and chat rooms." (These "relationship management" techniques are in reality mostly one-way communication vehicles.) Third, a group of fairly strategic client relationship and account planning methods, including issue-

Client relationship management is one of the most popular methods respondents use to become more market driven.

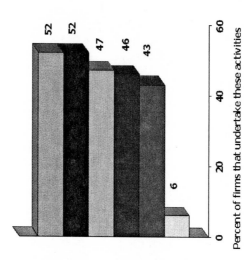

Software applications (e.g., customer relationship management or contact management)

Implementing client retention activities

Tracking and proactively working to build "share of customer"

Using new technologies to get closer to clients (e.g., extranets, opt-in e-mail, pagers for our staff, etc.)

Creating strategic account management plans and/or assigning account managers

Other

Percent of firms that undertake these activities

0   20   40   60

52
52
47
46
43
6

Figure 3.6 Client Relationship and Account Management Methods

oriented meetings that result in booking or developing new services. A management consulting respondent noted, for example, "We have semi-annual or annual, non-billed, planning and 'think tank' sessions with clients." A few accounting and management consulting respondents reported using a "client advisory board."[30]

- Many respondents equated the terms "account planning" and "relationship management" with the notion of "cross-selling." For example, a human resource management consulting firm respondent said, "[We have a] planned program to target certain clients to introduce new services." An accounting firm described how "Partners and marketing director use [a] client matrix to evaluate what services we need to offer clients. Staff [is then] encouraged to look for opportunities." A law firm reported, "[We undertake] active research among current clients for additional work opportunities outside current practice."[31]

- Many respondents equated "relationship management" with the notion of "client responsiveness." Several offered client access on a "24 hours/7days a week" basis; they used a broad variety of technologies to do so, including hand-held communication devices, intranets, digital cameras, instant messaging and interactive video conferencing.[32]

- Many responses indicated that account *service* was more the focus of "account management" than was account *development*. Account managers whose purpose is service delivery appeared to be assigned to manage work flow, handle relationship problems, and to oversee billing and fee collection. For example, a construction management firm noted, "Management team members are assigned to specific clients and are responsible for managing those accounts." An accounting firm added, "Every client has a client service team that is headed up by an in-charge."[33]

- Only a handful of respondents appeared to realize the role of *profitability* in account management. For example, an accounting firm noted: "Partners and senior staff should have profit accountability for client relationships. Unprofitable relationships need to be addressed with partners and then with the clients." An architecture firm added, "More billing and collection responsibilities are being pushed to [the] local studio level; additionally, staff are being empowered in respect to their impact on profitability."[34]

None of these initiatives is wrong, yet collectively they reveal the still-nascent stage at which client relationship management and account planning exists in the professional service arena. The majority of firms have made laudable progress. However, keen competitors will go farther. For example:

- *Building a deeper—more strategic—way of thinking about client relationship management and account planning.* Fortunately, these two practices have enjoyed the heightened interest of professional service firm leaders. Yet it appears that the professional service sector is once again rushing too tactically at a powerful digging-deeper competitive practice. Strategically astute professional service firms will realize the appropriateness of building account plans to attract and retain clients that most readily help the firm achieve its strategic and financial goals. They will begin to map out the specific criteria that will help them identify strategic clients—companies that reward them for the increased level of relationship investment that managing such accounts requires. They will stop giving knee-jerk obeisance to the large-revenue clients, simply because they are "big." They will start planning for—and implementing—their investment in clients that support the strategic goals of the firm.[35] Simply put, they will reject an all-too-quick embrace of a one-size-fits-all and overly tactical response to these two high-potential practices. They will think more critically and broadly before taking steps.

- *Balancing internal and external perspectives as part of client relationship management and account planning.* First, astute firms will begin their thinking about client relationship management and account planning from an *external marketplace perspective.* Among other issues, they will question themselves about their chosen targets and segments. What client segments appear to be growing, shrinking, or shifting? What will decisions about these segments and targets mean to the eventual growth of the firm? With which clients does the firm want to build its share-of-wallet? How are any of these decisions affected by competitor activity, and how might these decisions affect competitors' responses? These are just a few of the external perspectives that firms will want to examine. Second, these firms will begin to think strategically about their *internal* approaches to client relationship management and account planning, asking the following questions and more: What aspects of the firm's "culture" could reinforce these initiatives? How many—and which—of the firm's professionals should be involved? What kind of operational backing will the firm give to these programs? What kind of professional development could the firm offer? How will the firm adapt its performance measures to guide the professionals toward the successful implementation of client relationship management and account planning?

- *Doing more to link account planning with client relationship management.* Professional service firms will become more incisive about the strategic linkage between these two initiatives. Does it make sense to apply the same relationship management techniques to *all* clients? Probably not. If a firm conducts an account-planning exercise first, however, it will likely be able to take more appropriate and customized relationship management steps with its various clients. Account planning informs relationship management, and relationship management informs account planning.

- *Taking relationship management deeper than a software application.* Already, professional service firms have at their disposal a powerful array of software applications to help them manage their client relationships. These technological tools are being upgraded continuously. However, a software application cannot drive strategic perspectives, only illuminate them. There is danger that professional service firms will rely too much on the technological capabilities of a software package while neglecting the all-important strategic elements of a relationship management program. Competitively intelligent professional service firms will avoid this fate.

The practices of account planning and client relationship management, though still relatively new in the professional service arena, are destined to become increasingly integral to the way a firm manages and markets itself. As digging-deeper practices, they will require organizational collaboration, visionary leadership, resource investment, and much more. The result can be competitive effectiveness and the successful realization of critical goals.

USING MEASUREMENT TO INCREASE STRATEGIC FOCUS AND COMPETITIVE ADVANTAGE

Measurement has long been considered a vexing challenge in the professional service arena. First, there are challenges regarding the identification of what needs to be measured: intellect-based "intangible" professional services, like management consulting or civil engineering, for example. These professional services are certainly not like products, which can be tracked from the moment of their production to the moment they are launched into the marketplace and the moment they are scanned at a cash register. Even "tangible" services, like hospitality or air travel, which involve physical enablers like hotels and airplanes and revolve around recognizable steps in a service process, can be measured more easily than a professional service.

For the majority of professional service firm leaders, a mention of the topic of *marketing* measurement is likely to produce a distressed look.

What aspect of marketing should we measure? The development of our service? Its purchase by our clients? How it stacks up vis-à-vis our competitors? Not only that, but how should we measure? What are the right techniques? How do we know if our benchmarks are good ones? And while we're at it, how do we know that our efforts to measure *anything* related to our marketplace will make a substantive difference to us in achieving our business goals?

All too often, at this point, professional service firm leaders simply throw up their hands and give up on the whole idea of measurement. It is deemed too much work for the benefit it can deliver. And if the economic environment for professional service firms appears favorable, as it did during the 1990s, the need to measure anything in order to improve a firm's marketplace advantage seems small. Who needs the hassle?

Our 1998 study corroborated this view. We began by exploring the approaches professional service firms used to evaluate the effectiveness of their promotional tactics. From our research of nearly one thousand professional service firms, we learned that:

- Methods to measure promotional effectiveness were generally rudimentary. Most of the respondents' approaches were informal, passive, nonanalytic, limited in scope, and internally focused.
- There was no single, universally used quantitative or qualitative effectiveness measurement method. "Tracking" was viewed as both a quantitative and qualitative activity. Other quantitative and qualitative measures weren't solidly defined, and even overlapped.
- There appeared to be no overarching respondent understanding of an acceptable return on investment (ROI) for promotion.
- Measurement as a *process* had not yet generally become an integral piece of professional service firm promotional programs. It appeared to be applied for specific initiatives rather than for entire programs.[36]

We also learned that professional service firms assessed the effectiveness of their promotional efforts based on thin evidence. First, we asked respondents to rank their promotional vehicles by their frequency of use. Then we asked them to rank their *most effective* promotional vehicles. However, when we asked them how they knew their "most effective" promotional vehicle was successful, only one-third of all respondents could say they actually gained new clients or brought in revenue from that activity.[37] (See Figure 3.7.)

In terms of implementing quantitative measurements of their promotional vehicles' effectiveness, responses were highly fragmented and

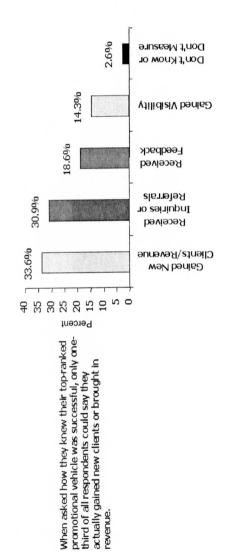

When asked how they knew their top-ranked promotional vehicle was successful, only one-third of all respondents could say they actually gained new clients or brought in revenue.

Figure 3.7 Professional Service Firms Assessed Promotional Effectiveness Based on Sparse Evidence

indicated that professional service firms hardly went far enough to determine real effectiveness. For example, only 23 percent of all the study respondents calculated a monetary ROI from their promotional vehicles. Moreover, this type of ROI appeared to include only actual cash outlays. Only 2 percent noted that they calculated both the *time investment* and *actual cash expenditures* into their ROI, which is more likely a truer measure of the effectiveness of a promotional vehicle. In addition, this measurement approach was one of eleven methods cited; none held sway as a widely endorsed measurement technique.[38] (See Figure 3.8.)

Qualitative measurements (of subjective impressions, personal opinions, and the like) did not appear to hold much greater favor. Only 27 percent of the study's respondents determined the effectiveness of their promotional initiatives through a formal survey or evaluation of qualitative client or prospect feedback. Focus groups, the only other formal qualitative technique cited, was used by only 6 percent. There were a number of other informal qualitative efforts, mostly revolving around a casual playback of clients' or prospects' anecdotal comments about a particular firm's promotional initiative; sometimes this was simply a professional's secondhand interpretation of those comments.[39] (See Figure 3.9.)

Next, we wondered about the relationship between a firm's professional service sector (for example, law, architecture, and the like) and

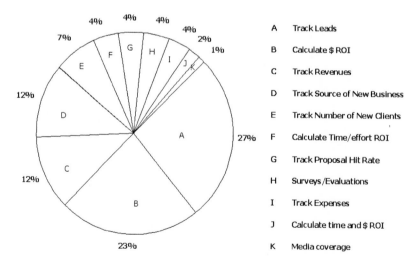

Figure 3.8 Quantitative Measurements of Promotion Effectiveness Were Fragmented and Superficial

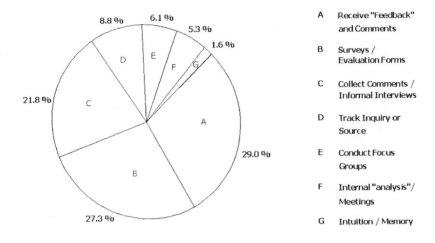

A	Receive "Feedback" and Comments
B	Surveys / Evaluation Forms
C	Collect Comments / Informal Interviews
D	Track Inquiry or Source
E	Conduct Focus Groups
F	Internal "analysis"/ Meetings
G	Intuition / Memory

Note: Numbers do not add to 100 percent due to rounding.

Figure 3.9 Qualitative Measurements of Promotion Effectiveness Were Largely Anecdotal

its embrace of marketing measurement. Which sector was most able to tie promotion to the bottom line? When we asked respondents to tell us how they knew their top-ranked promotional vehicle was successful, we found that law firms ranked highest in their certainty that they had gained new clients or revenue from their top-ranked promotional vehicle. Accounting firms came in a close second, followed by health care consulting, management consulting, and a combination of architect, engineering, and construction. The IT professional service sector ranked last.[40] (See Figure 3.10.) Why did law firms appear so much more ROI-oriented than IT consulting firms? Could it be that this sector simply *had* to mind its revenues and profit margins more rigorously than other sectors? Our 1998 study did not delve more deeply into this line of questioning. Nevertheless, these findings offered tantalizing hints about the economic state of a "mature" sector (featuring well-known and possibly commoditized services and numerous well-established competitors) and its relative influence on that sector's apparent acceptance of marketing measurement. It was clear that further examination of measurement in professional service marketing was warranted.

However, three years later, in 2001, it appeared that little had changed. When we researched professional service firms' client attraction and retention methods, our 2001 respondents did not demonstrate

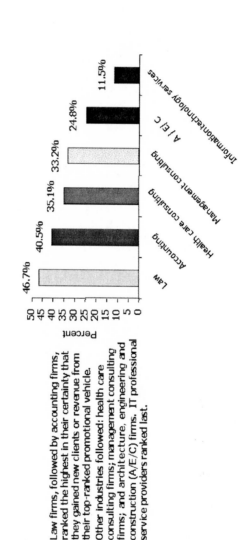

- Law firms, followed by accounting firms, ranked the highest in their certainty that they gained new clients or revenue from their top-ranked promotional vehicle.

- Other industries followed: health care consulting firms; management consulting firms; and architecture, engineering and construction (A/E/C) firms. IT professional service providers ranked last.

Figure 3.10 Tying Promotion to the Bottom Line

a much heartier embrace of marketing measurement than those in our 1998 study. For example, when asked to describe the various methods they used to manage their professionals' behavior so that they would get closer to their clients, only 28 percent of the more than five hundred responding professional service firms reported that they were adapting their performance measures in order to do so.[41]

A review of the respondents' verbal comments on this topic revealed that many were taking distinct steps toward linking their firm's client satisfaction measures to their professionals' performance reviews. For example:

- A respondent at an architecture firm said, "Client survey information is a part of our staff's performance evaluations."
- A respondent at an accounting firm commented: "Satisfaction surveys are systematically sent, responded to, and tracked. Reward systems are linked to customer satisfaction/retention."
- A respondent at a law firm reported: "Providing outstanding client servicing is a high priority at our firm. This is taken into account for all attorneys and staff at the annual reviews."[42]

These are laudable and very necessary measurement steps in a firm's efforts to succeed with clients. Nevertheless, these comments reveal that these particular respondents were not really *adapting* their performance measures at all; they were simply applying basic client satisfaction measures to steer their professionals toward retaining the clients they already had. These respondents weren't using any kind of newer measurement approach that would help them achieve a new marketplace advantage or competitive edge.

A few respondents did describe some interesting performance measurement adaptations, however. For instance, a management consulting firm reported that it was "Working toward a fully integrated balanced scorecard where numerous issues related to interaction and responsiveness to clients will be measured and rewarded." An accounting firm described that it had "developed a nine point performance measure including Resilient Empathy to signify the importance of staying close to clients."[43]

Thus, our 1998 and 2001 studies revealed at least two ways in which a professional service firm could use measurement to achieve a competitive advantage: (1) establishing and then benchmarking an ROI for its external—and internal—marketing expenditures and (2) using measurement as a means to help it push the boundaries on its tried-and-true strategic marketing methods.

Let's take a look at why both approaches are critical for achieving marketplace mastery.

1. The age of marketing ROI is upon us. A firm's outwardly directed ("external") marketing investments have multiple objectives: stimulate a prospect's inquiries, increase the depth of a client's loyalty, block a competitor, attract new talent, and much more. Firms hope to achieve their objectives as efficiently and effectively as possible. As the professional service environment grows increasingly competitive, marketing spending will become more judicious. Firm management will request more proof that external expenditures will be worth it. Anecdotal measurement simply will no longer suffice. It will be imperative, therefore, for firms to develop and consistently use formal marketing measurement tools that can capture a distinct ROI on their firm's external marketing spending. Moreover, they will have to utilize more integrated measurement techniques than they have used before (for example, going beyond simply tracking out-of-pocket costs and moving toward the inclusion of staff and professional time and other resources). At a minimum, firms will work to arrive at their own one-to-one benchmark for comparisons. For example, suppose the question is, "What was the ROI of our recently-concluded seminar series?" (The answer will be: "This year's seminar series measured better than last year's because we added the following features. . . .") Beyond this, firms will move toward a more multidimensional aspect of marketing measurement, where they will compare their measurement of distinct initiatives (like a seminar series) with their measurement of other initiatives (a published article, for example). Once they do this consistently, they will begin to perceive the *relative effectiveness* of various approaches. In this manner, marketing leaders will know the answer immediately when their firm is asked, say, to sponsor an expensive table at a professional association's annual awards dinner: "Yes" (because we have learned that our ROI on sponsoring a table with this particular association's awards dinner, which is 17 percent, is better than the ROI we realized on a four-color brochure tailored for the same targeted client group, of only 6 percent). Eventually, by making a deep commitment to marketing measurement, professional service firms will be able to answer an even more significant ROI question: "What were the aspects of *that particular* seminar that caused our prospect's buying switch to move from Off to On?" With these external marketing ROI benchmarks more solidly defined, professional service firms will be able to more effectively plan their marketing budgets ("Our requested 7 percent increase in the firm's marketing budget will generate at least that much more in revenues; here's how we know it will do so"). External marketing ROI benchmarks will also help them spend their budgets more wisely and, if necessary, justify them.

In addition to increasing the effectiveness of their *external* marketing spending, professional service firms will work to increase the effectiveness of their *internal* marketing expenditures. Groundless investments in internal staff marketing resources are simply no longer acceptable. Many professional service firms have long been ambivalent about paying for internal marketing staff. When economic times permit, these "overhead" expenditures can be tolerated, but when revenues and profits dwindle, as they did for many professional service firms in the early part of the new millennium, many firms look inside, to root out any staffing that they suspect might be unprofitable. Layoffs of internal marketing staff are not uncommon, but are layoffs justified? What if a firm's marketing staff, properly focused and deployed, is the *very* resource that can help a firm hold on to its competitive leadership? On the other hand, when economic times are good are hiring and funding a marketing staff justified? How do we know the appropriate amount for a compensation investment? The bottom line here is that professional service firm leaders are too uncertain about how to determine an appropriate ROI from their payroll expenditures for their marketing staff. They have too little idea about the optimum proportion of marketing staff to professionals. Moreover, when making compensation decisions for their marketing professionals, they have too little conviction about what is "worth it" and what is not. And, for their part, marketing staffers have too little ability to justify their salaries as ultimately profitable for the firm. When going forward, strategically astute professional service firms will take the time needed to develop measurement mechanisms that will allow them to establish these internal marketing benchmarks and to measure against them. ("We can demonstrate clearly that our marketing department of 17 people last year contributed $XXX to revenues.") They will have a better feel for the optimum levels of internal resource allocation for their firm. They cannot afford not to do so.

2. Marketing measurement will be the means to achieve a stretch goal. Measurement is supposed to reveal areas where improvement can occur. For professional service firms, measurement can create critical benchmarks that today most sorely lack. Once baselines are established, though, measurement can become the mechanism by which firms can increase their success at achieving strategic marketing ends. Observe what happened at ACNielsen, a case presented later in this book. Its effort to set a baseline was deep, wide, and organizationally integrated. The goal was simple and bold: to achieve significant new competitive heights. Professional service firms that want to win in the marketplace will implement marketing measurement methods that are formal, proactive, analytic, and externally focused. They will harness their marketing efforts and resources, evaluate them with an eye to compete more effectively, and fine-tune them on their way to marketplace mastery.

I've said that the digging-deeper building block is all about process. The good news is that professional service firms are increasingly capable of instituting processes. We can thank the 1990s wave of alliances, mergers, and acquisitions and the continuing rise in business globalization for helping firms grapple with—and get better at—using *processes* to achieve goals. Now they know that implementing processes is a surmountable challenge. The payoff is a more toned, smoother running, and more deeply distinctive business engine.

Embedding Innovation

The three competencies in the embedding-innovation building block illustrate a firm's resolve: "We are *not* powerless in our ability to manage our response to the challenges the marketplace throws at us; we will create *our own* new opportunities." The competencies are building an R&D process, using technology to build new services, and using incentives and rewards to stimulate innovation. Embedding innovation underscores a professional service firm's wholesale acknowledgment that its service portfolio has a finite shelf life, that it is powerless to stop the inevitable march of commoditization, and that it will take responsibility for its own survival.

BUILDING AN R&D PROCESS

R&D—research and development—these are words that spark instant recognition in most business sectors. Global leaders like 3M and Procter & Gamble have long dominated the products arena, in large part because of their high-powered R&D engines. Even in the U.S. manufacturing sector, which was hard-hit by the economic downturn in the late 1990s and early 2000s, "Research and development spending has remained remarkably resilient . . . and is expected to increase . . . [in the current] year. More R&D spending means new product development, which could generate greater revenue."[1] For companies in these and other sectors, R&D is the process through which innovation is driven, and innovation ultimately drives the survival of the business. The commitment to R&D remains stable through good times and bad.

Despite these maxims, however, for most firms in the professional service arena, the notion of a structured R&D process—monitoring and managing the shelf life of a service and taking steps to innovate it—has not yet become deeply ingrained. Moreover, the entire school of thought about innovation in professional services is still emerging. What we *do* know is that the very nature of professional services requires mental agility and creative problem solving. Our studies uncovered evidence that professional service firms generally do have some familiarity with at least some level of innovation, that they are pursuing it, and that they are having some level of success with it. We found an example in our 2000 study of differentiation. When asked about their top-ranked approaches to differentiation, 68 percent of the more than four hundred respondents reported that they had improved or evolved their current services in the past year.[2] In our 2001 study, 46 percent of the more than five hundred respondents reported that they were becoming more market driven by codeveloping or piloting new services with their clients.[3] Some of their comments follow:

- A management consulting firm: "We frequently partner with our clients to utilize our methodology in unique ways to support their customers. Example: training sales managers on business process reengineering for an Internet firm so the sales managers can work with their clients to design an overall solution utilizing the Internet."
- An accounting firm: "Have created several Strategic Alliances in the past year with technology firms, insurance firms, banks, etc. Have piloted several new services for our clients in conjunction with these strategic alliances, especially in the area of technology."
- An executive search firm: "We have developed [a client service Web site] to help satisfy client needs."[4]

While none of these respondents represents a tidal wave of enthusiasm for innovation, certainly they appear to understand the meaning of service customization: adapting a service or method to the specific needs of a client. Nevertheless, our research went on to reveal strong evidence that professional service firms are pursuing innovation only superficially, passively, and half-heartedly.

- *Superficiality:* In the 2000 study, "repackaged our services" was a "high-use" (top ten) but "low-success" differentiation activity.[5]

"Repackaging services" means not making any substantive change to the services but simply rearranging them into different groups of offerings (and sometimes renaming them). Some firms might consider repackaging a set of services to be "innovative," but the reported low effectiveness of this method revealed it for its truly shallow nature. Painful examples of this "innovation lite" approach abound: Remember when the e-commerce craze swept professional service firms in the later years of the 1900s? A noticeable number simply added an "e" at the front end of the names of their fatigued services. After a fanfare of visibility-enhancing activities, they waited for the calls to come. They waited in vain: clients know when they are looking at the same old thing. "Repackaging services" was not the only superficial innovation technique revealed in our study findings, however. In some cases, improvements in "service delivery" also masqueraded as real innovation. For example, in the 2000 study, 42 percent of the respondents used new techniques and tools to "deliver" their services (i.e., printed reports now delivered via CD-ROM).[6] As with repackaging services, respondents reported this was a low-success differentiation technique. It is clear that these professional service firm respondents were trying to do something new that they thought would bring added value to their clients. It is equally clear that using new techniques and tools to deliver professional services, while laudable and probably even necessary for the sake of competitive parity, is not a demonstration of genuine innovation. And clients know it.

- *Passivity:* The 2001 respondents' comments regarding their work on "codeveloping or piloting new services with clients" indicated just how passive most professional service firms actually are. For example, many respondents cited "client requests" as the basis for codeveloping new services. A health care consulting firm respondent remarked, "A number of our recent service line expansions were largely driven by clients' requests for services."[7] In addition, engineering and human resource consulting respondents proclaimed that their innovation activities featured, as one put it, "Surveying clients to look for new/innovative services which they would like for us to offer." Arguably, this innovation listening exercise, while commendable, simply encourages clients to articulate something they have probably already seen elsewhere. The clients' responses are not likely to be highly innovative.[8]
- *Half-heartedness:* Some of the 2000 study's professional service participants pursued innovation by trying to buy it. For example, a supply chain management consulting firm reported that its innovation approach was through "Acquisition. Hiring the expertise or

buying the knowledge is how our firm develops innovative service offerings."[9] Other 2000 respondents appeared to give up quickly on even the *possibility* of innovation. This sentiment, although voiced by a law firm respondent, could have been articulated by any one of the study's participants: "As far as co-developing new services with clients, there may be conflicts of interest to consider."[10] Our 2001 study findings did not reveal a much more enthusiastic stance on innovation: it was among the more than five hundred professional service firm respondents' *least used* methods of becoming more market driven.[11]

These gloomy portrayals might suggest that the professional service arena is simply not ready to take innovation seriously. Perhaps many firms *are not* ready. Nonetheless, our 2000 study resulted in three findings suggesting that at least some professional service firms see innovation as a competitively astute move.

- First, 22 percent had added new-to-the-firm services that blend into the services of another industry (i.e., accounting firms offering litigation support). This approach was one of the very few that respondents deemed effective in terms of differentiation. It certainly requires firms to "look out" beyond their current service portfolio to spot emerging opportunities that could help them address their clients' unmet needs. It also requires firms to "dig deeper," creating and implementing organizationally innovative processes.
- Second, 15 percent had eliminated services. This signals that professional service firms grasp a number of vital principles about innovation: Services have a life cycle, and service fatigue *does* exist. Moreover, the firm does not have to offer a particular service forever and its leaders can deliberately choose which services to offer. This is an indication of a marketplace mastery perspective. Finally, a firm can eliminate one service and still retain others. This signals an ability to think about services from a portfolio perspective. Overall, this step signifies that a firm comprehends the real reason it is in business: to serve the marketplace.[12]
- Third, 13 percent developed what they believed were new-to-the-world services.[13] This means the services had never before been offered *by anyone*. Pessimists may call 13 percent a paltry number that deserves little celebration. But it is a significant number when considering that respondents are reporting their development of services so innovative that they are truly unique. Doubters may question the actual newness of these reported services, yet professional service firms develop new-to-the-world services frequently

enough to prove this kind of innovation exists. Examples include management consultants Michael Hammer and James Champy's 1993 manifesto about business process reengineering,[14] Robert Kaplan and David Norton's 1996 methodology (called the Balanced Scorecard),[15] and Economic Value-Added (EVA), a new measure for corporate performance that was coined in the mid-1990s by its inventors at Stern Stewart & Co.[16] We have seen new methods emerge in other professional sectors, too, such as design-build project delivery in the architecture, engineering, and construction sectors and investigative or forensic accounting.

Our past research findings on innovation found reasons to celebrate and reasons to be concerned. But what about the question of *how* professional service firms innovate—do they use a formal research and development process? In our 2001 study, only 36 percent of more than five hundred respondents said they had created or improved the firm's new service development pipeline in order to become more client sensitive.[17]

However, only a subset of this 36 percent appeared to be implementing anything approaching a formal innovation process for developing, testing, and launching new services. For example, a management consulting respondent declared, "Annually, [we] select two development areas and charge small teams to work out how to break into these markets." An information technology consulting firm explained, "We have currently launched our strategic consulting service as a result of internal service development over the past 6 [months]." A law firm reported that it had an "Incubator with outside sponsors."

Most firms may report that they are "constantly innovating," but the new service development process is largely restricted to "looking" and "listening" activities; it doesn't actually embrace the subsequent formal development of a new service. An example comment from an architecture firm described that its "involvement in client organizations usually consists of our staff members being on committees that look at trends and future developments within that industry." A management consulting firm commented that innovation efforts were "Not formal such as [an] R&D department. However, our Partners listen to clients and are willing to adapt our services and our strengths to fit our clients' needs."

Others report that they have individuals assigned to champion the cause of innovation and actual new concepts within their firms. An accounting firm study participant said, "We have a partner in charge of R&D." An engineering firm reported that it had "personnel assigned to looking [sic] for new applications for technologies." Another engineering firm added that it was currently "Only evaluating new service opportunities for which there is an internal advocate/champion of the cause."[18]

The quantitative and qualitative comments from our studies make it clear that the majority of professional service firms have yet to grasp the value of creating a formal innovation infrastructure. Anecdotally, from my years of consulting with professional service firms, I have observed that many are trying to innovate as if from a standstill, without an organizationally supported process framework. In the not too distant past, this approach worked quite well; professional service firms could enjoy a steady stream of strong revenues and profits, reasonable competition, and a stable share of fairly loyal clients. Now, fresh from the still-painful experiences of turbulent economic times, they are searching for ways to improve their ability to weather any such future maelstroms. It makes it easy to understand, then, why some firms are adapting versions of the tried-and-true R&D processes that helped so many products and manufacturing companies to innovate to help them ride through their own economic ebbs and flows.

I can imagine my readers saying: "Oh, great. Now you're telling me I should commit virtual hara-kiri within my firm by telling my colleagues that they aren't innovative enough and that they should institute an excruciatingly detailed R&D process that will probably wreck the service mix we've depended on since the firm was founded. No, *thank you!*" These are legitimate concerns. Nevertheless, professional service firms must get serious about formally supporting innovation. Moreover, the payoff from establishing a defined R&D process comes in two forms. The most tangible (and firm-specific) is the easily tracked ROI from a firm's monitoring of investments in R&D time and money and from analyzing the returns, over time, of the newly launched services. Of course, some new services will be disappointments. Some will be outright failures. The point is to *start* and begin to fine-tune things from there.

The real payoff, however, is much less tangible and far superior. It is the value of a dispassionately managed service portfolio that allows a firm to proactively maximize its profit margins. It is the ability to engage a firm's prospects and clients in a collaborative exploration that truly addresses their unmet needs and brings a form of empowerment for all parties, to offer a set of services that are compellingly attractive and unquestionably unique. It's the ability to be competitively preemptive. Gone are the days when professional service innovation could be allowed to happen serendipitously. As this sector continues to mature, especially with technology's impact dramatically reshaping its landscape, innovation will become mandatory. Innovation, the lifeblood of marketplace mastery, *can* be managed. A clearly defined R&D process is the way to do it.

USING TECHNOLOGY TO BUILD NEW SERVICES

Technology has changed professional services in at least three ways: first, in the way services are *promoted*, and second, in the way services are *delivered*. In these two, technology has served as an exciting, but not always valuable, evolution of the traditional way of doing things. A third frontier is the way technology will *innovate* the professional services themselves. As professional service firm leaders contemplate innovation and the use of technology to drive it, they might do well to heed some of the findings from our recent studies.

First, let's examine the way professional service firms *use technology to promote their services*. Do the lyrics "I can't live—with or without you" sound familiar?[19] These words from rock group U2 neatly sum up the sentiments about technology that were revealed in our 1999 study. We asked more than three hundred professional service firms about their use of external technologies in their marketing programs.[20] Respondents reported that their external marketing technologies were generally meeting their expectations.[21] (See Figure 4.1.) Upon further analysis, though, we discovered that they were *least satisfied with the technologies they used the most*.[22] (See Figure 4.2.) The reason is that they rushed too fast to implement their marketing technology plans:

- Without having a clear articulation of the expectations the technology must meet in order to be deemed a success. "We didn't spend the time, nor money, 'to do it right,' we just 'did one' [a Web page]."
- Without having realistic expectations of the support required or the technology's ability to deliver "performance." "[We should have] moved Web site responsibility from the [Information Services] dept to [the] Mktg dept."
- Without formulating a solid rationale for implementing the plans except "because we should." A telling comment was that "technology was internally considered a 'must have' but [with] not much confidence in [the] medium doing more than keeping up with the pack."
- Without knowing what would best attract clients and prospects and why. For example, comments on one firm's Web site included "boring," "I expected more from a large company like yours," "too basic," "no real reason to re-visit."[23]

Some of these comments are downright painful to read. The respondents all but admitted they were implementing their marketing-technology decisions in a knee-jerk fashion. With little or no strategic underpinnings for these initiatives, it is small wonder that their efforts

Professional service firms were generally satisfied with their external technologies.*

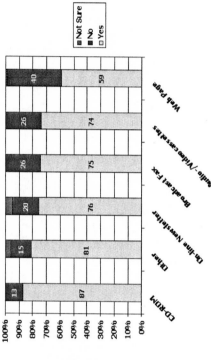

Has this technology met your marketing expectations?

Technology	Yes	No	Not Sure
CD-ROM	87	13	
Other	81	15	
On-line Newsletter	76	20	
Broadcast Fax	75	26	
Audio- / Video cassettes	74	26	
Web page	59		10

*External technologies are defined as technologies that are used to build a firm's visibility with its target audiences—those that are directed toward a firm's outside publics, including clients and prospects. Studied vehicles included on-line magazines or newsletters, broadcast faxes, Web pages, CD-ROMs, video- or audiocassettes, as well as others independently mentioned by respondents.

Figure 4.1 Satisfaction with External Technologies

Respondents were the *least* satisfied with the external technologies they used the *most.*

Use of and Satisfaction with External Technologies

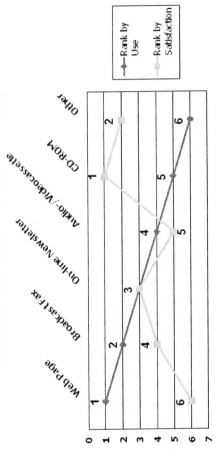

Figure 4.2 The Most-Used External Technologies Were the Least Satisfactory

delivered less-than-thrilling results. Unfortunately, even today, this scenario is being repeated in many professional service firms.

Instead of enduring the disappointments encountered by these respondents, professional service firms should define the expected outcomes from their development of awareness-oriented technologies in terms of a meaningful competitive advantage, not in terms of low costs, efficiency, or an amorphous notion of "looking cutting edge." They should plan and provide for necessary support. They should make long-term commitments to their marketing-technology program, with plans for its continuous improvement. Simply put, they should start with a strategy.

Of course, these points are directed toward the use of technologies to build a firm's external visibility and to develop or cement its client relationships. Nonetheless, they also have implications for firms that are contemplating service innovation.

Next, let's review how professional service firms have enthusiastically employed *technologies to help them deliver their services*. Recall the findings about our 2000 study respondents' application of new techniques and tools to deliver their services (one of their top-ten most frequently used methods to differentiate).[24] This pattern continued with our 2001 study participants, whose firms employed a number of service delivery technologies.

- Respondents in architecture, construction, engineering, environment and energy consulting, law, and management consulting reported that they used "Extranet[s] to allow clients to download reports, presentations," "shared document archiving systems," and "Web-based project delivery."
- A construction firm said it employed "Jobsite webcams that provide 'round-the-clock monitoring of project progress and activity" and videoconferencing.
- An accounting firm said it was "giving clients access to their financials online."
- Accounting, architecture, law, and financial planning respondents reported using chat rooms.[25]

Professional service firms are to be commended for the variety and added value of these and other service delivery technologies. Their enthusiastic embrace, however, might lead them to form an unfortunate misunderstanding, based on a potentially blurred distinction between the service itself and its delivery. Let's take a look at an example of how this can happen. We'll use one of the examples cited in our research, client-oriented extranets. Whether in law, executive search, construction management, or other fields, firms that reported their use of this tool in our research used extranets to allow clients to monitor the work they have purchased and to communicate and collaborate more effectively with their professional service providers.

When a technological tool like this is introduced, it is usually heralded by the providers and welcomed by the clients, with good reason. Both sides benefit from increased efficiency and effectiveness. But does an extranet actually affect the intellectual underpinnings of the service itself? In all likelihood it does not. The work itself (law, executive search, construction management, and the like) can still be delivered, whether it is monitored through an extranet or not. This kind of litmus test also can be applied to other service delivery technologies. In their introduction of these very appropriate technological tools, unfortunately, all too many professional service providers fail to see the truth: they did not innovate their service, they simply improved its delivery.

Why is this distinction so important? Professional service skeptics will say: "Really, who cares where a service 'ends' and the delivery of it 'starts'? Isn't it enough that we found a new way to delight the client?" Well, no, it's not, because *service-delivery techniques—even those based on dazzling technology—are eminently reproducible.* If one professional firm can deliver its services through an extranet, so can, and so will, another. In their 2000 book, *Market Leadership Strategies for Service Companies,* Craig Terrill and Arthur Middlebrooks call this the "Be Better Trap." It won't be until the first firm develops an innovative professional methodology that the value comparison between the two will begin to diverge; this is because intellectually based service processes are extremely difficult to copy exactly. Terrill and Middlebrooks explain, "While most companies are trapped trying to do things better with their existing business, the true competitive advantage lies in redefining the business and the benefits provided to customers."[26] Technology-oriented service delivery tools are reproducible "be better" tools; the unreproducible competitive advantage lies with technology-based or -supported intellectual capital innovations. Clarity about this distinction will be critical for professional service firms that want to use technology to innovate.

For my final point about the use of technology in professional services, the U2 theme again strikes a chord, as singer Bono croons, "I still haven't found what I'm looking for."[27] He might as well have been singing about the role of *technology in the innovation of professional services.* Yes, professional service firms have been disappointed with the performance of their promotionally oriented technologies. Yes, many might believe their service delivery technologies are innovating the services themselves. Moreover, all too many professional service firms think that incorporating technology into their services means that they should take an existing, fatigued service and productize it into a software application. Unhappily, this is a step that all too often nets no more than mixed results.

None of these approaches to incorporating technology into services will bring professional firm leaders what they are really looking for—solid competitive opportunity. As long as they hold on to their superficial improvement mindset and view technology as a wraparound to their core services, they will not achieve technology-integrated innovation. However, it can be achieved. Take the example of Ernst & Young's award-winning "Ernie," an online consulting program introduced in the mid-1990s, whereby subscribers gained answers to a given number of managerial questions fielded by a virtual team of Ernst & Young knowledge providers. When it was launched, Ernie was a powerful example of a technology-based new service. Directly targeted to entrepreneurial clients with revenues of under US$250 million, by fall 1996 Ernst & Young's Ernie-related revenues had surpassed US$1 million.[28] Ernie was not simply a glorified frequently asked questions Web site. It offered clients significant benefits, and simultaneously it offered Ernst & Young the opportunity to help these clients after their Ernie question was answered. "One of the major benefits of Ernie has been the ability . . . to see certain trends develop, identified through Ernie TrendWatch, as a company goes through various stages. By understanding what issues their clients have gone through, [Ernst & Young analysts and consultants] can apply this knowledge and proactively provide consultation to new clients on similar issues."[29]

In a 2001 case study about Ernie, Brian Baum, then Ernst & Young's director of market development for online consulting services, said, "Ernie is serving an entirely new market—the market for assisting managers to make timely and accurate decisions." By 2002, Ernie had morphed into Ernst & Young Online, an interactive gateway that Ernst & Young clients use to access the firm's global knowledge resources, and business tools.[30]

When it comes to using technology to compete more effectively, for professional service firms, the future is right now. They must take a considerable step back to ask themselves, "What totally new technology-enabled service can we invent?" Only then will they have the opportunity to achieve marketplace mastery.

USING INCENTIVES AND REWARDS TO STIMULATE INNOVATION

Mine is not the only voice urging professional service firms to pursue innovation; the call is being sounded in a number of professional sectors. For example, in a 2003 article from its client newsletter,

Report to Legal Management, consulting firm Altman Weil Inc. noted: "It is difficult to think of any industry, other than the legal industry, where companies have been able to operate successfully under essentially the same business model for decades with no complaints from consumers and fairly consistent increases in profits. Law firms have been able to avoid innovation, even in a global economy that is constantly changing." The author goes on to assert: "Law firms that successfully utilize innovation . . . are the most likely to achieve market dominance. . . . Innovators essentially create temporary monopolies with the introduction of a new capability, and competitors can do nothing but react."[31] Accounting firms have begun to hear the drumbeat of innovation too. At the 2003 annual conference of the Association for Accounting Marketing, for example, one of the sessions was entitled, "Expand Your Service Offerings: How to Successfully Launch Services into the Market."[32]

How will professional service firms respond to this call? As we've seen with our findings on cultural groups, at some organizations the practice of innovation will naturally rise to the forefront. However, other firms will need to discover a way to inspire their professionals to pursue innovation. This means using incentives and rewards. Professional service firms appear generally unused to the idea of offering incentives and rewards to encourage their people to engage in marketplace-focused behaviors. In our 2001 study of how firms are trying to get closer to their clients, only 31 percent of more than five hundred participants reported that they used incentives to try to manage their professionals' behavior.[33] (Rewards were both direct—cash and additional compensation—and indirect—gift certificates, days off, names on plaques, and the like.)

Within that 31 percent of our samples most of the incentives or rewards were given for behaviors such as delivering excellent client service, selling or cross-selling new business, implementing a firm's quality processes, revenue contribution (billability), profit contribution, and leadership in marketing initiatives. Stimulating innovation appeared to be only a distant thought. There were only three specific citations of this practice. They included an executive search firm that gave out "an award for idea of the month. . . . This is typically a gift certificate to a local restaurant." A health care consulting respondent said it offered annual awards for "innovation in service delivery." The third and most compelling example was presented by a management consulting participant: "We have annual innovation awards judged by an external committee made up of clients and business management professionals."[34]

Why are behavior-oriented incentives and rewards—especially those related to encouraging innovation—not used nearly as much as they might be? My research, and the work of other respected professional service industry observers, point to three possible reasons:

- *Incentives or bonuses generally are not structured to focus on innovation:* The compensation practices at most professional service firms are largely focused on rewarding revenues related to rainmaking (selling the firm's services) or billability (performing the firm's services). Research conducted in at least one of the professional service sectors—management consulting—supports this point. In its August 2002 issue, *Consultants News* (CN) reported that "on average, a consultant's ability to win new work is valued twice as much as client satisfaction, according to an exclusive review of almost 50 consulting firms' compensation packages conducted by CN."[35] This scenario also exists beyond the management consulting sector. In their 2002 book, *Aligning the Stars*, Jay Lorsch and Tom Tierney stated: "Professional service firms' incentives tip toward clients because PSFs are top-line driven; their short-term financials hinge on revenue generation and utilization. Therefore the natural orientation is to recognize and reward rainmaking above all else."[36] Perhaps this "natural orientation" was acceptable for the professional service arena of yesteryear. In the future, however, as professional service competition becomes increasingly keen, we will see firms expanding their rewards programs for qualitative behaviors like satisfying clients or managing client relationships. Astute professional service competitors will go even further toward seeding their long-term marketplace success: they will incorporate incentives and rewards for innovation.
- *Incentives require the measurement of performance, and professional service firms don't handle measurement well.* Measurement means work, especially as the behavior being measured moves from easily quantified to more subjective. In their call for professional service firms (PSFs) to be more "inventive about the measures they use to evaluate performance," Lorsch and Tierney wrote: "On this topic, PSFs are no different than any other organization: You get what you pay for, and what you pay for is rooted in what you measure. The problem is that it's easy to measure revenue, billable hours, and other 'hard' indices of short-term financial performance. But it's hard to capture the subtler aspects of partners' contributions (such as mentoring young people or idea development)."[37] Professional service firms simply must wrestle this beast to the ground, and doing so incrementally is a commendable approach. First, they could start with *a program that measures and rewards the "quality" of new ideas.* The qualitative measurements could feature a series of subjective assessments of, say, the relative

newness, uniqueness, or potential value of an idea. Other measures could include how much effort it would take to incorporate the new idea into the firm's everyday operations. For the next step, firms could begin to *reward their practitioners for well-documented and vigorous "thought leadership."* Qualitative measurements could include the successful publication by a "thought leader" in respected journals or book publishers. Over time, the practitioner would be rewarded for publishing in increasingly rigorous, prestigious, or broadly distributed publications. Another qualitative measurement could be the development of a clearly documented methodology: How thoroughly was it supported by marketplace research? Did clients pilot test it as a methodology? How did clients assess its short- and long-term value? Both of these suggested models are targeted toward individual incentives. The next incremental step should be toward *an incentive program for a team-driven new services development function,* involving qualitatively and quantitatively measured milestones that result in incentives and rewards for teams that conceive and launch new services into the marketplace. The bottom line is this: If innovation counts, it should be counted—and rewarded.

- *Only a minority of professional service firms have created a defined R&D framework.* Without a formal "managed innovation" process, it may be hard to reward for the desired behaviors that would fit within it. There *are* some professional service firms that have created a defined R&D framework. Take the example of Deloitte's Innovation Zone, a coordinated program launched in 2001 to manage innovation from Deloitte's hundreds of thousands of employees worldwide. The programmatic elements of the Innovation Zone include a mechanism to balance external insights and internal ideas; multifunctional resources to screen ideas, manage projects, and launch new businesses; a formally defined process and technology; and internal practices that sustain the progress of innovation throughout the firm. John Kutz, senior manager of the Innovation Zone, said: "We wanted to tap into the global innovation that we knew was underway, albeit separately, in many of our global offices. So we devised a viral marketing campaign to communicate that the Innovation Zone was the avenue through which ideas should be funneled. We used give-aways and key prizes and other techniques that 'prime the pump' for innovation." Kutz and his colleagues didn't stop there. They created an incentives and rewards program to encourage ever-wider participation. This program, which includes elements of a frequent-flyer point system, is offered as a supplement to Deloitte's existing rewards program. It includes a framework for an idea competition, followed by a system to recognize implemented ideas as well as those not adopted, and culminating in a group award and, ultimately, a grand prize (a complimentary team trip to the Olympic games, for example). "The Innovation Zone is now part of Deloitte's corporate DNA—an integral part of our growth strategy," said South Africa–based Louis Geeringh, Executive Director of Deloitte's Service Innovation & Growth unit. "Our incentives and rewards program helps make it so."

Unfortunately, other professional service firms will try to hang on to the belief that innovation cannot be harnessed or managed. Without this infrastructure, their practice of rewarding innovation will probably mirror their internal situation: lightweight rewards for trivial innovations that will occur only by happenstance. Trivial innovations will earn trivial rewards, and so the cycle will continue. As illustrated so effectively by Deloitte's Innovation Zone, a defined, well-supported, and broadly communicated innovation machine—with clearly defined analysis parameters featuring predetermined quantitative and qualitative measurement points—can allow firms to reward for new services that increase their value or competitive advantage. A formally managed new service development function can also make incentives and rewards more easily observable, comprehensible, and internally desirable.

There is a fourth reason why professional service firms may be less than assertive in their encouragement of innovation. It's called inertia, and it comes in many insidious forms. Over the years, I've heard numerous versions of the following composite remarks:

- "I'm not convinced we have to develop a separate scheme to reward our people to innovate! Our promotion and profit-sharing program has served us well; there's no need to screw it up."
- "Change our compensation structure to foster innovation? That will never happen here; the partners couldn't agree on it."
- "It would simply 'cost' us too much [time, effort, money, whatever] to ramp up on this type of initiative. And I doubt this effort could deliver the kind of immediate ROI we'd need to see."

"People are afraid that they will lose something that's worthwhile," said Ronald Heifetz, founding director of the Center for Public Leadership at Harvard University's John F. Kennedy School of Government, in a 1999 *Fast Company* magazine article.[38] Unfortunately, at some firms, there may be an additional—and unflattering—subtext to their resistance to programmatic innovation: providing incentives and rewards, especially if they are structured to require a long-term innovation investment with a long-term ROI, means taking money out of the pockets of those who have it now. In the same *Fast Company* article, Heifetz continued, "They're afraid that they're going to have to give up something that they're comfortable with."[39]

It remains to be seen whether professional service firm leaders will heed the call to take bold new steps. Providing incentives and rewards for innovation *will* require them to encounter resistance from their colleagues; it will require their energy, professional passion, and commitment to overcome the inertia that contemplating change inevitably produces. Heifetz asserted that a leader's new role is "to help people face reality and to mobilize them to make change."[40] For the professional service marketplace, change is already underway and the competitive landscape is being altered radically. A firm's survival will require the commitment to pursue service innovation, the leadership to create a distinct internal structure for it to thrive, and the rewards to bring it to fruition and sustain it.

As they establish any of the competencies in the embedding-innovation building block, professional service firms will be required to acknowledge a critical marketplace dynamic: The moment a firm offers its services, the marketplace's "clock" begins to tick away on their eventual demise. The firm promotes its services, clients consume them, and competitors copy them. Add in a few other "events" like technology and globalization. Inevitably and irrevocably, these actions will substantially alter the marketplace in which those services must survive. The consequences of ignoring these marketplace dynamics are grave. In order to thrive, professional service firms will have to pursue innovation, and they will have to do so with a deeper acceptance of, and real passion for, the market's fluidity and economic conditions. They will have to be fervent about stoking up and steering their firm's internal intellectual engines. Think about it. If a professional service firm genuinely applies a set of processes to embed innovation, the result could be the most intellectually stimulating moment any professional could ever hope for: witnessing the enthusiastic consumption by a client of a newly created solution that was built on a shrewd anticipation of the emerging direction of the marketplace.

We have reviewed the evolving competitive landscape for professional service firms. Increasingly discerning clients, new technologies, globalization, and more create an environment that undoubtedly will increase the pace of competition. The research findings we have just reviewed illustrate that they are taking steps to develop new approaches to their marketplace but, in all likelihood, without a broad and genuinely strategic marketplace framework to guide their efforts. With a market-driven infrastructure that is built on the competencies of looking out, digging deeper, and embedding innovation, professional service firms can more adroitly address the shifting business environment and increase their chances of business success. Small steps and great gains amount to marketplace mastery.

Part II

Portraits of Marketplace Masters

Let us turn now to case studies—accounts of real professional service organizations that are well on their way to becoming masters of their marketplace by applying the competencies within the three building blocks of looking out, digging deeper, or embedding innovation. These case studies do not present *exact* portrayals of the research findings; rather, they are intended to serve as effective illustrations of the way the eleven competencies are being applied.

Case Studies: Looking Out

Four firms are featured in this chapter, all examples of how professional service enterprises can use the looking out competencies as a starting point to master their marketplace. The first two cases explore two types of client research, qualitative and quantitative. The final two cases illustrate broader marketplace research: economic forecasting and trend analyses, and competitive intelligence.

STUDYING A FIRM'S CLIENTS USING QUALITATIVE AND QUANTITATIVE RESEARCH

Winstead Sechrest & Minick P.C.

Many legal marketing professionals believe that law firms are hopelessly behind the curve in their embrace of modern marketing strategies and tactics. Winstead Sechrest & Minick P.C., one of the largest law firms in the southwestern United States, offers a great example of a firm that used forward-thinking qualitative and quantitative research to study its clients. This case shows how one law firm employed the kind of successful research and marketing strategies that corporations have used for years to reveal buyers' underlying motivators and value-based purchase criteria. From a seemingly simple mandate to build a new Web site, the Winstead management team had the foresight to implement sophisticated research techniques to significantly improve its understanding of clients' motivations and needs.

But Winstead's story is remarkable because of its coordinated use of these techniques to build a brand image that appeals to both its clients and its own professionals. It is remarkable also because it created a Web site that helps Winstead professionals truly deliver on their brand promise, with visible and behind-the-scenes capabilities to serve those targeted buyers in increasingly effective ways. This is what successful competitive strategy looks like—in action.

The Winstead Story: Context and Background. "Let's build a Web site." By now, most professional service firms (even the smallest ones, regardless of professional sector) have built a Web site. Some of these sites look like a graphic designer's dream, with gorgeous visuals, nifty color schemes, and flashy buttons. These sites, however, were probably not developed from research about what real clients and prospects find useful or respond to with action.

The attorneys at Winstead Sechrest & Minick had in mind a much more competitively savvy strategy when they redesigned the firm's Web site in 2001. Those simple words—"Let's build a Web site"—set in motion the development of a well-targeted creative strategy that was made possible by a qualitative research initiative that used cutting-edge interviewing techniques and analysis.

From its 1973 beginning, Winstead Sechrest & Minick enjoyed a solid reputation and steady growth. From its start as a three-attorney boutique, it grew to 20 attorneys in multiple offices in major Texas cities and to recent office openings in Mexico City and Washington, D.C. It now comprises more than 340 attorneys and 400 professionals. Its premier practices in real estate, real estate finance, and banking are augmented by a host of other business-oriented practices, including, but not limited to, business restructuring and bankruptcy, corporate law, litigation, securities and taxation, labor and employment, technology and intellectual property, and wealth preservation.[1]

The Winstead management team knew that the firm's competitors had Web sites, and good ones. They knew that rival law firms were touting capabilities in the very same areas in which Winstead had long held sway. They knew that the stakes for communicating effectively to their marketplace are growing each day. As they began their planning to develop the Web site in 2001, then, they appreciated the importance of gaining strategic perspectives about their clients. They knew that they would have to craft the Web site's text and imagery to communicate effectively about Winstead's uniquely valuable differences.

Until then, though, Winstead, like many professional service firms, had relied on the perceptions of its client-facing practitioners (in this case, the attorneys) about how its clients had decided to engage the firm, what they considered to be its strengths and weaknesses, or how they perceived that it differed in any favorable way from other law firms. The Winstead management team wanted to determine if the attorneys' perceptions did, in fact, match the clients' perceptions.

Conducting an Internal Client Analysis. Winstead's then chief marketing officer, Kathleen Yeaton, began the project by building a profile of the firm's client base. Looking at the firm's top one hundred clients, she reviewed:

- Revenues for each year over the past three years, watching for changes from one year to the next
- Repeatability and turnover (Which clients came back year after year and which ones did not?)
- Each of the top one hundred clients' Web sites (In what industries did these clients do business?)
- Corporate organizational structure, business locations, contact information, officers and the kind of company (public or private)
- The business background of each client (their rankings and reputation within their industries and business in general, their intended plans, legislative impacts, presence in geographical areas in which Winstead had a presence)
- The Winstead background with each client (the date Winstead began working for the client, the client's annual billings with the firm, the Winstead contact and his or her location within Winstead offices, other attorneys that worked with that client, the client contact and contact address, and the like)
- The primary work, by service offering (for example, real estate), that Winstead did with the client, and the matter (corporate real estate transactions, for example)
- The percentage of total revenues that the client represented for Winstead (for example, "If our service portfolio is 100 percent, this client uses of 32 percent of it")

This activity allowed Winstead to get a clear, overarching view of who its clients were demographically. Mike Baggett, Winstead's chairman and chief executive officer (CEO), explained further: "We've made a public promise to our clients: 'we promise to know you, your industry, your company and your objectives.' Since we were founded, we have defined our success by our ability to impact the success of our clients. This kind of formal fact gathering helps us help our clients take their business to the next level."

Implementing External Qualitative Research. Market research experts tell us that qualitative research is invaluable for uncovering nuances and emerging opinions and for revealing complex relationships between issues or perceptions. Winstead decided to convene a series of focus groups and individual interviews to capture qualitative information about the way its clients generally became aware of, and subsequently made decisions about, engaging a law firm. The focus groups were openly sponsored by Winstead, but the interviewees understood that they were not going to discuss their impressions of Winstead specifically.

Completed in just over one month's time, the interviews began by seeking the following, fairly factual, information:

- How many law firms have you dealt with?
- How did your law firm relationships begin? (That is, what were the circumstances that triggered these relationships?)
- Do you conduct reviews ("beauty contests") of law firms (like many companies do with their advertising agencies or financial service firms)? If so, what prompted that review? Was there a review process? What were the steps in that review process? How formal is the process? In this process, who were the decision makers?
- How did you first find out about the law firms that you eventually engaged?
- Have you ever used a Web site for a law firm, or have you accessed other professional service firm Web sites, like a management consulting or accounting firm, for example? On what occasions, for what information, and why?
- How might you use a law firm Web site, even if this involves new applications (for example, billing online, tracking your transactions online, checking your lawyers' schedule, etc.)?
- Under what circumstances would you fire or eliminate a law firm?
- What is the size of your legal budget? How does this budget break down in terms of the type of law? What percent of that total budget does each of your law firms have?

Taking a Research Lesson from the Products and Packaged-Goods World. The answers to these questions revealed valuable information that Winstead staff knew they could use in all its branding and communication strategies, including its Web site development. Nevertheless, that information, by itself, leads to fairly shallow insights. Yeaton recommended using the focus groups and interviews to look beyond these comments, to learn about what would motivate these clients to hire a particular law firm. The goal was to reveal clients' deeper, actionable insights. She employed three techniques: (1) a projective interviewing method, (2) an iterative interviewing approach called laddering, and (3) a hierarchical value map. "These qualitative research techniques are as yet under-utilized in the professional service world but are well-known in products and packaged-goods arenas," Yeaton commented. "They are designed to help reveal purchasers' underlying psychological end-states. These end-states or beliefs are particularly relevant when clients make decisions to purchase complex intangible services like finance and law."

1. *Using a projective interviewing technique.* A series of internal interviews with Winstead attorneys was conducted. The goal was to set a baseline: to understand how the attorneys perceived their own firm. "Some of the things we wanted them to articulate were the personality of the firm, and why they thought their clients chose Winstead. These are critical elements of a creative strategy brief," Yeaton recollected. "We asked, 'If Winstead could be a famous personality, who would it be? What could it be in the future? If Winstead were a car, what kind of auto is it, and what could it be in the future?' There was a good degree of commonality to the answers, which helped us eventually to shape a brand message that effectively dovetailed with how the clients perceived the firm."

2. *Using a laddering interviewing technique.* For the firm's external research, focus group and individual interviewees were asked to describe the characteristics they look for in a law firm. In this phase, Yeaton used a laddering interviewing technique to probe the links between their values and the attributes of their preferred law firms. She started by eliciting the attributes that interviewees sought or avoided when soliciting an attorney or law firm. She also asked about the attributes that interviewees perceived were unique to Winstead. Next, she asked why those attributes were important (that is, the consequences of choosing those attributes). Her questioning continued—like going up a "ladder"—until the interviewees' underlying desired values or end states were identified.

3. *Creating a hierarchical value map.* From the feedback obtained in the focus groups and interviews, Yeaton created a series of hierarchical value maps (also known as benefit chains) to illustrate the relationships or links that were identified. From this graphic illustration, Winstead could visualize why its clients took certain steps toward what they perceived would be favorable consequences and why they avoided a certain set of undesired consequences. The theory, first applied in marketing in the 1950s by the

founder of motivational research, Ernest Dichter, postulates that both tangible (physical) and intangible (psychological) characteristics influence purchase behavior. The theory posits that the link between attributes of a product or service and the clients' (or consumers') social or intangible needs or values is a predictor of purchase choice.[2]

Research Reveals Common Psychological Links. Winstead's use of projective interviewing, laddering, and hierarchical value maps helped it gain a crucial understanding of its clients and their reasons for choosing a law firm, and Winstead in particular. These techniques also revealed the common areas where the desirable end-states of two seemingly disparate sets of clients were similar. Senior-level clients—those on the "fast track," facing high risks and high rewards and shouldering tremendous responsibilities—needed to feel a sense of control and authority, even though they looked to their attorneys to give them insight and to steer them in the right direction. Middle management clients, however, preferred a more team-oriented role. They enjoyed helping others in the limelight; they felt a sense of purpose and satisfaction in actively helping their company to move forward.

As pleased as Winstead's leaders were that they had uncovered a common psychological link between targeted client groups, however, they knew their analysis would not be done until they found a link to the perceptions of their own attorneys. Baggett recalled, "Our firm was founded in 1973 with a mission to empower its business clients by seeking creative solutions to their business challenges. It was critical that our attorneys' desired self-perceptions were reflected in the way we communicated about our firm."

The Results. The answer lay in matching up the findings from the internal interviews with the hierarchical value map from the external interviews. They found a message and a brand image that worked for all of these targeted audiences.

"The motif that resonated with all our audiences was a sailboat navigating through tough waters," said Mike Baggett. "In the photograph we chose for the home page, the members of the sailing team illustrate the crucial and discreet roles that our attorneys and our clients play for each other." The firm also trademarked a positioning phrase—Seize the power—and prominently featured verbiage throughout the site that underscored the visual image from the sailboat photograph. "By doing what we do best—practicing law—we empower our clients to do what they do best. Winstead attorneys and counselors will provision your crew with the momentum and direction to make your dreams a reality. Seize the power of Winstead and together we'll chart a course for success—no matter which way the wind blows."[3] (See Figure 5.1.)

Winstead's qualitative research brought about three notable results:

1. From its sophisticated and highly analytical research effort, Winstead was able to create a notable Web site that features astutely crafted messages and images that effectively communicate the firm's brand promise to its primary and secondary targets. In fact, the new Web site won the 2002 Platinum Internet Marketing Award for excellence in areas such as design, content, usability, and interactivity (and a gold award from the same organization in 2003). Using the research findings and the creative strategy brief, those graphic designers and computer programmers did wonderful work.

Figure 5.1. Part of the Winstead Sechrest & Minick P.C. Homepage, June 2003

2. From its queries to clients about their preferences for the type of information they seek and the usability they expect from their law firm's Web site, Winstead learned that it had new opportunities to serve its clients. For example, it learned the circumstances under which clients would like anonymity when accessing their law firm's Web site. It also learned what aspects of its services clients would like to have shared with their own outside team members (as an extranet with the clients' ancillary audiences) and what they would pay for this offering.

3. From the information gathered from its internal research, Winstead was able to develop its Web site to have behind-the-scenes capabilities that quickly support attorneys who are engaging in marketing or business development activities. Brochures, biographies, and proposals—all updated at once on the Web site—can be instantly generated. This feature gives Winstead the ability to respond more effectively to client needs.

QRST Associates

This case study is an illustration of how a firm can effectively learn about clients and potential clients with quantitative and qualitative research. It features a venerable global professional service firm that I am obliged to "cloak," using the pseudonym QRST Associates. The case involves pricing research, and it's a "no guts, no glory" tale. The story is impressive for two reasons.

First, QRST conducted research *seriously*. Too many firms do superficial research, implementing incomplete or overly casual efforts, on which they make significant strategic decisions. QRST's example is powerful because the firm had the perserverance to get substantive marketplace information. Practice leaders of other professional service firms will be pleased to learn that QRST's research helped it go far beyond offering a service that would merely satisfy its clients. Its embrace of a rigorous, phased project of qualitative and quantitative research helped it eventually offer its clients significant value: an optimum set of service attributes, the most equitable brand qualities that they had come to expect from QRST Associates, and at a most advantageous price. Everyone's notion of value was met. This could not have been done without a willingness to conduct substantive research.

Second, the firm successfully overcame the potential derailment of the research project (professionals' queasiness about having an outsider involved in client interactions) with rational communication about the reasons for having an objective observer attend client meetings. By overcoming this obstacle in order to exploit an outsider's perceptive, its research findings ended up being much more potent and competitively preemptive.

The QRST Story: Context and Background. The science of pricing has long been a murky abyss for most professional service firms. Even as we begin the new millennium, the majority of professional firms still largely determine their prices from a products-oriented time and expense model. Unfortunately for these professionals, clients, as they encounter an ever-expanding array of service providers, have found it increasingly easy to compare one firm's prices to another's. Profit margins, already challenged (especially on commoditized services), threaten to erode further.

In response to this conundrum, some firms have stopped overtly expressing their prices as based on a time and expense model.[4] Yet in one form or another, most still rely on it heavily. Other firms believe they can stoke their clients' positive perceptions by rolling out highly creative branding campaigns or exerting massive effort in the pursuit of the engagement, yet these endeavors still leave too many professional service firms on the short end of the straw in a pricing contest with their rivals. Too many firms still find themselves undervalued, anxious about needing to change the formula but unsure about how to do it. In fact, clients seek value pricing from their professionals. Marketing research guru William D. Neal succinctly framed this notion in his 1998 article "Satisfaction Be Damned." Neal stated, "Buyers who are considering a purchase in a particular product or service category scan their product/service options and develop a consideration set. Within the consideration set, they develop a hierarchy of products based on their assessment of value. They then choose the product at the top of their value hierarchy, if available." Neal went on to explain how value can be measured through the elements of price, product or service deliverables, and brand equity.[5]

Simply put, Neal and a host of pricing experts tell us, the optimal pricing of a product or service can be developed from an assessment of the clients' perception of its value.[6] Arguably, developing the price for a static, well-known, and probably commoditized service is harder to do than for an innovated service. However, innovators must beware: the pricing of new services must be considered as carefully as their very creation. QRST Associates not only innovated an element of its service portfolio, but also figured out how to break out of a time-and-expense pricing mindset for this service. It did so by employing both qualitative and quantitative research techniques.

In the early 1990s, QRST had conceived a new professional method that could complement its core service offerings in one of the firm's global practices. QRST's management wanted to understand what types of clients, if any, would be interested in using the new method. The practice's partner in charge remembered, "We wondered if this method could offer any benefits for our clients or prospects. If so, what would be the demographics of the target audience that would buy it? And how would we price it?"

Working with Kathleen Yeaton of Dallas-based Marketing & Research Partners, QRST Associates embarked on a two-pronged research effort that featured qualitative methods and a powerful quantitative technique called dynamic price sensitivity modeling.

Qualitative Research to Assess the New Service's Attractiveness. In order to determine who the target clients could be, and what they perceived would be the benefits of the method, Yeaton conducted a series of exploratory focus groups. Then, during a six-week period, she accompanied a number of QRST's partners as they made presentations to clients to describe the new service. After the observation, Yeaton contacted the clients to ask a series of follow-up questions. The follow-up conversation included their general reactions to the new method; their descriptions of the qualities of the method that they liked or disliked; and when and under what circumstances they might use it. This initial concept research helped further define the target audience, revealed that they *were* significantly interested in the service, and helped refine key messages about the method's attributes.

Quantitative Assessment of Pricing Scenarios. Once the target audience and occasion for use were identified, the firm still needed to know how to price the service. To determine the optimal price range, Marketing & Research Partners and QRST's practice leader decided to use the dynamic price sensitivity model. This research technique is based on a statistical model developed in 1976 by Peter van Westendorp, a Dutch economist. Van Westendorp developed a set of four simple questions designed to identify a product's or service's optimal price points.[7] The technique assesses a respondent's perception of the relationship of quality to price.

In this phase, QRST used a five-step quantitative research and analysis process directed to the proposed service's targeted buyers, CEOs, and chief operating officers (COOs):

1. *Asking four questions:* (a) At what price would this service be so expensive that you would not consider purchasing it? (b) At what price would the service be expensive, but you would still consider purchasing it? (c) At what price does the service become inexpensive? (d) At what price does the service become so inexpensive that you would question its value or quality?

2. *Mapping the indifference price:* The answers to the first and third questions intersected at what van Westendorp called the indifference price (the price at which the "maximum number of respondents are indifferent"). Yeaton mapped a visualization of this point (see Figure 5.2).

3. *Graphing the optimum pricing point:* Yeaton graphed the cumulative distribution of answers to the second and fourth questions, which intersected at the optimum price point (the price at which an equal number of respondents saw the service as "too cheap" and "too expensive") (see Figure 5.3).

4. *Visualizing the stress points:* The data were then combined into a graphical representation of the pricing stress points (see Figure 5.4).

5. *Mapping the range of acceptable pricing:* Finally, Yeaton mapped the range of acceptable pricing. "Experience has shown that pricing outside this range will generate little new business," she said (see Figure 5.5).[8]

This quantitative approach allowed QRST to value price the service well above an hourly-fee pricing approach and also meet the prospects' demand for value pricing. The pricing study also confirmed that clients who were interested in using QRST's method to evaluate a particular

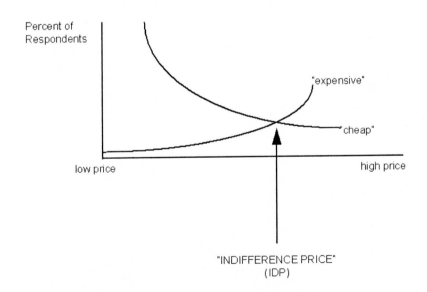

Figure 5.2 The "Indifference Price" Map

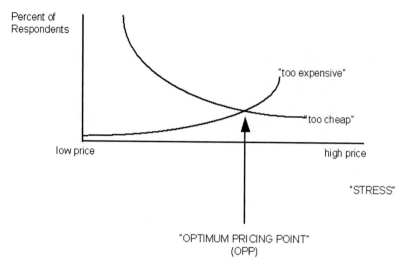

Figure 5.3 The "Optimum Pricing Point" Map

opportunity were more likely to pay higher fees and to use the method than those clients not considering the same opportunity.

The Challenge of Being Watched. QRST Associates and Yeaton had to overcome a critical obstacle in the early qualitative stage of this research project: having Yeaton observe the QRST partner interacting with cli-

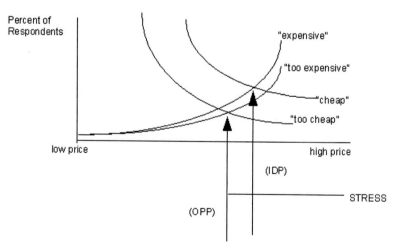

Figure 5.4 The "Price Stress Point" Map

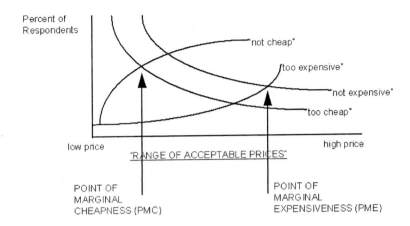

Figure 5.5 The "Range of Acceptable Prices" Map

ents in the introductory presentation about the proposed service. Understandably, the partners felt uncomfortable being watched. For what reason exactly, they wondered, was a market researcher there? Partners weren't the only ones who experienced some level of discomfort at first. The clients themselves needed an acceptable explanation about why a market researcher was attending the presentations.

QRST's practice leader called for QRST to explain to its professionals that they weren't being measured, just observed by a trained, impartial market research professional. He stressed to his colleagues that QRST was simply trying to get a valid, unbiased interpretation of the clients' attraction to or avoidance of certain aspects of the proposed service. He and Yeaton coached the firm's partners on the optimum way to introduce the presence of a researcher at the meetings. It is interesting that once he was able to provide a reasonable explanation of the appropriateness of this step, both partners and potential clients welcomed the approach. Once the potential clients had met Yeaton and had established a sense of rapport and trust, they were more willing to participate —candidly—in the follow-up interviews.

The Results. QRST's research effort resulted in the successful introduction of a new service with a price point that equaled its clients' value perceptions *and* simultaneously allowed the firm to realize a much higher profit than it could have with a standard hourly billing approach. This initiative also paved the way for new processes for developing new services within the firm.

RESEARCHING THE MARKET USING ECONOMIC FORECASTS AND TREND ANALYSES

YaYa Media Inc.

The YaYa Media case study illustrates the second competency of firms that excel at looking out. Some readers may wave their hand at this case, dismissing it as too technology focused, or perhaps not relevant to their venerable professions. However, many professional service firms have yet to give trends analysis and forecasting the credence that they deserve. Too many professionals believe they already *know* the trends in their profession. They may believe that their own educated guesses about the future are more than adequate. Also, especially if they have increased their efforts in researching clients, they may believe they have more facts than ever to help them make strategic decisions. But conducting client research—by itself—may not be enough. It can be compared to flying at 6,000 feet; trends analysis and forecasting are more like flying at 41,000 feet. This is the kind of looking out that can give a professional service firm a perspective that client research projects cannot provide.

Alternately, if professionals conduct competitive intelligence they may believe that this information is illuminating enough. Yes, competitive intelligence is increasingly critical, but competitive intelligence is not the same as understanding and mining trends in the economy and business or observing broader marketplace shifts. Competitive intelligence is not the same as exploring forecasts of future potential threats or opportunities.

YaYa's case is intriguing because it revealed how a group of regular folks could brainstorm their way beyond the edges of a traditional professional service field, in this case, advertising. Like the field of advertising, many professions are brushing up against commoditization. Ad agencies could take steps like YaYa did—to consider trends and to forecast opportunities by examining a blend of hard facts and softer, yet equally illuminating, commentary. You never know—there might be an entirely new professional service category waiting to be born.

The YaYa Media Story: Context and Background. The newly appointed managing partner of a midsized law firm was pleased. He had just finished leading his first annual strategic planning review for the firm. For the most part, it was a successful showcase of his capabilities in consensus building. His colleagues were enthusiastic about the firm's new initiatives. Revenues were not spectacular, but they appeared to be steady, and the stable of clients appeared to be mostly satisfied. He felt good that his firm was headed generally in the right direction.

Nevertheless, a niggling voice of doubt persisted in his ear. "How much do you *really* know about the marketplace changes ahead, for the legal industry and for your clients' industries?" "How confident are you *really* that your new initiatives will succeed?" He realized he was not at all confident that his firm was headed generally in the right direction. He wished he could stop worrying.

Whistling in the Dark. The manager was right to worry. Many professional service firms, even those that conduct research on their clients and prospects, give short shrift to examining the wider arena in which they work—their business, economic, and market environment. Mostly, they rely on an overly anecdotal and too fragmented system of internal information sharing about the past shifts or future opportunities in their marketplace. This "whistling in the dark" approach is pervasive across professional service sectors, firm sizes, and lengths of tenure in the marketplace. It is underway right now in firms that are happily conducting general strategic planning exercises and excitedly rolling out new initiatives.

The example of YaYa Media will serve to illustrate how to avoid this myopia. In order to launch this new organization and develop its flagship services, its founders researched the firm's market using economic forecasts and trend analyses. Their goal was simple: make the case to create a new business from a germ of an idea hatched by a few individuals, make the case to develop a new and unique set of services, make the case for the growth of a market segment, or make the case for not bothering to do any of it.

Los Angeles–based YaYa Media Inc. is an online interactive gaming company. It was formed in spring 2000 to provide services at the intersection of the gaming, entertainment, and advertising industries. In its development of Internet games for Fortune 500 advertisers, YaYa Media pioneered a completely new category: *advergames*. Its early roster of clients included such household names as DaimlerChrysler, Siemens, Honda, Burger King, PepsiCo, and IBM, and its early steps were covered extensively by the likes of *Forbes, Fast Company, Advertising Age, American Demographics*, the *Wall Street Journal, Business 2.0, Brandweek*, the *New York Times* and *USA Today*.[9]

Putting On a Game Face. In the late 1990s YaYa cofounders Knowledge Universe and Sandy Climan of Entertainment Media Ventures LLC began brainstorming about forming and investing in a company that could take advantage of emerging opportunities in technology and media. They were particularly interested in exploring the nexus of two seemingly disparate segments: the computer games industry and the business-to-business sector.

The computer games industry, they knew, had experienced phenomenal growth. The market capitalizations of industry leaders like Activision and Electronic Arts were huge. The business-to-business sector was solid too. They wondered, "What kind of an opportunity could be forged where one could apply games in a business-to-business environment?" They wanted to avoid creating a traditional entertainment entity ("Let's *not* make it just like the movie business"), and they wanted to avoid the hits-driven Internet arena ("Let's *not* make it a simplistic, clicks-tracking business)." However, they *did* want to build a company that could tap the availability of greater bandwidth and increasingly rich media, maximize the use of enabling technology and next-generation infrastructure, and hasten the evolution of broadband communications and entertainment.

They tapped Keith Ferrazzi, who came on-board as a YaYa advisor (and became its chief executive officer), to conduct a formal exploration of market opportunities. They needed hard facts about the economic, demographic, and industry trends and forecasts for any arena that touched the areas of broadband communications, the business-to-business sector, and games.

Ferrazzi had just concluded two successful stints as chief marketing officer, for Starwood Hotels and Deloitte Consulting. In both roles, he had become well known for pushing the marketing envelope. He had developed new businesses, new turf, new revenue streams, new clientele, new brands. The goal was to push the envelope here, too. What if games could be used to help businesses build brands and relationships? It was time to build the case.

Trend Analyses of Current and Past Business and Economic Events. Trends are started by things that have already happened. Rooted in the past and seen happening *now*, trends push consumers toward their future purchasing choices. Trends can be seen as predictors of near- or longer-term behavior. YaYa initiated an intensive examination of trends in three initial areas: (1) computer and online or interactive gaming, (2) the business of branding, and (3) customer relationship management technologies.

A simple step was to collect as much relevant secondary data as could be found. The YaYa team tapped well-known technology research sources like Forrester Research, Jupitermedia, Peter D. Hart Research Associates, and ACNielsen; industry associations like the European Leisure Software Publishers Association and the Interactive Digital Software Association (IDSA); and publications like *Advertising Age*, the *Wall Street Journal*, and the *Christian Science Monitor*.

1. *Online or interactive and general gaming trends:* YaYa wanted to know about three things: the economics of the online or interactive

gaming industry and the computer game industry in general; the demographics of the customer base; and data about their usage of games. Ferrazzi found "the growth rate for gaming . . . simply astounding."[10] Here are some of the data points the YaYa team found (all currencies are in U.S. dollars):[11]

a. Economics:

    i.   A full 35 percent of players on the top ten games sites earn $50,000 to $100,000 annually, while 16 percent take home more than $100,000 (comScoreNetworks, 2002).

    ii.   Sales of videogame hardware, software, and accessories increased 43 percent in 2001, to a record $9.4 billion. The movie industry (which also had a record year), generated box-office receipts of only $8.35 billion (NPD Group, 2002).

    iii.   In 2000, overall demand for computer and video games in the United States generated employment for 219,600 people; wages of $7.2 billion; federal and state personal income tax revenues of $1.7 billion; and a $10.5 billion market for game software publishing, wholesaling, and retailing, as well as transporting, wholesaling, and retailing of some, but by no means all, complementary game hardware (Interactive Digital Software Association, 2001).

b. Usage:

    i.   The number of monthly online game players increased 43 percent in the past year, with a 92 percent increase in total gaming minutes. In July of 1999, it was estimated, online gamers spent 250 million monthly minutes online; in only three years, this number grew to 5.7 billion (*Electronic Arts*, 2002).

    ii.   During peak hours (6 P.M.–9 P.M.) about 100,000 people worldwide are playing Yahoo Games alone (IDC).*

    iii.   About three times as many Americans (60 percent of all Americans ages six and older, or about 145 million people) played computer and video games in 2000 as went to the top five U.S. amusement parks in 1999 (56.1 million). In addition, about twice as many played computer and video games as attended Major League baseball games in 1999 (70 million; Interactive Digital Software Association, 2001).

    iv.   Games have gone Hollywood; there may be no better illustration than the *Hollywood Reporter*'s decision to begin

---

*In-text reference citations in this section are in the YaYa "Value of Games" document of 2002.

full-scale coverage of the industry in 2001 (*Philadelphia Inquirer*, 5/19/02).

v.   Games are the fastest-growing segment of online entertainment (Jupitermedia Metrix).

vi. Online gamers play games an average of 13 hours per week, which is more than people spend reading newspapers or magazines and about the same as TV watchers.[12]

c. Demographics (by Age and Gender)

i.   More than one-third of online gamers are between the ages of 35 and 49. The average age of a game player is 28 years old; a decade ago, the average age of a game player was 18 (Jupitermedia Metrix).

ii. 90 percent of all games are purchased by adults over the age of 18 (Interactive Digital Software Association, 2001).

iii. Gaming is most popular in the 25–34-year-old range (European Leisure Software Publishers Association).

iv. A full 32 percent of Americans who play computer and video games are age 35 or older, with a remarkable 13 percent age 50 or over (Peter D. Hart Research Associates, 2000).

v.   Close to half (41 percent) of people who frequent online game sites are women and 43 percent are ages 25 to 49 (Nielsen//NetRatings 2002).

vi. Women ages 24–49 and older are the fastest growing online audience (*Advertising Age*, 5/28/02).

vii. Demonstrating a swift increase in female gamers, the *Christian Science Monitor* reports that more than 60 percent of those who have played videogames for less than a year are women (*Christian Science Monitor*, 6/10/02).

viii. More than half (55) percent of computer game buyers are women (Interactive Digital Software Association).

YaYa also tapped game research being conducted by the University of Wisconsin, which found that when people played computer games, the retention rate was ten times higher than the retention of information in a movie. People (children and adults) remembered content better when they were *engaged* in it. This news had implications for another of YaYa's service offerings: training and education.

2. *Trends in the business of branding:* Trends can be identified from statistically significant data and researched facts, but they can also be discovered by simply talking to people with relevant perspectives. Ferrazzi, with his background in marketing, had his own

views about the potential of gaming and branding. Nevertheless, he sought to validate his assumptions by conducting an organized set of one-on-one meetings with CEOs and chief marketing officers (CMOs), advertising agency executives, potential competitors and users. He confirmed that:

a. "Advertising, a major revenue stream for traditional media companies, is undergoing a major scaleback, forcing companies to reinvent how they present themselves to their consumers. [There is a] current downturn in ad spending, which has been dropping precipitously since the tech bubble burst."[13]

b. Interest in technologies that challenge the basics of broadcast ads (TiVo) is on the rise: "consumers have heightened radar and cynicism for advertising, plus tools to filter out unwanted messages";[14] "it is ever harder for brands to break through the sensory clutter. New technologies like TiVo and ReplayTV hold the looming promise that turned-off consumers may someday have the choice to bypass commercials altogether."[15]

c. "Broadcast advertisers don't know how many consumers actually saw their ad or how many were in the kitchen getting a drink when it aired."[16]

d. Media outlets are highly fragmented.

e. Advertisers want to use games to market to their key targeted audiences: "analysts believe that about 5 percent of the average person's leisure time is spent playing video games in one form or another. The video game business now takes in $9.4 billion a year, $1 billion more than Hollywood movies collect at the box office. . . . Advertisers are well aware of this, and have made the decision that they want to be right alongside their customers as they're playing."[17]

3. *Trends in customer relationship management technologies:* "The big brand companies wanted to build relationships with customers on a one-to-one basis," said Ferrazzi. "They turned to customer relationship management solutions (CRM). They've spent a lot of money on CRM, mostly buying big technological systems." From his conversations, Ferrazzi confirmed what his YaYa teammates had suspected: CRM systems, built by information specialists and technologists, had brought marketers the capabilities to connect with customers. But their data sets remained largely empty. They coveted content, but they had not yet satisfactorily obtained it. Banner and pop-up ads on the Internet didn't give advertisers the customer information that they craved, like demographic information or the all-important information tracking through to a purchase. Advertisers were ripe for the idea of using games as an underlying database tool.

Economic Forecasts of Potential Future Business Scenarios. Forecasts are intelligent guesses about the future. Forecasting is not a new discipline. A number of professional service sectors already rely on their trade associations, industry watchdog groups, the government, or for-profit organizations to help them assess future business opportunities. For example, engineering and construction professionals can obtain U.S. national, regional, and sector-specific industry outlook reports from McGraw-Hill's Dodge division. For the management consulting sector, Kennedy Information Inc.'s Research Group publishes both global trend analyses and industry outlook reports by sector. Hunt-Scanlon's Market Intelligence Report is targeted to the global executive search landscape, and so on.

Once again, YaYa Media serves as a good example of forecasting beyond one's professional backyard. YaYa compiled data-driven forecasts from many of the same secondary sources from which it found trends.[18]

- Revenue from online gaming will increase from $670 million in 2002 to $2.9 billion in 2005 (Datamonitor, 2002).
- Revenue from subscription and advertising on sites such as Microsoft's Zone.com, which has 29 million registered users, is projected to grow to more than $1 billion by 2006 (Interactive Digital Software Association, May 2002).
- By 2004, marketers will spend $61 billion on interactive projects (Jupiter Media Metrix).
- As brands and companies embrace the entertainment platform for its marketing value, online gaming will continue to grow exponentially (Forrester Research, 2002).
- The U.S. video game market will grow to $29 billion by 2005 (Forrester, 2002).
- By 2005, the online gaming audience will rise to 80 million, from 58 million today (IDC, 2002).
- 60 percent of gamers today expect to be playing games as much 10 years from now as they do today (Interactive Digital Software Association).
- 53 percent of all female gamers are likely to play games online, compared to 43 percent of all male gamers (Interactive Digital Software Association, 2001).

These data-driven forecasts are important, but so is prediction-oriented commentary from respected national publications like the *New York Times*, the *Wall Street Journal*, and *Newsweek*. YaYa founds quotes in all three:[19]

- "The growth isn't going to slow down anytime soon. . . . No site attracts and keeps users like a game site" (Billy Pidgeon, an analyst at research firm Jupitermedia Metrix, quoted in the *Wall Street Journal*, 3/26/02).

- "The time has come to take games seriously as an important new popular art shaping the aesthetic sensibility of the 21st century" (Professor Henry Jenkins, Director of MIT's Center for Comparative Media Studies, quoted in the *New York Times*, 10/14/00).
- "In the century to come, the medium producing the most dynamic, vital, and exciting new art will be ... video games. Games will be more entertaining than movies, more profitable than movies, and yes, more moving than movies. For where the moving image was cinema's bold new advantage over previous media, video games boast interactivity, an even better way to engage the emotions of the audience" (Seth Stevenson, *Newsweek*, as quoted in the IDSA "State of the Industry Report 2000–2001," p. 4, 2001).

The Results. Advergames are clearly a powerful phenomenon; the number of gamers is growing exponentially. From Ferrazzi's trend analyses and forecasting data, YaYa Media went on to be officially formed in spring 2000. From a start-up with two founding organizations, YaYa became a twenty-person company with more than US$8 million in revenue.[20] It was acquired by American Vantage Companies in April 2003.

With its unique integration of its proprietary database customization tool (Consumer Dialog Technology, an integrated application that tracks and measures consumer involvement and lets advertisers mine data to reach consumers more effectively), along with creative gaming scenarios and branding strategies, YaYa quickly emerged as the leading developer of advertiser-driven Internet games.[21] For example, a game that YaYa launched for Chrysler attracted more than 40,000 players in its first week, and the average age of these players was 45 years old. Another YaYa game launched for Kmart had even bigger numbers.

In addition to Consumer Dialog Technology it also developed proprietary technologies like Zoomlet™ (which enables viral e-mail campaigns that allow users to play the game and then e-mail it to friends to challenge them to play). YaYa's Zoomlet™ technology is already a winner, achieving "double digit click through rates and compounded viral growth reaching over 100%."[22]

Armed with confirmed knowledge about the trends that were shaping its customers' desires, and confident from the future predictions and the forecasts it had collected and generated, YaYa Media was able to hit the ground running with strongly attractive new services and a value-added technological infrastructure.

RESEARCHING COMPETITORS BY GATHERING COMPETITIVE INTELLIGENCE

Towers Perrin

This case, the final one in this section on firms that excel at looking out, illustrates a "best practice" approach to researching competitors by gathering competitive intelligence. Towers Perrin also gets the "Competitive Intelligence Award" for:

Not being like other big fish: The firm's story illustrates a key principle in the marketplace dynamics of professional services. Large firms—like Towers Perrin—are the big fish in the professional services ocean. Smaller fish—the boutiques—dart among them, often sporting attractive colors and patterns. All too often, these big fish fail to take seriously the competitive inroads being made by smaller, niche-oriented rivals. They lumber along, confident that their existence will be unaffected by these smaller pests or by other oceanic undercurrents that are forming. It is refreshing to see a larger firm that takes its marketplace seriously, instead of summarily ignoring the sea changes around it. This happens less often than one would assume. Also, it is laudable to watch a firm of any size make deliberate decisions about exactly how it wants to exist in the "ocean" with the many other large and small rivals that it encounters.

Not having marketplace myopia: Unrelated to the issue of a firm's size, but sometimes accompanying it, is the issue of marketplace myopia—the kind of myopia that is at the heart of competitive missteps like those presented at the beginning of this story. Towers Perrin was able to see the market's shift toward compensation methodologies like Economic Value Added (EVA). Even better, it chose to take a closer look to see exactly what was the marketplace's attraction to this and other branded compensation techniques.

Seeing competitive intelligence for what it is: Old traditions die hard. Even as they begin to embrace market research more broadly and deeply, and even if their research includes an examination of competitor activity, many professional service firms still shy away from saying they are conducting competitive intelligence. If so, they will miss the opportunity to truly name the most important aspect of the activity—intelligence. By helping themselves get smarter about their marketplace in relation to other providers, the firms that engage in real competitive intelligence are in a better position to know what their clients truly value and which firms are best equipped to deliver it.

Having the courage to not fall in love with a methodology: Too many professional service practitioners still cling to the romance of their craft. Too many firms listen harder to the passions of their partners than to the voice of the marketplace. For Towers Perrin, it was, for a time, its own Value-Based Management methodology. Being the author or the early proponents of a new methodology can be heady, but with the intelligence gained from its competitive assessment, Towers Perrin understood that making a good business decision ultimately benefits the clients more than being overly devoted to an intellectual pursuit.

Being a market-driven business whose mission is bigger than the sum of its practices or service lines.

The Towers Perrin Story: Context and Background. Increasingly, professional service firms are beginning to see competitor intelligence for what it can be: a business-appropriate, ethical, and focused analysis of information about competitor initiatives, relationships, marketplace perceptions, and the like. More firms are engaging in programmatic analyses of competitors as a way to shape their business and marketing strategies.

Top-tier management consulting firm Towers Perrin provides an excellent example of how a professional service firm researched its marketplace through a formal competitive intelligence-gathering initiative, and then incorporated its findings into a well-defined go-to-market strategy. With more than nine thousand employees in 78 offices worldwide, and at $1.5 billion in revenues, Towers Perrin is one of the world's largest management and human resource consulting firms, assisting its clients in managing people, performance, and risk. Founded in 1934, its clients include three-quarters of the world's 500 largest companies and three-quarters of the *Fortune* 1000 largest U.S. companies. On the human resource consulting side, the firm offers human resource (HR) strategy and service delivery, benefit and compensation design and implementation (including retirement, health and welfare, and executive compensation), employee and organizational communication, HR technology, and outsourced HR administration. Its Tillinghast–Towers Perrin division provides actuarial and management consulting to financial services companies worldwide, and its Towers Perrin reinsurance unit provides reinsurance intermediary services and consulting expertise that focus on the creative blending of traditional and nontraditional risk-transfer vehicles.[23]

Towers Perrin's executive compensation practice is consistently ranked as one of the largest in the world. The size of this practice is not simply happenstance; rather, it is the by-product of the firm's senior management commitment to leadership in compensation practices and methodologies. Being "the best" in executive compensation design—a field that exists between intense secrecy and intense attention—is a critical, ongoing Towers Perrin objective.

As expected, then, the firm took heed in the mid-1990s, when the technique known as EVA burst into the public arena. Coined by New York–based consulting firm Stern Stewart, EVA, strictly defined, is a metric representing a company's net operating profit after taxes, minus the cost of capital.[24]

Its introduction sparked an outpouring of public discourse. Journalists and pundits had a field day discussing their perceptions of its merits and shortcomings. Consulting industry observer *Consultants News* said: "Although widely thought of as a valuation technique, EVA is really an incentive compensation system for management. Its central idea is simple—and powerful: managers should be rewarded based on the actual profitability of their business unit relative to the economic cost of the assets under their control which generated the profitability."[25] Corporate strategy expert Gary Hamel was more critical; he questioned whether EVA was an adequate technique to measure a company's wealth creation.[26]

Towers Perrin had its own "subpractice" of highly sophisticated practitioners that focused on value-based executive compensation design: It was called Value-Based Management (VBM), and by 1997 it represented almost 10 percent of the executive compensation practice's revenues. The VBM practice was comprised of a group of about a dozen specialists that had formed themselves into a kind of SWAT team; their mission was to keep Towers Perrin at the leading edge of financially intense executive compensation design and to serve as a resource to colleagues working on financially sophisticated pay projects.

"Who Are Those Guys?" Devotees of the 1969 film classic *Butch Cassidy and the Sundance Kid* will remember one of the more memorable lines in the movie. Butch (Paul Newman) and Sundance (Robert Redford), while being chased throughout the western United States by a band of horse-riding lawmen led by a mysterious man in a white hat, repeatedly ask themselves "Who *are* those guys?" They grow more exasperated as the movie progresses. Eventually, "those guys" are responsible for the duo's demise.

In 1997, Gary Locke was the head of Towers Perrin's North American executive compensation practice and responsible for the development of its intellectual capital. He saw the hype about EVA as a signal from the marketplace, and he wanted to take advantage of the market's strong response. He had to find out who "those guys" were, what they were doing, and why. He had to find out who else knew "those guys" and what they thought of them. He needed to know how "those guys" could affect Towers Perrin's future.

Locke had other reasons to be on heightened alert about marketplace shifts: some of Towers Perrin's executive compensation consultants had left the practice to work at Stern Stewart. In addition, even though he believed EVA was simply the latest in a continuing line of new approaches claiming to have won "the metric war," he was concerned that Towers Perrin's clients were vulnerable to EVA's siren call. "We wanted to grow our practice," he recalled. "But in order to do that successfully, we had to get a handle on how the marketplace perceived EVA and other increasingly sophisticated measures as determinants of executive compensation. We had to understand more about the firms that provided these methodologies and their executive pay expertise."

He and the practice's leadership group agreed to conduct a competitive intelligence assignment for its executive compensation practice. A secondary purpose was to explore opportunities for new business. He prepared to carve out a piece of his practice's budget to begin such an engagement. Almost before he knew it, Locke was approached by his boss who told him the firm was going to make this initiative a "high-impact study." At Towers Perrin, this term had cultural significance. It meant that the firm's most senior managers believed an initiative represented significant strategic importance to the firm. For Locke, it also meant the project would be funded out of the corporate budget and not the practice's.

In 1997, Locke brought in Fuld & Company, a Boston-based competitive intelligence consulting firm, to conduct the research. The objectives of the assignment were:

- *Assess market maturity:* Determine the shelf life of branded executive compensation approaches like EVA and VBM. Where were these and other concepts in their marketplace life-cycle? Were they still gaining traction? Had they hit their peak? Were they dying? How did the marketplace react to a firm's claim to own the gold standard on a concept (the way Stern Stewart did with its registration of the trademark of EVA)?
- *Determine the role of outside executive compensation experts:* How much of this work was moving in-house? To what extent were clients going to continue to tap outside experts? Who might be the typical buyer for these services? What did these companies *really* want from their professional service providers: convenience, speed, knowledge transfer, or what else?
- *Evaluate Towers Perrin's competitive standing:* Who were the executive compensation professionals that clients deemed most capable of providing them with sophisticated and financially rigorous

executive compensation models? How did these clients perceive Towers Perrin vis-à-vis other executive compensation providers?

- *Listen to the voice of the client:* What were the "lessons learned" from those companies that had employed a value-based executive compensation model, whether it was a branded approach like EVA or their own in-house variation of the concept? How much time did it take to implement? What areas of the company were affected?
- *Make a "go/no go" decision:* Should Towers Perrin dive into the metrics battle and ramp up its investment in making the VBM team a full-fledged practice?

The Framework of a Competitive Intelligence Project. The research fell into two broad phases: preparation, followed by direct market contact. In the preparatory phase, Locke focused on building internal consensus and enthusiasm for the project. "The goal was to give the project a feeling of inclusiveness, and not exclusiveness," Locke said. Members of Towers Perrin's VBM team, as well as other executive compensation practitioners, agreed to join the project team.

Lenore Scanlon led the project for Fuld & Company. In the preparatory phase, Scanlon and her teammates collected the names of companies that were known to have used a value-based compensation approach. They gathered these names by accessing publicly available press releases and finding citations in published articles. They conducted word searches on publicly held companies' proxies for reference to EVA, ROI, or any other value-based technique. They gathered other secondary research on these techniques. Finally, they tapped Towers Perrin's own prospecting and client database.

The next step involved scripting an interview guide that would capture the information that Towers Perrin wanted to learn. "We spent a fair amount of time thinking about what we'd ask the sources," Scanlon recalled. "Normally, we would employ a much more conversational interviewing style. In this case, because we wanted input as a proxy for the market, we ended up developing a fairly scripted interview guide."

Scanlon and the Towers Perrin project team agreed that Fuld & Company would conduct one hundred interviews, evenly split between companies known or believed to have implemented EVA or another value-based measure and companies in the Fortune 1000 whose activities related to VBM were unknown. The functional purview of the sample covered a variety of areas—some in the financial side of a company, some in compensation, and some in human resources. The interviews lasted anywhere from 20–30 minutes to 1 hour. Towers Perrin was not mentioned as the source of the inquiry. "We noted it when there was unprompted mention of Towers Perrin," remembered Scanlon. "But we also had a formal section of the interview where we asked the interviewee's perception of eight specific firms." These firms were classified into four groups: HR or compensation consulting firms, strategy consulting firms, the Big Five accounting firms, and others (boutiques that specialized in value-based compensation consulting).

Each week Scanlon provided Locke and his team with a summary of the interviews and an update about progress on the research. They discussed whether to revise the interview guide, and in some cases did so, in order to capture the most viable competitive intelligence details. Fuld & Company also provided Towers Perrin with unexpurgated (not interpreted) interview findings.

Do Not Pursue a Branded Metric! The end result was a thirty-page document containing Fuld & Company's articulation of the thematic streams that it had uncovered. Two critical findings emerged. First, it was clear that the already crowded market for EVA and other metric-based methodologies was not expanding; companies had either implemented a program and thus considered the work done or had evaluated some form of VBM and decided not to implement. The second key finding was that Towers Perrin was perceived as a highly valued source of broad-based, unbiased, and nonbranded executive compensation design and counsel. "We concluded that the pursuit of a branded metric for executive compensation would *not* be a smart competitive move for Towers Perrin," Scanlon declared. "Specifically, we encouraged Towers Perrin to incorporate its elite VBM SWAT team back into its main executive compensation practice—to let VBM be one of the many arrows in its quiver."

"The competitive intelligence research helped us see that, over the long haul, our clients preferred us to continue to excel in *all* of the latest thinking on executive compensation, to be sophisticated enough to develop our own new concepts but also to grasp all of the other new and equally viable methodologies, and to recommend to them the best approach for their circumstances," confirmed Locke. "Essentially, the marketplace told us not to become narrowly focused on only one concept." Locke, the project team, and most of their Towers Perrin colleagues were gratified to hear Fuld & Company's recommendations. They had watched management consulting fads come and go. The story line was familiar: a subset of clients would be seduced by the siren song of the newest panacea; soon, many would sour. For Towers Perrin, it was best to let the boutiques sing their one-note songs. They concluded that Towers Perrin *would not* invest any more deeply in a branded value-based executive compensation model—this was like putting too many of its eggs in one methodological basket. More appropriately, it would play in an executive compensation marketplace where it could achieve its global growth goals. It would brand itself as a true executive compensation consultancy, not as pitchmen of a productized service.

The Results. These conclusions meant that Locke had to take two critical steps:

- Integrate his team of twelve VBM specialists back into the firm's overall executive compensation practice. This would be a challenge, since they had enjoyed their focus on value-based management work; they had hoped that the firm's competitive intelligence research would lead to a decision to grow their part of the practice into more prominence. Ultimately, Locke employed a mixture of diplomatic finesse and unabashed personal respect for his partners. In 1998, at a partner conference, he announced the full integration of VBM back into the practice.
- Raise the bar (dramatically) on Towers Perrin's grasp of the latest executive compensation thinking that could be learned. "Our folks have never wavered from wanting to be the best practitioners working for the best consultancy; we all welcomed the challenge to raise the caliber of our financial acumen," reported Locke. "We embarked on two years of intensive financial training. The goal was to ensure no consultant was left untouched. Each consultant participated in two-to-three days of intensive training and case study work on rigorous financial metrics and cutting edge incentive plan design." The training became a core curriculum—the lifeblood of the Towers Perrin executive compensation practice.

Case Studies: Digging Deeper

This chapter features seven superb illustrations of how professional service firms apply digging deeper competencies to establish marketplace mastery.

EMBRACING COMPETITIVE DIFFERENTIATION

Malcolm Pirnie, Inc.

The case of Malcolm Pirnie, Inc. (Pirnie), an environmental engineering, science and consulting firm, embodies my call for professional service firms to dig deeper. While not letting go of its core services or leadership position vis-à-vis its competitors (as a provider of environmental engineering consulting services), it found a way to evolve in order to capture a share of an emerging market—performance enhancement for organizations in the environmental engineering arena. Put another way, the firm identified—and pursued—a powerful way to differentiate itself: by becoming an environmentally focused firm that would go far beyond providing commoditized technical services to solve traditional engineering challenges. As a result of its efforts, it is now able to apply its engineering and technical expertise toward a more valuable, higher-level client need: improving their performance, which would include not only improving their physical facilities, but also their operating, business, and even political functionality.

Think of the client's options before and after Pirnie's embrace of competitive differentiation:

- *Nondifferentiated scenario:* "We need to fix up our wastewater collection systems, because they are always breaking down and are causing us unnecessary expense. Let's put out a request for proposal (RFP) to fifteen environmental engineering firms and pick the lowest price provider."
- *Differentiated scenario:* "We need to manage our assets better; our costs are outstripping our revenues. How can we get the biggest bang for the buck in terms of where we put our future investment and energy? We see where one of our traditional service providers, Pirnie, a company that understands what we do, has dedicated itself to guiding municipalities like ours to improve their performance. Let's use *their* services!"

Sounds pretty simple, but in order for this outcome to be accomplished in the external perceptions of the marketplace, Pirnie had to risk the consequences of being out too far ahead of its market. Leadership can be lonely. Nevertheless, Pirnie dared to transform itself—differently—and did so ahead of an industry that has only recently begun to catch up. Now that's an impressive competitive strategy, especially for a firm that is more than one hundred years old.

The Malcolm Pirnie Story: Context and Background. Consider two ends of a spectrum: On one end are the war stories about professional service firms that embark on huge initiatives to make systemic changes and then stumble badly in the process. From these stories, we get the notion that doing *big* things—like differentiation—is *bad.* Yet, on the other end of the spectrum, we've reviewed our research findings, which suggest that the most successful differentiation strategies are so unique and complex that they cannot be easily copied, are deeply integrated into the fiber of the organization, and are challenging to implement. We're left with the impression, then, that the only way to succeed competitively is to go ahead and do those very *big* things that we were warned are so dangerous.

It's true that differentiation is not for the faint of heart. It requires a significant commitment to forge ahead into uncharted competitive waters. Yet its conception and implementation do not have to look like a tsunami. Indeed, the story of Pirnie's journey toward its own differentiation strategy is a perfect illustration of the "small changes, great gains" concept. This is a firm whose leaders were looking out for the kinds of marketplace shifts that would allow them to dig deeper. They then proactively and repeatedly pursued strategies that required the firm to make incremental yet transformational internal changes. In doing so, they learned the pitfalls and power of organizational change, which is at the heart of effective differentiation.

Malcolm Pirnie, Inc., was founded in 1895 by two Boston sanitary engineers. With an early focus on cleaning up water and wastewater problems, the firm's focus expanded over the years to include environmental management and restoration projects, including air pollution and solid and hazardous waste management. At this writing, close to 1,500 engineers, scientists, consultants, designers, architects, and technical support personnel in fifty offices provide services that include planning and feasibility studies, pollution control designs, construction observation, and facility management. With annual revenues of more than $200 million, Pirnie has a repeat client rate of 80 percent from organizations such as the U.S. Environmental Protection Agency; the Army Corps of Engineers; numerous village, city, and state agencies; and a host of private clientele.[1]

Through numerous separate strategic differentiation decisions that spanned fifteen years, Pirnie's leaders took incremental steps to create what is today a recognizable, competitively distinct differentiation platform: a privately owned consulting enterprise whose exclusive focus is on continuously improving its clients' performance, doing so by employing a discrete set of policies and organizational structures that demonstrate its independence and objectivity.

Internal Initiatives Set in Motion an Intentional Transformation toward Being Different. Beginning as far back as 1988, Pirnie management set in motion a cascade of internal initiatives that resulted in the firm's transformation toward becoming an increasingly consultative enterprise, more than just providers of requested engineering services. Each decision was intentional. Each step, while not at the time viewed as part of a comprehensive overarching differentiation strategy, was logically connected to the next. Each had a discernible role in propelling the firm toward differentiation. Here is how it happened.

In 1989, after it had conducted client research and taken its management through internal workshops to map out its approach to customer satisfaction, Pirnie committed to a solid goal: to exceed customer expectations. Its wake-up call was an exercise that showed that the firm's reputation for high quality and a respectable degree of "client service" only earned it a grade of C+ in clients' eyes. The whole concept of "points-of-impression" became the centerpiece of developing a client service culture. Suddenly everyone had a role in pleasing clients. Telephone systems and computer systems were totally replaced with the customer in mind. The internal customer also became important as the "supply chain" concept became understood.

As a natural outgrowth of this awakening, Pirnie also established, in 1989, a formal quality program to attend to all areas that ultimately contributed to client satisfaction. Historically, said Eric Dodge, recently retired vice president for quality management, Pirnie was well known for its technical quality. But the firm's leaders realized they were going to have to be intentional about upgrading all aspects of the firm's approach to quality—beyond technical quality—as part of their dedication to exceed clients' expectations. Dodge spearheaded the firm's adoption of a hybrid of the Malcolm Baldrige model and led the firm's formal commitments to improve its quality in the areas of process and leadership.

Change did not come easily. "We began hitting walls," recalled Dodge. "We needed strong leadership and people skills throughout the organization, and we needed ways to measure and then recognize abilities and performance." Pirnie leaders realized they had to build a solid performance appraisal system in order to encourage, recognize, and then reward improvements. In 1994 Pirnie benchmarked itself against several best-in-class Fortune 500 companies to develop a performance feedback and appraisal system. By 1995, Pirnie adopted a 360-degree performance feedback program for its entire management and leadership (20 percent of its population). Through this data, Pirnie learned that it was strong technically, in project management, and in the business management of its own business, but that it was not as strong in areas of leadership (communication, developing others, vision, setting a direction, strategic thinking, etc.). Dodge remembered: "These are also the skills that our clients expect us to exhibit *for them.*"

Saying "No." In the mid-1990s, under the leadership of then president and CEO Paul Busch, another step that would propel Pirnie toward competitive differentiation occurred when the firm informed its clients that it would be adopting its own "Declaration of Independence." Busch declared that Pirnie would say "no" to directly participating in two emerging trends, privatization and design-build. He confirmed that Pirnie would welcome the opportunity to offer its objective perspectives to clients that wished to evaluate and decide whether and how to embrace these trends. But Busch insisted that Pirnie would be an independent objective advisor, in the future "saying no" to any associations with a privatizing team or a design-build team.

Here's why this decision was so strategically important and how the declaration supported Pirnie's journey toward effective differentiation.

- *The privatization trend:* Utilities run water plants that deliver clean water to citizens, transport wastewater away, and treat it. Most are public entities, run by municipal government employees. Responding to citizens' pressure to "do more for less," and with a perception that the private sector can operate things more efficiently, some municipalities became intrigued with the possibility of selling their water and wastewater facilities to private operators. Most of the private sector teams that compete to take over these facilities still need on their teams an engineering firm like Pirnie. Busch argued that Pirnie must not accept participation in these alliances; it would be an unacceptable ethical compromise to be hired to help manage and operate a client's utility while also still providing it with objective performance counsel.

- *The design-build trend.* Another phenomenon was the rise of the design-build approach, in which clients purchase design and construction services from a single provider, to be carried out concurrently, rather than in a stepwise approach, with traditional design followed by construction. The argument is that a project can be carried out more efficiently, in less time and for less money. To join this market, Pirnie would have to partner with construction companies. Busch and other Pirnie colleagues voiced concerns about the potential for a conflict of interest, because so much of the firm's traditional client work is in the oversight capacity. Rather than having the client ask Pirnie to judge whether a contractor was providing the agreed-to services (the same contractors Pirnie might have to partner with if it engaged in a design-build project!), Pirnie preferred the role of an independent engineer to monitor the work of a design-build team.

It was evident that "saying no" would cost Pirnie some business (i.e., as a participant on design-build and privatization teams). However, the firm's leaders planned that their declaration of independence would also create other business opportunities that its competitors (especially if they had chosen design-build or privatization opportunities) might lose.

With this in mind, in 1996, Gary Westerhoff, then Pirnie's director of marketing, surveyed the firm's clients to determine the importance to them of working with an objective advisor that would be independent of any relationship with a contractor or private operator. One subset of clients said, "I don't care. I trust my engineering firm to keep everything straight." Another subset of clients *did* express concern over the potential for conflicts of interest. "This survey showed us, however, that our differentiation choice would cost us some work. It's the inevitable consequence of making a bold choice to be different from competitors,"

Westerhoff said. "We realized we'd have to be proactive in educating potential clients about what a 'conflict of interest' looks like, how it could hurt them, and how our independence and objectivity was a preferred approach." "What we also came to realize," added Dodge, "is that our independence stance would facilitate our transition into becoming a big-picture consulting resource for our clients."

As Pirnie's commitment to its differentiation strategy was being solidified, the firm made two more external moves. First, in 1998 Gary Westerhoff spearheaded the publication of a book, called *The Changing Water Utility: Creative Approaches to Effectiveness and Efficiency*. He pulled together a broad cross section of experts from within Pirnie itself, plus from a number of utilities, as well from competitors. The book was published through the American Water Works Association, the leading professional society in drinking water management.[2] Essentially, the book served as a manifesto for how water utilities could improve their performance and, among other things, gave utilities an alternative option to privatization. Westerhoff stated, "The book enabled us to hold something up and say, 'This is what we mean about effectiveness and efficiency in running a water utility.'" Dodge put it directly: "It was a strategic way to develop an operating manual for the services we were providing." The sequel to this book, focusing on management issues like strategic planning, leadership, and organizational effectiveness for the water utility, was published in mid-2003.[3]

Second, Pirnie publicly named a subset of its services "Performance Enhancement Consulting." Dodge remembered, "These services had not been named before. But we saw that some of our client work was evolving in much the same way our own internal work had evolved: managers were at the point that they had to look at their operations from a holistic, total point of view. We told a certain subset of our professionals, 'Your work now is as much about management consulting as it is about engineering.'" Pirnie rearranged these professionals into practices that overtly supported municipalities with their management of large programs and their operations. The firm added experts in finance, program management, and information technology to its cadre of operations specialists.

All during this time, Pirnie continued to work on improving its own leadership development capabilities. "We asked ourselves, 'How can we improve our leadership and consultative skills?'" Dodge recalled. "We tried a number of the standard approaches to leadership development: internal workshops, external retreats with gurus, and the like. While these were good awareness-builders, they didn't change behavior much. We began hitting another wall."

And so, in 1999, again as the result of an external benchmarking exercise, the idea of offering executive coaching was embraced. Performance-improvement coaching was first offered to a small group of Pirnie's key up-and-coming executives. "It was an 18-month process, involving another 360-performance feedback exercise, complete with personal interviews by a professional coach, with the individual's business colleagues, as well as clients and even family members," Dodge recounted. After the first three months, the individual and the coach decided improvement areas on which to focus. After that, coach and coachee consulted two-three times per month (four to six hours total per month) for the next year, and then prepared a plan for the individual to follow for the next part of his or her career.

Increasingly, Pirnie professionals reported an improved ability to relate to each other and to clients. The program was regarded as successful within its first six months. It has been continuing ever since, with a total of 50 persons so far enrolled as of this writing. According to Dodge, the key lesson was that to achieve the desired level of developmental change, a highly personalized and customizable approach was necessary.

As Pirnie's internal performance improvement work continued to take shape and more emphasis was put on leadership activities, a series of marketplace epiphanies began to occur with the firm's leaders. "We were still in the paradigm of providing our clients with technically oriented services," recalled Dodge. "But in the latter 1990s, we began to see an opportunity emerging where we could help our municipal clients to improve their operating performance." It became clear that the kind of management consulting Pirnie was doing so effectively on itself internally could help its clients to improve their own business performance. The firm successfully worked with a few established clients to test their receptivity to work with Pirnie on their municipality's organizational effectiveness and leadership development.

By 2002, under the new leadership of Jerry Frieling, chairman, and Bill Dee, CEO and president, a Pirnie strategic committee was appointed to decide how to market the firm's management consulting practice. One of the considerations was the formation of a separately named unit under the Pirnie banner. What exactly could be the merits—and risks—of starting it as a new company, they asked? What could we gain? What could we lose? Could those potential gains and losses ultimately provide an appropriate growth opportunity for our firm in the marketplace? What are the consequences of further differentiation? What are the consequences of *not* pursuing further differentiation?

In early 2003, Pirnie established a separate division, Red Oak Consulting, into which about fifteen percent of the firm was transferred and which would begin hiring to fill in the necessary competence gaps to provide all the management consulting services that the firm's municipal clients should need. Care was taken to maintain a strong liaison with the remainder of the company, so as to maintain and benefit from the firm's client base in traditional engineering work. The goal was to become the municipal sector's most sought after management consulting entity, by providing the combination of management *and* technical services that these clients need and want, all while maintaining its independence.

Speed Bumps. The preceding accounts of Pirnie's journey toward differentiation are not meant to imply that the firm encountered a completely smooth ride along the way. Far from it. Making changes of this significance never does. One of the speed bumps included the challenge related to an organizational reorganizing in order to properly serve the new direction that Pirnie had set for itself. In order to smooth this reorganization, Pirnie used its own executive coaching programs to help executives assume their new corporate roles.

Another obstacle was managing the organizational paradox between two types of partners: those who would adopt a quick-fix approach to solving organizational problems, and those who wished to be more deliberate in decision-making for the long term. "It took us a while to realize—and accept—that we benefit by the tension their varying viewpoints creates," explained Dodge. "The 'quick-fix' partners help by urging us to keep pushing ahead, and the other folks challenge them to think carefully through their proposals. The result is that we now realize the benefits of trying to change, as well as the inherent risks of doing so."

The third speed bump was related to overcoming resistance to the changes that were underway. The firm engaged a change consultant who helped Pirnie management to stay the course even amidst internal pushback. Eventually the firm improved its internal communication efforts by communicating more often and using a broader variety of techniques. "Our leaders learned that they had to *lobby* for change, over and over and over," smiled Dodge. "'Tell 'em 8 times' became a mantra."

The Results. Like any continuous change effort, Pirnie's transformation to becoming substantively different from its competitors has featured a series of mini-victories that add up to a bigger picture: preemptive competitive advantage, even against larger rivals. Here are some examples of these victories.

Pirnie has become one of the most honored firms in the environmental profession. In the last ten years, directly related to its dedication to exceed clients' expectations by delivering forward-thinking solutions, more than 100 Pirnie projects have been recognized for engineering excellence in competitions nationwide.[4] Many of these projects reflect the firm's differentiated performance consulting approach.

Pirnie, already viewed as a thought leader on municipal utility leadership, organization, and management issues, is increasingly being sought out to make presentations at numerous professional society gatherings. Pirnie has partnered, for example, with the International City Managers Association (ICMA) in delivering several webcasts on leadership and management issues, with these webcasts available to the management of cities and towns across the United States. The Association of Metropolitan Sewerage Agencies (AMSA) and the Association of Metropolitan Water Agencies (AMWA), representing management of America's larger wastewater and water facilities, respectively, frequently invite Pirnie to address their gatherings.

Through all this change, Pirnie has maintained financial stability (always in the black). Also, its employee retention has been higher than industry norms (under 10 percent for the most part). The firm has doubled in size since its initial forays into organizational change back in 1988. Finally, in the wake of the post-Enron ethical debacle, Pirnie has rededicated itself to its pledge of independence. It has formed an Independence Policy Committee to carefully evaluate each consulting opportunity that the firm thinks might have potential for conflict with its public clients. In an article, Gary Westerhoff wrote, "our concerns and our position on independence are looking wiser and wiser. We believe strongly that our decision clearly provides added value to many of our clients in the way we deliver specific services that help them and their clients, the public."[5] For Pirnie, the transformation to "being different" will continue.

MINING CLIENT DATA

Numerica Group

The second case in this section about how professional service firms dig deeper explores data mining—the practice of analyzing raw data in a database to describe past trends and obtain future perspectives on strategic marketing issues. It is a competency that is in its infancy for most professional service firms. The story features a look at Numerica Group, a new company that built its entire competitive plan around data mining.

Numerica's strategic approach to data mining signals a new shift in the management of professional service firms. In the "olden days," a firm's human resource department had the responsibility to integrate new employees into the fabric of the organization. Numerica's model requires that the information technology unit is as much involved, if not more so, in that integration. Why? Because a professional firm's core competency is expertise and knowledge; therefore, taking formal steps to collect evidence of new employees' knowledge and expertise, and to inculcate them into the firm's philosophy of information sharing and management, must of necessity become an element of the integration of new hires. We will see more firms taking this approach, as they become more market and technology driven.

I should note before I tell Numerica's story that it could be said that Numerica's data-mining strategy has worked because it became a public company and is no longer a partnership. Some observers could claim that it would be much more difficult to select this strategy and successfully implement it if the firm was still a fusion of equity-based colleagues. Perhaps this is so, but the argument ignores the reality that Numerica has been shrewd to embrace: with increasingly robust technological capabilities, most professional service firms—regardless of their corporate structure—*will* move to initiate data-mining strategies. Numerica's early-mover advantage offers significant opportunity for its successful achievement of its growth goals.

The Numerica Story: Context and Background. Data mining: there has never been a market-driven practice that causes quite as much of a thrill—and simultaneously such a pit in the stomach—for market-focused leaders in professional service firms. At the pit-of-the-stomach level, data mining represents the ultimate in behavioral change for professionals. It requires information—the more the better. And capturing data means *work*. Indeed, professional information cannot be captured as easily as it can with products (scanning bar codes at the checkout lane) or in retail ("May we have your telephone number and postal code?").

For professionals, the practice of data mining means they must embrace database and other technological applications fully; they must overcome whatever reticence they may have about them. It requires them to understand and make use of the ever-expanding capabilities of most of these tools. It also requires them to slow the normal rhythm of working on client problems, just to make sure information gets input into a common repository of facts and figures. In a small firm, this may mean professionals typing information themselves. In a large firm, this may mean reviewing reams of client and project information that someone else has entered (possibly incorrectly) into a database.

Finally, the practice of data mining requires a behavioral change that goes much deeper than resistance to learning new things, or the dislike of boring and time-consuming tasks. It requires professionals to share their deep knowledge of and exclusive access to clients. In most professional service firms, these are areas that historically had been sacrosanct.

But, ah, the thrill of the competitive gains because of data mining! The profit potential of astutely managed client relationships! The promise of data mining runs deep. In fact, data mining touches upon every one of the market-driven competencies that are discussed in this book: as part of a looking-out initiative, the data mining of client research can reveal the nuances of clients' perceived value. As part of a digging-deeper initiative, the data mining of client preference patterns can lead to competitively advantageous differentiation strategies and increased client retention and attraction success. As part of an embedding-innovation initiative, data mining can drive the development of new services that solve clients' latest problems.

Many professional service firms are beginning to use data mining as a part of their client research function, and many are taking early steps to build the systems and processes that will support effective data-mining initiatives. But, as our research has shown, much of their data-mining work is in its early stages; many firms do not yet broadly consider data mining to be an integral element of their marketing strategies.

They would do well to read the following case about Numerica Group plc. The story of this U.K.-based accounting and business consultancy offers a fascinating look at a professional service enterprise that built its entire go-to-market strategy around client data mining: making data mining itself one of the company's core competencies, and using that competency to make competitive gains.

Numerica Group plc was established in July 2001 as an organization dedicated to providing high quality business services to entrepreneurial organizations, high net worth individuals, and other professional firms. For entrepreneurs and high net worth individuals, its services include corporate finance, fundraising, flotations, mergers & acquisitions, transaction support, tax planning, Value Added Tax (VAT) services, consultancy, corporate advice, outsourcing, insurance, internal audit, international tax, personal wealth management, and tax investigations.[6] For other professional service firms, including lawyers and other accountants, its services include business recovery, corporate finance, corporate insolvency, financial planning, forensic accounting and dispute resolution, international tax, tax planning and investigations, training, VAT services and investigations, and wealth management.

Calling itself "the business for business," Numerica's objective is to be the preferred choice of business service provider in the United Kingdom for the entrepreneur. The strategy is to build a single national integrated business through acquisition and organic growth. Using this approach, Numerica acquires businesses that provide business services and that already have strong synergies and shared cultures.[7] The firm's goal is to grow rapidly, and so it did. On October 30, 2001, Numerica acquired the nonaudit business of Levy Gee, which was then the thirteenth largest accounting practice (outside of the Big Five) in the United Kingdom, to be the "cornerstone firm" for the group. (Since then, it has integrated more than a half dozen firms.) Numerica also successfully raised £30m on its admission to the London Stock Exchange's Alternative Investment Market. By September 30, 2002, Numerica's turnover was £20.5 million (approximately US$33 million).[8]

As a result of these integrations, by 2003 Numerica was the eleventh largest accountancy in the United Kingdom (outside of the "Big Four," the world's largest accounting firms). It employs about 1000 people in nine locations and has six key service lines and multiple areas of developing industry profiles.

Critical Considerations. The decision to design Numerica to be a data-driven professional service company was rooted in the marketplace experiences of the firm's founders. Chief operating officer Julian Synett, formerly Levy Gee's managing partner prior to its integration into Numerica, recalled four key areas of focus on which he and his colleagues were determined to concentrate as they prepared to join the new organization. They were: exceeding client expectations that continuously evolve, increasing the ROI of marketing, competing more effectively, and integrating people's knowledge as rapidly as possible.

- *Exceeding client expectations through knowledge management:* "Our targeted clients expect us to have deep familiarity with their commercial sector and a keen understanding of their particular business, so we knew that knowledge management would be a crucial element to growing our firm successfully," Synett said. Numerica leaders decided that the firm would need to adopt platforms and processes to organize, manage, and extract its knowledge. Moreover, these platforms and processes had to be able to help the company catch early signals of how clients' expectations were evolving. From this operational base, they reasoned, Numerica could go beyond merely *claiming* to be a knowledge-rich firm; it could *actually* demonstrate its knowledge about particular industry groups and sectors.
- *Increasing the return on marketing investments:* "At Levy Gee, we realized we had put a lot of money into marketing, but we felt we were not getting an appropriate ROI," Synett declared. "I came to the conclusion that spending money promoting your business is fine, but that it wasn't enough simply to create a profile in the marketplace that is warm and comfortable." Numerica's marketing initiatives would have to be better tracked and more productive.
- *Competing more assertively and with more acumen:* "We can't operate like 20–30 years ago, where you could wait for new business to

come to you," Synett acknowledged. "Now you have to go get the business, and you have to give your people the knowledge to be effective." Numerica decided to bring a sales function into the business. Synett continued, "In order to make the sales function work, we had to provide the appropriate tools—access to information and knowledge."

- *Connecting and integrating professionals' knowledge:* Numerica's strategy is to grow by integrating other firms, not consolidating them. "We mean integration literally, across service lines and industries and sector groups and offices," said Synett. "The key to bringing this together is to align the entire business around the most effective technological tools." Numerica's leaders believed that the firm couldn't compete effectively if it relied on an increasingly far-flung group of professionals to exchange information about their work with clients and prospects. They believed their efforts, however heartfelt, would be too unorganized and anecdotal to allow the company to address clients' needs and marketplace shifts proactively. They resolved that Numerica would acquire integrated software packages that could enable it to work across internal lines, connecting its people together as they collaborated on marketing, selling and serving clients. "We decided that flexible and scalable software applications would be the glue for our strategy," said Synett.

In order to meet its goals for each of the four focus areas above, the firm acquired a robust client relationship management database application, InterAction (developed by Interface Software in the United States). Numerica uses InterAction to monitor, organize and report on its ongoing relationships with clients and contacts.

Client Relationship Management. "Our business model is premised upon each business unit being able to leverage the resources of the collective whole, such as contacts, relationships, experience and expertise," said Ross Mullenger, Numerica's chief technology officer. "This is why we had to have the IT infrastructure that makes this business model possible." The day Numerica debuted on the London Stock Exchange, the firm began a rigorous process to implement InterAction. The software application had the ability to support three critical areas. First was sales and new business opportunities. Mullenger pointed out that the sales cycle for intellectual assets such as consulting, financial, insurance, and other services is not about sales force automation, but about managing complex relationships. "If one of our professionals is able to uncover a strategic relationship connected with a sales opportunity, the chances of closing that deal rise exponentially," he said. "Inter-

Action can track the complex relationships that our company members have with those contacts, and the relationships contacts have with one another. This capability means we manage information such as who knows whom, the subtle connections existing among contacts, and which relationships are essential to closing business."

Mullenger described an example that underscores the importance of this capability to the firm's standards for a high level of service quality:

> In 2001, we acquired a firm based in Bristol, west of London. One of the focus areas for our London office is our Business Recovery Group (liquidations, receiverships, turnaround management and insolvency advice). This business recovery unit's clients are typically banks and lending institutions. When these banking clients become concerned about the financial health of their clients, they ask our Business Recovery Group to investigate or to act as their investigating accountant. Historically, many of these services had been delivered by our founding firms through their long-standing relationships with Bristol-area banks and lenders. Levy Gee had successfully developed standards of service that were adopted upon the creation of Numerica. These had become the Numerica format. Therefore it was essential that the newly joining firms worked at the same standards. Our new Bristol office, before our formal acquisition, had just inked a contract to provide detailed investigation support for one of our Numerica banking clients. Our relationship management system flagged this, and not only helped us communicate together about our mutual relationships with this bank, but also helped us deliver our service at the Numerica level of quality. Without our IT infrastructure supporting a relationship- and service-delivery connection, our new colleagues' reports not only might have diverged from Numerica standards, it is possible the entire client relationship could have been compromised.

Numerica's marketing director Catriona Russell also relies on the data mining capabilities of InterAction. One of her responsibilities is to discern patterns and monitor performance on the company's sales and new business in its multiple industry focus areas. "Even prior to implementing InterAction, we tracked the company's gains and losses and sources of business," she reported. "But now, I can examine which of our industry groups has a high conversion rate" (the number of leads the company garners compared to the rate at which it converts them into engagement letters and then into clients). She can also review client retention and prospect inquiry rates.

Numerica also monitors its profitability by client and by sector. This data mining approach gives the company the ability to be strategic and competitively savvy about managing its accounts and targeting its hottest prospects. "We have identified a watch list of approximately

1,000 hot relationships," Russell affirmed. "We alert our professionals as to exactly where to direct their focus on these relationships."

The second critical area was cross-selling. For Numerica, cross-selling is seen as an imperative. It can be especially challenging to effect, though, especially within an organizational structure that resembles a "diverse confederation," and is complicated by the fact that the company is continuously acquiring new business units and perpetually evolving its inventory of service offerings. "Tax clients might naturally be interested in wealth management, insurance and other services, provided our professionals can spot the opportunity and understand the inventory of services available to that client," Mullenger cited as an example. "Our relationship management software provides our users with immediate access to the firm's collective expertise and experience, which information is then used to identify new opportunities and upsell to clients." Numerica sales director Douglas Shanks described how Numerica uses the application to motivate its selling teams and directly aide them in their conversations with targeted clients:

> InterAction helps our team members to recognise all of their collective sales, marketing and networking activities. Team members know that if they record these activities properly, they will be recognised and rewarded. Also, access to this information will give all our directors the confidence to pursue opportunities, and give the younger ones a significant head start when it comes to developing their own networks and client lists.

The third area is rapid staff integration. Numerica's concentrated acquisition and integration of new organizations and their staff forces a constant learning curve and repeated ramp-up periods during which new employees become familiar with the resources of the larger organization, and the existing staff become familiar with the new business units joining the group. "We wanted to avoid the cycles of disruption we've seen when other organisations have acquired companies," said Mullenger. "We see our relationship management database as the equalizing infrastructure capable of providing immediate visibility into people, companies, relationships, experience and expertise." For newly acquired firms, Numerica embarks on a program of immediately bringing into its database the contacts, relationships and profile information of each entity's staff. "As a result, users are right away tied into the resources of all our business units," noted Mullenger. "They are therefore capable of leveraging the knowledge base of our entire integrated organisation as soon as possible." Mullenger underscored that new staff people are highly motivated to get information about their personal experience and expertise into the system, because Numerica client managers mine the database to find the capabilities of particular professionals when they staff up for a project. It means specialized professionals can be tapped for projects sooner, and can increase their profile within Numerica more effectively.

Integrating Three Systems. With its embrace of a comprehensive relationship management software application, Numerica took a significant step—one that many other professional service firms also have begun to take. However, by itself, a relationship management database cannot deliver professional service firms a powerful competitive edge. The real strategic marketing leverage from such a step is applied when the software is integrated with a firm's financial and practice management infrastructure.

Upon its formation as a new company, Numerica expanded its use of its practice management system, Novient (developed by Solution 6, a public Australian company). Novient, a highly scalable application, supports the details of the professional and commercial side of Numerica's work on client engagements, such as developing budgets and monitoring the company's performance against project budgets, recording professionals' time, amounts billed to the client, and engagement write-offs. A third system, sitting "behind" the other two systems, is Numerica's accounting system, Sun Accounts (developed by an English public company called Systems Union). This application handles the financial accounting elements, including purchases, ledgers, net profits, overhead costs, and the like.

Data mining occurs primarily between the practice management and client relationship management systems. Mullenger offered an example of how the two work together: "If we are making a pitch to a new client, we might want to know who else we know in that market sector (this would be a relationship management query). If we want to know how many of our managers have done this type of work before, the value of their hours, the value of any write offs, or even Numerica's market share in that sector, this would be a practice management query." Queries begin through a Numerica-specific portal; the systems "figure out" from which application to pull information, which can be pumped into a set of reports.

True Grit: The Challenge of "Living" an Information-Sharing Manifesto. For its employees, Numerica has drawn a metaphorical line in the sand. In essence, Numerica says, "If you work here, you will divulge professional information as a routine part of your job. The ownership and analysis of information is so deeply critical to the achievement of our strategic growth goals that we will do everything we can to emphasize this practice and to enable it."

A declaration like this, even obliquely delivered, would make many professional service practitioners run for the hills. But Numerica expends time and effort to communicate the personal and business value of its information-sharing philosophy and technology-heavy infrastructure. Here is how the firm has done it.

- *Use the database to give everyone credit for selling new business:* "We have shifted our behavioral requirement," said Russell. "We tell our people, 'Please let us give *you* credit for helping the company win a new project! To get this credit, you must input all the relevant data into our database.'" In order to encourage full participation across project and selling teams, Numerica drives this behavior deep: everyone who had a part in bringing in the business gets credit, not just a rainmaker. But they must share the required information first.
- *Apply liberal amounts of elbow grease:* Julian Synett recalled the magnitude of the logistics required to bring all the desired data into a centralized location. "To date, we have integrated 19 principal databases operated by the different firms that have joined Numerica; also, we have brought in more than 300 individual contact databases," he confirmed. "We knew this would be a big issue: cleaning and validating data and maintaining its integrity. In hindsight, we should have started this effort sooner, and worked faster." In order to move faster, Numerica resolved to apply even more elbow grease. It designated a data steward who will make sure that data is entered properly and validated.
- *Influencing the information guardians to let go:* Numerica implements an assertive and ongoing internal promotion campaign that emphasizes the soundness of its information-sharing ideology. "We were prepared to address the resistance of those people who have guarded their contacts jealously over many years," remembered Synett. "We actively sold this conceptually throughout the organization, promoting the 'greater good' that all could enjoy with information sharing, and what they can get out of it if they do this." Second, the company tries to keep the collection of information as uncomplicated as possible, by linking the relationship management system to the contacts and calendar applications that people were already using. The idea was to keep as much control as possible in the hands of the fee earners. "When you make a business appointment in your calendar software, or a change in the address of your client contact, our system flags this information for inclusion in our relationship management database," said Mullenger. Russell added, "We knew that this had to work without adding any time to the already frenetic life of professionals. Also,

we wanted to avoid the messy process of having information get
bottle-necked in the marketing department." Third, even before it
has the opportunity to apply these internal methods, Numerica
works to ensure that it integrates similarly-minded firms to begin
with. The company actively seeks a good cultural fit with target
firms that appear willing to embrace its information-sharing
mindset and software application infrastructure. "Building up
trust amongst like-minded professionals is a lot easier than forcing
integration on those who don't want it," said Shanks.

- *Giving information in order to gain information:* There are two aspects
  to this approach. The first is formal reporting on marketing and
  sales progress. Russell developed a series of marketing and sales
  progress reports using InterAction. From a basic master report, she
  can slice and dice the information in several ways to analyze
  patterns and to gain new perspectives. During her monthly meetings with the company's industry group leaders, she uses these
  reports (the living results of the data mining she has done) to
  manage the industry groups toward marketplace opportunities or
  to forewarn them of unfavorable shifts. Even beyond these formal
  reports, however, is Numerica's commitment to give people plenty
  of information back. This includes giving staffers adequate notice
  about how and when the company plans to collect their information. For example, Numerica will announce to its people, "Next
  week, we will download your contacts; make sure you mark those
  contacts that are private (like your dentist or your grandmother)."
  This demonstration of consideration goes a long way to helping
  people feel respected.

- *Encourage information sharing by making it a performance issue:* A
  senior management appraisal initiative that motivates cross selling is planned. In the interim, most Numerica directors clearly
  see the value of recording their efforts, for the common good.
  "By and large they accept that they can hardly claim credit for
  contributing to a new client, or winning a new instruction cross-
  sold into an existing one, if they don't use the system to document what they've done," said Shanks. "And we're training a
  new generation of senior managers and associate directors in a
  variety of sales and marketing techniques—including knowledge management software."

The Results. In the later years of the twentieth century and the early
years of the new millennium, the U.K. business environment began to
undergo dramatic changes: concerns about auditor independence, reg-
ulatory developments, heightened client expectations, and increased
pressure for professional firms, entrepreneurs, and financial institu-

tions to be more effective in serving their clients. Numerica's move was to respond to these environmental changes by delivering an even better quality of expert service to its clients at prices that are cost-effective. Data mining is the vehicle.

Its practice of data mining has allowed the company to realize strong results.

- *Profitability:* Since its public debut, when Numerica Group began to implement the three integrated systems together, especially the relationship management element, it has outperformed the market and is operating profitably despite its high acquisition expenditures. "Our rate of growth couldn't have been achieved without our IT infrastructure," said Shanks.
- *Streamlined marketing and sales processes:* "Our integrated use of InterAction and Novient has become second nature to the whole process by which we go to market," stated Mullenger. "Without these tools, conducting our business would be impossible. We'd just be an amalgamation of disparate offices."
- *Service quality:* In addition to the example cited earlier, there have been many times that Numerica professionals have been able to spot and avert potential service quality lapses that could have hurt the company. But as important as averting disaster is the focus on the positive. Numerica's data mining orientation has allowed it to discern the subtleties of evolving client needs; it has supported the development of increasingly creative and valuable service offerings.
- *Sales and marketing ROI:* These days, Julian Synett likes what he sees. He has increased capabilities to track Numerica's marketing and selling investments and their results. "With our data mining practices, we are managing our marketplace more effectively— literally."

The firms we researched reported about their use of and success in implementing a number of methods to attract and retain clients. Our analysis found that their self-reported most effective methods clustered into what I call cultural groups. That is, the methods they used reflected certain values, perspectives, and behaviors that were already ingrained in the firms.

Culture is a squishy topic. It's difficult enough to identify definitively a behavior as being a cultural reflection of a firm, much less make that same identification for a marketing initiative. From our analysis, though, we surmised that our professional service firm respondents indeed *did* employ marketing techniques that have a cultural underpinning, but that they may not necessarily have done so from an overarching strategy or discernible program.

That said, I do believe that the alignment of culture with marketing strategies can and should be deliberate. The three case studies I include here, Kepner-Tregoe, Marakon Associates, and Egon Zehnder International, are good examples of that deliberateness.

All organizations have multiple facets of culture, but many professional service firms' awareness of their cultures is simply so big and broad and generic that it is amorphous. Kepner-Tregoe, Marakon Associates, and Egon Zehnder International—each with a different size, origin, and global presence—successfully distilled a key essence of their cultures into a focused market force. Each firm homed in on one critical aspect of its personality, and then made it a central part of its processes and go-to-market infrastructure.

Arguably, the Eureka moment ("Let's align our marketing strategy with our culture!") occurs frequently at most professional service enterprises. It may be hard to imagine that other firms don't also find a way to build a key aspect of "firm personality" into their marketing processes. (It makes a lot of sense to do so.) In fact, however, most professional service firms have yet to establish the strategies, processes, or marketing infrastructure that truly harnesses their cultural leanings for the express purpose of achieving a competitive advantage.

Even beyond this, though, our three case firms understood more: that their actions could also *reinforce* their cultural ethos. They committed, not to a simple onetime implementation of a single program, but to ongoing action, monitoring, and recommitment. This made their choice of a culture upon which to align their marketing strategies even more crucial, especially since the incremental implementation of their strategies would have a deepening effect on the cultural norms that they chose. Even for those firms that, perhaps because of their founders' strong principles, "fell into" their cultural choice, there came a series of moments when they chose *once again* to reinforce their key cultural norms in a market-driven way. This is the essence of aligning marketing strategies with culture.

ALIGNING MARKETING STRATEGIES WITH CULTURE

Kepner-Tregoe: The "Practical Results through Process" Culture

The story of management consulting firm Kepner-Tregoe serves as the first case of three about the competency of aligning marketing strategies with culture. It offers a compelling example of a firm that dug deep below the surface of its academic credentials, professional experience, and collective intellectual capital to align its marketing strategies with its "practical results" culture.

Since the very beginnings of what we now recognize as the professional service arena, practitioners have struggled with the question of how much to "show" their intellectual capital. It's the age-old professional service marketing paradox: Should we give away some of our knowledge before we ask clients to buy? Should we talk about our methodologies when we write articles or make speeches? Will our competitors steal our knowledge?

Some professional service firms never clearly answer this question. Others blow hot and cold on it, depending on the economy or their leadership's opinion. In the case of Kepner-Tregoe, however, this is a question that has a clear, culture-based answer: "Let's communicate our processes to as wide an audience as possible. And let's make them as practically applicable as we possibly can." It's one of the cultural platforms on which Kepner-Tregoe has effectively competed.

The Kepner-Tregoe Story: Context and Background. In the mid-1950s, Chuck Kepner and Ben Tregoe, conducting research for the Rand Corporation in California, found that an individual's successful decision-making did not result from his or her reliance on experience or seniority. Instead, it resulted from employing a logical process of gathering, organizing, and analyzing information to support that "gut feel" or experience. In 1958, from these findings, Drs. Kepner and Tregoe developed a rational set of problem-solving and decision-making processes, and offered them as their newly formed firm's proprietary method to help clients effectively manage their organizations. Now a US$40 million global firm with 200 professionals in 22 offices worldwide, 12 of which are wholly owned subsidiaries, the firm specializes in strategic and operational decision making. Using its proprietary processes, Kepner-Tregoe helps clients examine their businesses in depth, formulate a vision for the future, and equip their people with the skills necessary to make it happen.[9] It serves clients on five continents and in just about every industry.

All along, Kepner-Tregoe has made the company's culture the cornerstone of its interface with the marketplace. It has intentionally aligned its culture with its go-to-market strategies. "Our commitment to share our knowledge to help clients improve their effectiveness was—and still is—a conscious, strategic choice," said Kepner-Tregoe executive vice president William Shine. "Chuck and Ben's founding principles now pervade all of our internal and external initiatives." These principles include:

1. *Process is as important as content:* Consultants at Kepner-Tregoe acknowledge the significance of having reams of information or deep-bench experience or unparalleled expertise. Indeed, the firm

conducts numerous cutting-edge research initiatives. But, they argue, if you have a flawed process, you will get a bad result.

2. *"Enable" instead of "do"*: "This is at the root of our culture," remarked Shine. "We believe it is far better to teach people how to fish than to catch the fish for them."

3. *Produce practical results*: Kepner-Tregoe consultants have long maintained that the training and development industry was content to settle for simply increasing people's awareness, with the expectation that a change in behavior would be forthcoming. But improved awareness and even a deeper level of skill proficiency were not enough. They believed that the Kepner-Tregoe methodologies had to demonstrate a noticeable, measurable result—and do so quickly. This emphasis on practical application serves as the third leg of Kepner-Tregoe's cultural approach to its marketplace.

The "Practical Results Through Process" Firm. In discussing the idea that a firm could align its marketing strategies with its culture, it is important to remember that the concept requires a firm to first comprehend the central aspect of its own cultural vein, and then, beyond this, to deliberately use it as a marketing strategy to build a competitive advantage. From a number of overarching principles set forth by its founders, Kepner-Tregoe successfully drilled down to a simple and powerful cultural core. It is a "Practical Results through Process" firm. It believes in transferring critical thinking processes to help clients solve their own problems, make important decisions, and achieve optimal results. This notion became the firm's true cultural foundation. Everything Kepner-Tregoe says and does in its marketplace and in its competitive strategies is intentionally designed to mesh with this persona.

Here's how it manifests:

- *Service portfolio:* Kepner-Tregoe's longtime services and new offerings are all built from its founding mantras. "Enable"; "Think clearly"; "Process, not content"; "Problem solving"; "Actionable results." An early example is Kepner-Tregoe's origination of the "Train the trainer" methodology, which it packaged and offered in workshops worldwide. Another example is the firm's development of operational improvement services for clients globally. For example, Kepner-Tregoe's approach to cost and complexity reduction is not the typical, "Let's show you how to reduce head count and inventory" consulting intervention. The company works in partnership with clients to understand the cost basis for the business, then shares a "True-Cost" process with them, and then works along side managers while they implement the process. Still another example is E-Think, Kepner-Tregoe's new process-support software. The firm continues to develop and roll out services that mesh with its practical results culture.

- *Targeting:* By hewing to its most critical and central cultural theme, Kepner-Tregoe is able to concentrate on targeted clients whose business challenges match the firm's "Practical Results through Process" cultural bent. "Our processes transcend any vertical market," Shine recalled. "Nevertheless, we maintain a special focus on industries in which we can help produce significant, practical results. For example, we approach healthcare and pharmaceutical markets, where the research and development and deployment of new products are especially important—and where we have a track record of producing major bottom-line results." This is a classic segmentation strategy, but done with a cultural foundation, rather than a narrow exercise of matching up a firm's services to its market's demand.

- *Client satisfaction:* Kepner-Tregoe intentionally uses its culture in its approach to client satisfaction. In delivering its client training sessions, for example, the firm creates actionable solutions in real time, right there in the session. Clients love it. They come away from the sessions with a real sense that they have received value. For its marketing workshops or speeches for prospective clients, Kepner-Tregoe transfers its knowledge right away. It explains its methodologies up front, rather than cryptically tiptoeing through a jungle of jargon and consultant-speak. Its consultants do not fear giving away too much. The firm's prospects find this approach very attractive; they begin getting a sense of Kepner-Tregoe's cultural foundation even before they formally engage the firm. This ethos of delivering real-time client satisfaction in fact helps Kepner-Tregoe successfully differentiate itself from others.

- *Promotion and business development:* Kepner-Tregoe also effectively implements a culturally aligned system for marketing and selling. "We have identified market teams that each contain three types of people: a relationship manager, a process engineer (the expert of the particular methodology), and a content expert (the authority in a particular subject)," reported Shine. "These three types of people work in tandem to market and promote our firm, and to develop new client opportunities." The configuration of these teams and the way they work together is a highly effective demonstration of the firm's "Practical Results through Process" ideology. Imagine the panoply of marketing or business development situations these folks might face: a question-and-answer (Q&A) session, a speech, an article for a trade journal, or a proposal to a new prospect. No matter. Kepner-Tregoe professionals dedicate themselves to deliver real-time, process-driven solutions that have immediate application for the recipient's effective use. "For example, at an invitational breakfast we may posit a critical question around a particular thinking process," Shine recounted. "Take decision-making as an example. With clients, we might ask: 'What does it really take to drive effective decision-making processes throughout an organization?' Our aim is to probe issues relating to strategy, structure, systems, capabilities, and culture—and not just training. The content of the breakfast is about using process to effect results. Together we arrive at the answer."

- *Marketing communications:* The content, usability, and visual presentation of Kepner-Tregoe's promotional material and research reports are all focused on results-oriented critical thinking skills. An example is the firm's report, *Decision Making in the Digital Age: Challenges and Responses,* published in June 2000. The report provided an in-depth assessment of decision-making trends based on a national survey of almost nine hundred managers and workers, along with best practices and quantitative research on ten major business organizations.

- *Web site:* The firm's Web site, kepner-tregoe.com, also follows the "Practical Results through Process" guidelines. "We worked to make the Web site as client-focused as possible," said Shine. "We envisioned how to enable knowledge transfer and how we would deliver practical results on the Web site. Then we built it to do so." For example, Kepner-Tregoe's Web site enables easy retrieval of past articles from the firm's publication, *Forum.* Another example of this practicality is the inclusion of clear explanations of the firm's "Rational Process" method and "Five-Phase Strategy" model. Additional links are offered in a logical arrangement and a simple visual presentation.

- *Service delivery:* Shine reported, "We have created a blended learning environment, a coaching model where remote individuals throughout the country can get real-time advice." Essentially, the Kepner-Tregoe blended-learning model involves a unique combination of Web-based, self-paced training under the watchful eye of an online coach, with instructor-facilitated, hands-on skill transfer and application coaching in a classroom setting.

- *Recruiting:* Kepner-Tregoe believes that a firm's talent is an integral part of its marketplace strategy. It makes a special effort to align its recruiting with its culture and ideology. "We don't recruit on industry expertise. It's not that important," said Shine. "We look for people with past business experience, and we rarely hire freshly-minted M.B.A.s." The firm also tests potential hires on analytical skills, rational thinking skills, process experience, and client orientation.

The Ties That Bind. Kepner-Tregoe's example of intentionally using its main cultural norm to guide its marketing strategies is a strong one. Sometimes, however, the unconscious and inflexible application of cultural structures can be a hindrance to achieving marketplace goals. Kepner-Tregoe's example also serves here. It is an effective illustration of how tightly aligning marketing strategies to a culture leaves little room for making appropriate market-focused adjustments. Bill Shine explained: "With a culture that reveres process and focuses on doing things *right*, we found ourselves in a somewhat risk-averse mode. Our notion of producing real quality for clients has not actively hurt us, but, I believe, almost encouraged us to adopt unambitious growth goals. We're working to morph our culture to be more mistake-tolerant, more flexible."

But this doesn't mean the firm has left behind the strong norms that it established; rather, it is updating them to fit with a changing business environment. Shine gave examples of the firm's work to make its Web site become even more practically applicable. For example, by early 2003 it had debuted its new Web site, which will feature a processes-with-results array of client war stories, anecdotes, and case studies.

The Results. Kepner-Tregoe's work is recognized globally as being at the forefront of organizational design, research, and practice. As the first firm to focus on the critical need for training in problem solving and decision making, it is today an undisputed leader in the training industry. It has moved well beyond training in problem solving and decision making, though, to include process consulting and organizational development in areas ranging from strategy formulation and implementation to cost management. Kepner-Tregoe has developed processes that are used by millions of employees and managers around the world. Kepner-Tregoe enjoys an almost 75 percent retention rate among current clients. Its list of international clients that have been with Kepner-Tregoe for more than twenty years includes such companies as Fuji Photo, Hewlett-Packard, Honda, Kimberly-Clark, Procter & Gamble, and Xerox.

Marakon Associates: The "Challenge with Empathy" Culture

The next case, featuring Marakon Associates, provides another look at the competency of aligning marketing strategies with culture. It's a story about a firm that possesses a unique combination of competitive effectiveness: an acceptance of complexity, organizational prowess, and even courage. In the movie *The Wizard of Oz*, the Cowardly Lion sings "Life is sad, believe me, Missy, when you're born to be a sissy, without the vim and verve."[10] Despite a rather understated profile, Marakon Associates is no marketplace sissy. In its pursuit of a competitively advantaged positioning, this firm had the guts to dig deep into a complex, nuanced cultural platform. All too many companies, even those in other industries, tout their cultures of honesty, teamwork, responsiveness, or what-have-you. These cultural attributes, as important as they are, have almost become clichés. Yawn.

The following story illustrates that Marakon went deeper than that, identifying an ethos—"challenge with empathy"—that has real meaning for clients and for its own talent. It is a platform that is valuable, decidedly attractive, and simple for clients to understand. It is credible for Marakon to claim and, because of its complexity, would be extremely difficult for competitors to copy.

It's also highly sustainable in the marketplace—but with an effort. That's where having—or building—a market-driven infrastructure becomes so important. It's clear that Marakon intended its "challenge with empathy" positioning to have staying power. First, it arrived at a potent marketing strategy by taking itself through its own consulting process, with all the trappings of a client engagement. It was fact based and choice driven. It was also collaborative and milestone oriented. Second, to ensure the achievement of its goals, Marakon intentionally devised a series of internal and external processes that iteratively reinforce the choices it had made. This kind of organizational prowess is too rare.

The Marakon Associates Story: Context and Background. "How are we *different?*" Some firms will always be too afraid to ask this question, for fear of facing the painful truth: "You *are not* very different from your competitors." Some firms will ask it too gently, and will resort to shallow responses after that. Many firms find they indeed *do* possess elements of differentiation. These elements may lie buried, though, perhaps within the firm's processes, or knowledge base, or people, or elsewhere. These differentiators can be uncovered, deliberately chosen as platforms upon which to go to market, and then polished into view. Eventually, these differentiators can become a feature of the firm's competitive strategy.

But beware: asking the differentiation question *seriously* is not for the faint of heart. It means digging deeply, with courage, conviction, time, and resources. Meet Marakon Associates. One of its differentiators is a key aspect of its culture: "challenge with empathy." This culture-based differentiator has become a key piece of Marakon's plans to maintain—and develop—its competitive advantage.

The following case study describes Marakon's purposeful alignment of its marketing strategies with its culture. Over a five-year period, beginning in 1997 and then intensifying from 2001 to late 2002, Marakon followed a deliberate route of building a differentiated position in the marketplace. During an iterative process of internal and external information gathering, the firm's partners solidified their comprehension of the ways their firm was different, reinforced their internal comfort about these differentiators, and developed a vision about how they could be used to help the firm in the marketplace.

Marakon Associates is a $133 million international management consulting firm that advises top executives on increasing the long-term value of their companies.[11, 12] Founded in 1978 in San Francisco, the firm now has more than 350 employees (250 consultants and approximately 100 staff) working in a network of offices in Chicago, London, New York, San Francisco, and Singapore.[13] Over the years Marakon has expanded its service offerings in order to help clients get the most value from their strategies.[14] From an early focus on strategic planning, corporate finance, and investment management, it built new services to help clients tie long-term strategic planning to capital investment planning ("value-based management"). From there it again evolved its focus, adding a major organizational component to its service portfolio.

Today, Marakon's services, still focused on helping large multinational corporations maximize long-term intrinsic value, have morphed into what the firm calls "managing for value."[15] This is a holistic approach to managing that combines the disciplines of leadership, organizational effectiveness, strategy, and corporate finance into an integrated approach to long-term value growth. Marakon's results are impressive: According to its Global Client TSR Index, which tracks the total shareholder returns of current clients since they hired the firm, Marakon clients outperformed their peers by an average of 100 percent during the five years ended May 2002.[16] Its revenues per professional are among the highest in the management consulting profession, at about US$590,000 in 2002.[17] Its reputation is stellar. In 1998, *Fortune* magazine called Marakon "an absolute top-notch [management consultancy], among the half-dozen firms that form the elite in strategy consulting. Marakon is the best-kept secret in consulting. Its anonymity is not for want of accomplishment."[18]

"What Are We Good At?" Leadership in benchmarks like the ones cited here doesn't happen by accident. Marakon's thirty-one partners work at it. Each year, they and the firm's forty-five managers come together for a week-long planning meeting during which they discuss external issues such as ways to share practice innovations with new and existing clients, areas for further practice development and the firm's positioning and awareness strategy. They also discuss internal issues including diversity, knowledge management, and consultant training.

In 1997, as part of an ongoing exploration of how to grow the firm, Marakon partners hired an outside consulting firm to provide information on the firm's perceived positioning. Over the course of the next few years, Marakon continued to gather qualitative client feedback and quantitative market research data. One of the quantitative areas, for example, was the number of press mentions (positive, neutral, or negative) that referred to Marakon vis-à-vis its competitors. London-based former managing partner Dominic Dodd systematically pored over the positioning data, looking for themes. "We tried to frame the issue by looking at the facts behind it," Dodd remembered. "We looked at what clients said about us and how their comments compared to others. We looked at what kind of things our competitors were doing."

As he reviewed and analyzed the research, Dodd also assessed the issue's readiness to be brought to his peers. Marakon's partners take great care in preparing to present their colleagues with serious questions. The formal inclusion of issues like these on the agenda of Marakon's annual partner-manager meeting is the signal of their gravity and timeliness to the firm. A certain amount of preparation is expected to be applied, in order to have the issue deemed worthy of being featured on the agenda. Questions of import typically take Marakon's partners eighteen months to three years to resolve adequately. By June 2001, Dodd and Chief Executive Ken Favaro had crystallized enough of the data to be able to present the "Positioning and Awareness" issue at the annual meeting: "How can we best position ourselves so that we can help *ourselves* to grow? What are we good at? What about us makes us different in a better way than our top competitors?"

Dodd's presentation featured six themes that clients had reported about Marakon: (1) challenge, (2) focus, (3) passion, (4) being collaborative, (5) driving to the right decision, and (6) helping get to agreement. After the presentation, the thirty-one Marakon partners, armed with these themes and the other factual research data that Dodd had presented, broke up into groups to discuss their own perceptions about how their firm was different. By themselves, the six themes from Dodd's analysis cannot be said to be all that differentiated. Nonetheless, that very day in June 2001, the cultural theme of "challenge with empathy" emerged as a critical differentiator. Why it came up is a significant part of the story.

We Choose . . . the Middle. The partners considered the question of "How are we different?" from a number of angles. "When we looked at where we are on the consulting 'spectrum' in relation to our competitors, we understood that we have a uniquely collaborative consulting process," recalled Favaro. "On one end, one could argue, there are content firms that study and study an issue and then come back with a recommendation of what the client *should* do." Favaro characterized the other end as a more process-oriented consulting approach—consultants who simply facilitate, without a viewpoint on the client's final choice. The nature of these consultants' work is a series of questions.

For its part, the partners agreed, Marakon conducts its work transparently, guiding the client through a series of defined milestones during which content-backed scenarios are put on the table. "We do develop a view of our clients' strategy," said Favaro. "We present them with a variety of choices that they could make to grow the value of their business." How very collaborative this sounds! The client gets to consider, compare, and choose. How very rigorous this sounds! After all, Marakon's content is robust and methodologically sound. Sounds good enough, right? Not to Marakon.

The partners realized that Marakon was in the middle. "Our consultants' dilemma is not to get the clients to own the answer, but to get them to own the *best* answer," Favaro explained. "What happens if the answer they come up with is the wrong answer? We don't want that impact. We have to make sure that they own the *best* answer." The Marakon partners also recognized something their clients had not been able to tell them directly: That Marakon's ability to "challenge" was not, by itself, enough to create the perception of real value. It had to be balanced with another element in order for real success to be possible.

The unarticulated element was "empathy." "If we don't challenge them, we will not have the results that are necessary for their success," acknowledged Favaro. "And if we don't have empathy, we will be rejected." The thirty-one partners agreed that the "challenge with empathy" aspect of their cultural approach to consulting—already so highly valued by clients—was, in fact, a powerfully unique position to communicate to the marketplace. By the end of their meeting, Marakon partners determined they would move forward with this platform as one of the pillars of a newly articulated position for the firm.

Aligning Marketing Strategies with Culture: The Socialization Process. In the ensuing months, Marakon began to formally align its marketing strategies with its "challenge with empathy" positioning. It became a socialization effort, with distinct inside and outside elements that each reinforced the other.

To align the inside elements, Marakon pursued a set of steps to build internal awareness of and approval for its new positioning platform. By August 2001, Dodd had written and internally distributed a positioning statement. "Challenge with empathy" was included as one of the themes. At the next partner-manager meeting (May 2002), Dodd presented the positioning statement again, for further polishing and consensus building. Typical for Marakon, this consensus building consisted of: playing back the results of the discussion in the form of both what was agreed and what was not agreed; surveying the partner group for feedback via e-mail; developing what Marakon calls a series of "defenders" or strawmen statements of positioning and using that as the basis for focusing progress; and encouraging and learning from experimentation with new ideas from the positioning debate with existing and potential new clients.

To align the outside elements, the partners acknowledged that "challenge with empathy" had to be infused through all of the firm's processes. "We are interested in 'delivered positioning,' not in 'intended positioning,'" said Favaro. Marakon decision makers believed the new positioning did not need, and indeed was not appropriate for, a major branding campaign. But the market's perception of Marakon's position *would* have to evolve. The first way to do that, all agreed, would be to ingrain the positioning into the firm's awareness-building processes.

In November 2001, Marakon embarked on direct mail and Web site initiatives to build external awareness of its new positioning statement. The firm sent out a client mailing that included the new positioning statement with its "challenge with empathy" element. By the end of the next month, it was featured on the Marakon Web site. In October 2002, as part of a revamp of its Web site, Marakon created an entirely new "Our Difference" section featuring a refined version of the positioning statement and the "challenge with empathy" description.

Marakon also decided to embark on focused awareness building through the media. Partners agreed they would pursue relationships with key communication channels in the same manner that the firm invests in client relationships. But this was not an everyday media campaign approach. The firm deliberately targeted ten communication channels that fit with its culture and target audience. Dodd explained how Marakon selected one of its media channels, a top-tier business magazine with a respected conference and Web division. "Culturally it is quite like us—understated, rigorous, premium," said Dodd. "It is iconoclastic, and takes a slightly contrarian position; we are like this as well."

To align the inside with the outside involves monitoring and guiding an ever-shifting array of internal self-perceptions with perceptions from the outside world. The thirty-one Marakon leaders knew the delicate balancing act they had chosen; that although they had chosen to position their firm on the "challenge with empathy" platform, this cultural ethos could forever morph into something else, especially without their conscious reinforcement internally and externally.

And so Marakon began an intentional process of aligning its internal marketing strategies with its external marketing strategies. Of the ten communication channels mentioned previously, it chose some specifically for their ability to help the firm further deepen its "challenge with empathy" culture. "One of the magazines we chose is very experiential, as opposed to theoretical. This particular publication employs a lot of real-world examples and case studies," explained Favaro. "We tend to be more theoretical. But we know that our clients live in the real world. So we pursued a relationship with this magazine in order to pressure ourselves to further shape the 'challenge with empathy' substance of our professional service." Working with this publication in fact challenges Marakon consultants themselves to write more anecdotally, and teaches them empathy for working in a different way than they might have preferred. This is challenge with empathy in action.

"Living" the New Position. In September 2002, Marakon held its annual partner-spouse meeting. At this meeting—the third consecutive all-partner meeting at which the firm's leaders formally considered "Positioning and Awareness"—Dodd briefed his colleagues on the implementation of awareness-building initiatives, including progress on building relationships with the ten communication channels.

At this point, the focus was getting partners to further buy in, to allow them to provide additional input. This is classic consensus-building. But Favaro and Dodd wanted to lead their colleagues beyond this simple level. At this meeting, the tone of the discussion shifted to a new question: "How will we 'live' the positioning choice we've made?" "There have to be internal consequences in order to make it real," declared Favaro. "We are now in the process of making it real." There are three areas underway.

- *Train professionals to challenge empathically:* Marakon offers its consultants and managers extensive training during their first several years, including modules specifically designed to help them challenge and empathize. As one would expect, much of the training seeks to build an understanding of Marakon's distinctive approach, tools and techniques. These sessions cover a range of strategic, organizational, and financial topics. Consultants quickly learn that the insights derived from applying the firm's tools and techniques are frequently new to clients and therefore become a source of challenge. To deliver this challenge with empathy, consultants receive additional training on how to understand their own operating styles, diagnose client styles and needs, and tailor their interactions to meet client needs. In their client management modules, for example, consultants are encouraged to first understand client concerns before seeking to build support for Marakon's insights. These sessions are complemented by communications training to further develop consultants' interpersonal skills.

- *Measure the ROI of new positioning efforts:* Marakon will make its measurement broader, deeper, and more systematic. The firm will increase the range and scope of its research efforts, from global awareness to individual interactions on its Web site. "We learn from 'living our new positioning,'" said Dodd. "And we intend to manage our return on investment."

- *Recruit people who can challenge empathically:* Marakon has begun a deliberate endeavor to hire people who "challenge with empathy" well. (This is indeed a challenge.) "Some people are very good at empathizing, but they don't bring an edge to it; others are good at challenging, but with too much of an edge," remarked Favaro. The firm has begun a process of screening for just the right blend of the two cultural approaches. "You never really know if the people will have the right combination," Favaro concluded. "But if you are looking for it, you have higher odds of finding it." Marakon also places emphasis on *who* is doing the recruiting, in hope that the firm's current challenge-with-empathy personnel will recruit for the qualities they themselves possess.

Overcoming Challenges. The road to a new positioning for the firm was not straightforward. Different partners naturally had different views on what attributes to emphasize. Also, the firm had been content for many years to remain low-key and gain most of its growth through client referral. Why should it change now? It had to change to meet its growth ambitions. Resolution required substantial time to be invested in consensus building, together with a determination to face down the facts about where Marakon really was and was not different. In other words, Marakon partners found that they had to apply "challenge with empathy" to themselves to make progress on changing the firm's delivered positioning.

The Results. Marakon is well-known for its results orientation, especially among its key clients, including Barclays, Boeing, Cadbury Schweppes, Coca-Cola, Dow Chemical, Gillette, Lloyds TSB, and Prudential plc. According to Vault.com, "The 10 companies with which Marakon has worked the most have seen double the shareholder returns of their peers during the time they worked with the firm. (The typical Marakon client outperforms its peers in total shareholder returns by five percentage points over a 10-year-plus period.)"[19]

The evidence proves that Marakon also takes its own growth seriously: it has been able to grow an average of 28 percent over the last 25 years (more than double the industry average).[20] Its revenues grew by

15 percent from 2001 to 2002 at a time when many leading strategy consulting firms struggled.[21]

In 2003, Marakon began its formal measurement of the marketplace's response to its challenge with empathy positioning. The firm's internal pulse has revealed strong support among all associates to date. "This has been a real advance for galvanizing us both externally and internally," said Herman Spruit, Marakon's managing partner for Europe. "In serving clients, it gives us the right questions to ask: Are we being challenging enough? Are we really empathizing? Is the balance right? Internally, it has given guidance on how we should work together with all of our colleagues—something all professional services partnerships struggle with."

Added Jim McTaggart, Marakon's cochairman and cofounder: "I think the positioning has resonated with a lot of people internally because it is true to our cultural heritage. We were not an offspring of one of the established, East Coast–based consulting firms. Our origins were in corporate finance, so we had to make up our own product offering and client service model as we went along, by trial and error. Challenging with empathy has been a part of that for 25 years."

In 2002, Marakon's new positioning strategy began to show a real impact on its reputation:

- Marakon jumped from twenty-first place to fifteenth place in Vault's annual survey of the top fifty management consulting firms.
- It was cited as the only top fifteen firm in the Vault survey that saw more than a 1 percent increase in its reputation (*Consultants News*, October 2002).
- *Bank Director* magazine cited Marakon as one of top 4 "most respected" corporate strategy advisors to large financial institutions (October 2002).
- *The Economist* described Marakon as "the consultancy that has advised some of the world's most consistently successful companies" (July 23, 2002).
- The firm was favorably profiled in *Consultants News* ("Differentiation Helps Marakon Grow While Others Struggle," December 2002).
- The number of "quality" press mentions—those that the firm wanted to highlight on its Web site—increased by 50 percent in 2002.[22]

Egon Zehnder International: The "Collaboration" Culture

Egon Zehnder International (EZI) is the third of three cases about professional service enterprises that intentionally align their marketing strategies with culture. The EZI story is absorbing because it demonstrates that "marketing strategy" can exist at a much more systemic level than "promotion" (which many firms employ as an adjunct initiative). Indeed, the following story makes it clear just how deeply EZI integrates its marketing strategy with its collaboration culture—and vice versa. One could even argue they are one and the same.

"Collaboration" is increasingly important in the business world. As we have entered a "remorse phase" after witnessing professional ethics breaches from all too many supposedly world-class companies, we've been subjected to an increasing din: proclamations about new ethics guidelines, fanfares about professional standards, and crescendoes about trust. In the midst of all this noise, more and more businesses are touting their effective teamwork and their seamless collaboration. Yet in many cases these words simply add to the cacophony. Most likely, these words are part of the promotional programs that many firms employ to reassure clients or persuade them to return to the fold. In fact, most of us in the professional service world have only a dim notion of what true collaboration is. We say we understand, but beneath our all-too-quick nods of comprehension, most of us still expect professionals to behave like they did before.

Egon Zehnder International, with its heartfelt belief in the selfless goodness of people and its insistence on conducting itself accordingly, understands genuine collaboration. Collaboration is reflected in the way partners and associates behave. It is reflected in the way the firm is organized, in the way work flows, and in the way people are compensated. And it is reflected in the firm's unique approach to its marketplace.

The EZI Story: Context and Background. "Why don't you come to New York to meet our Executive Chairman, Dan Meiland?" said EZI partner Justus O'Brien in December 2002. "You could conduct your case interview in person." I was intrigued; seldom does a request for an interview generate an invitation to really "look inside" a firm. I traveled to New York, and there I witnessed a pitch-perfect demonstration of the very topic I sought to profile: the deep alignment of Egon Zehnder International's marketing strategies with its highly collaborative culture. During the interview, I watched Meiland and O'Brien embody all the aspects that make Egon Zehnder International's collaborative culture so seamless, so systemic, and so truly unique compared to those of its executive search competitors. There were no breathless fanfares about the firm's teamwork methods or chest-thumping proclamations about faddish collaboration technologies. Instead, there was a quiet, heartfelt account of an ethos on which the firm was founded and which today helps it thrive even in the face of profound economic disruption in its sector.

The Road Not Taken. In 2002, EZI was ranked the third largest retained executive search firm in the world.[23] With 2001 worldwide revenues of nearly US$300 million, its three hundred consultants operate in fifty-eight offices in more than 35 countries. Clients range in size; they include the world's largest organizations, emerging growth companies, government and regulatory organizations, and prominent educational and cultural institutions. More than two-thirds of EZI's engagements come from these existing clients. Industry practices include financial services, consumer, life sciences, technology and telecoms, energy and process, engineering and automotive, services, insurance, and private capital.[24] There are also professional practices including executive search board consulting and director search, management appraisal, and Venture Engine.

From the earliest days, since it was founded in Zurich, Switzerland, in 1964 by Egon P. S. Zehnder, the firm began building the fundamentals of today's true collaboration: equality, collegiality, noncompetitive internal sharing, and nonhierarchical organizational structures. In many ways, Zehnder's initial philosophy set the firm on a road not taken by its executive search consulting brethren. This philosophy, born forty years ago but continually renewed, serves as the firm's de facto marketing strategy, and has enabled EZI's achievement of its leadership position in the global marketplace. To understand how the promulgation of EZI's culture so deeply embodies its go-to-market approaches, let's look at how EZI does things: the five behaviors and practices that bring Zehnder's viewpoints to life.

1. Operating with a single, firmwide profit center rather than a matrix of separate profit and loss centers: By operating with a single profit center, EZI reduces the potentially negative effect of revenue and profit competition between practices or offices. (EZI employs this method even though it organized into sector specialties in 1997.) "We take the long view. If a particular part of the world or business sector is in a slump, that is not the fault of the consultants who are located in that geography or who specialize in that particular sector," Meiland explained. "We've agreed to be true colleagues; we will carry others when necessary."

2. The firm selects and retains employees whose interests dovetail with its own. Among its practices, the firm:

    a. Hires only those consultants who have significant business or consulting careers prior to joining the firm. This ensures a level of professional experience and maturity that true collaboration requires.

b. Hires only those with postgraduate degrees. EZI believes that intellectual collaboration, between its own consultants and with its clients, is of paramount importance.

c. Seeks multilingual or multicultural candidates who are comfortable working collegially across a host of invisible boundaries, with businesses that operate in the global economy.

d. Screens its candidates for an indication of certain behaviors, notably "evidence of a collaborative attitude." "We use a systematic interviewing approach to get beyond a candidate's 'resume-speak,'" said O'Brien. "It's very results- and details-focused." This screening is accomplished by arranging for candidates to be interviewed by 25 to 40 people in multiple countries and offices.

e. Pays EZI partners (equity owners) less in tough times in order to keep the firm's pre-partners (individuals on track to become equity owners) feeling secure and content. When the money is tight, partners would rather choose to tighten their own belts. "We have a strategy to grow organically," declared O'Brien. "We have historically tended NOT to lay people off; we don't believe it makes strategic sense." This practice—certainly a ringing endorsement for the long-term view—contributes to EZI's high retention rate.

3. Training to foster deep collaboration: EZI pegs its current investment in training as the highest among any of the global executive search firms. Presently pegged at more than US$5 million per year, EZI's training program is geared to inculcate new associates into its collaborative culture. The firm's training program is aimed at three junctures in the employee's early tenure at EZI. The first occurs within six months of joining the firm, when all new consultants go to Zurich for a three- to four-day training session. The primary purpose of this gathering is to orient the new people toward EZI's methods of conducting searches and management appraisals. Trainers employ a significant amount of role playing to emphasize the importance of collaboration. The second training program typically takes place by the new consultant's eighteen-month mark. At this two- to three-day session, they learn EZI's Performance Oriented Prediction (POP) interviewing techniques (which are based on a proprietary method developed at the University of Michigan). POP techniques are deeply grounded in the spirit of collaboration. At the third juncture, usually within a consultant's first two years, EZI offers a three-day training program, also held in Zurich, around interpersonal skills and "influencing" skills among consultants. Consultants are taught to recognize and interact with different person-

ality and preference profiles. EZI will soon offer a new element to this training: client relationship building. Other training programs focus on teaching EZI consultants the newest tools and techniques for collaborative problem solving and coaching techniques for office leaders.

4. Enacting open-book compensation. Every EZI partner knows every other EZI partner's compensation. For that matter, anyone who cares to ask will be told about EZI's open approach to compensation. Like others at EZI, this ideology—the ultimate illustration of collaboration—was Zehnder's brainchild. He reasoned that money is simply a by-product of one's work. In order to be focused on the most appropriate goal—solving the client's problem—one has to be focused on doing the best work. Money must be a distant consideration. EZI disdains the common professional service firm practice of compensating professionals on their individual performance (mainly, the size of their client billings and their selling prowess). Instead, compensation is seniority-based and transparent.

EZI pays its partners through a combination of salary, equity shares of the firm, and annual profits. "There is some variation among partner salaries across countries because of variations in the cost of living; people don't expect to be paid the same base salary in Kuala Lumpur, say, that they would be paid in New York," wrote Zehnder in a "First Person" article for *Harvard Business Review* in April 2001.[25]

Beyond salaries, the distribution of equity and profits is consistent across the firm. Regarding equity ownership, each partner has an equal number of shares in the firm's equity, no matter how long his or her tenure. Because 10 to 20 percent of the firm's profits are plowed back into the firm each year, the shares' value continuously rises. When a partner leaves EZI, the shares are sold back. (Departing partners keep the difference between the value of the shares they bought originally and the value of the shares on the day they sell them back.) In this fashion, seniority is rewarded.

Distribution of the rest of EZI's profit (80–90 percent) is also influenced by seniority. It falls into two pods. The first, divided equally to all partners, is a 60 percent distribution of profits. The remaining 40 percent is divided according to seniority (up to fifteen years of service). After fifteen years of tenure, the level stays the same.

5. Evaluating potential partners for their collaboration effectiveness: Everyone who gets hired to be an EZI consultant is assumed to be partner material. These "pre-partners," in order to have been hired by Egon Zehnder International in the first place, have already been pre-screened as excellent collaborators. Nevertheless, EZI's evaluation process further underscores the importance of collaboration. Each pre-partner is evaluated (annually and at the time they are considered for election to partner) on three fundamental criteria: execution excel-

lence, generating clients, and collaboration with EZI peers and clients. After five years of tenure, potential partners may be considered for partnership. A review committee of six people spearheads the process. At EZI's June partners meeting, the partners agree which pre-partners will go through the review process. In September or October a member of the review committee will be assigned to a subset of pre-partners. Each will spend one to one and a half days reviewing everything those pre-partners have done. The committee reviewer will collect references from anyone with whom the pre-partners have collaborated. With the appropriate information in hand, the partnership review committee then decides which pre-partners to recommend for a vote. Partners are elected by a two-thirds majority in January; from there, the process begins again.

6. Supporting collaborative effectiveness. A review process works well as long as everyone understands clearly what to evaluate. EZI has established multiple mechanisms to support collaboration effectiveness.

   a. *A collaboration timetable.* When EZI begins a new search, consultants are expected to share the position "spec" within practice groups, by e-mail. Within one week, the consultant is expected to convene a huddle of five to ten colleagues, by phone or in person, to brainstorm in real time about the search.

   b. *Technology that supports collaboration.* EZI uses a proprietary relational database (called ADAPT) that was developed in 1998. Every contact and every search is on this database. All field notes, e-files, calendars, and folders are cross-referenceable, open to all, and simultaneously viewable. But having a database and using it are two different things. At many companies, seeking to enable shared knowledge, the IT department or an IT committee has established an internal database or intranet designed to foster employee collaboration, but in too many cases, few people actually take advantage of the available technology. At EZI, however, using ADAPT is a norm, woven into the culture; people know they really cannot be successful without deeply relying on this database for their work with their colleagues.

   c. *Executive search "backups."* EZI assigns *two* people to every search—a lead and a backup consultant. This mechanism is derived from the firm's collaboration philosophy that a team is more effective than a single person.

   d. *Research collaboration.* Each office has a research capability and each practice has a practice specialist (researchers who have deep knowledge of a particular sector—retail or packaged goods, for example). These research teams are available across the globe; twice a week they participate in virtual gatherings with consultants and other researchers on conference calls to discuss specific searches, required capabilities, or the need for help.

e. *Bonding opportunities.* EZI fosters layers of opportunities for its consultants to develop collaborative bonds. While every practice group sets its own norms, a typical global practice group will meet off-site twice a year, usually during partner meetings, plus one other time a year for regional practice meetings. These meetings help EZI's consultants to build familiarity and trust together. Absolute confidentiality is required and in-person relationship building is deeply supported (with the firm investing significant amounts in travel). In addition, every three years EZI features a firmwide conference, usually tagged onto a partner meeting in June.

"And That Has Made All The Difference." EZI's marketing and business development strategies are designed to promulgate its culture. This is in contrast with many professional service firm leaders, who assume that the most effective way to align their marketing strategies with their culture would be to use external awareness-building vehicles. "We'll talk about our unique culture on our Web site." "Let's develop relationships with selected media that will reflect and further support our cultural theme." They would not be all wrong in making this decision: these are effective steps to take. After all, there's nothing like telling the world something to make you first "get it right" internally.

Arguably, though, promotion is the "outer ring" of other marketing strategies that must precede it. Egon Zehnder, already thinking globally about EZI's marketplace from the day he formed the firm in 1964, made three critical and deeply strategic decisions that serve as the ultimate alignment force behind EZI's culture. The net effect was to further sharpen the firm's cultural difference from its executive search rivals, and to more obviously attract the kind of talent that would embody the collaboration model that Zehnder had envisioned.

- *Fixed-fee pricing:* The vast majority of executive search firms invoice their clients a percentage of the successfully placed candidate's annual salary. In the 1960s, this percentage was about 10 percent; at this writing it hovers at around 30. Zehnder rejected the percentage approach. EZI therefore became the first retained executive search firm to charge a fixed fee for its professional services. No commissions. No bonuses. No matter at what level the candidate's salary was pegged.

  This practice was immediately more acceptable to EZI's European clients, skeptical as they were about the professionalism of search consultants who commission-priced their services. Their embrace of EZI's fixed-fee pricing helped it build a significant European-Asian base of business that remains a strong point for the firm.

EZI's no-percentage method also had an underpinning of egalitarianism and globalism that the firm's clients favored for two other reasons. "First, we want to demonstrate that we have no monetary interest in recommending a higher-paid candidate or excluding an internal candidate from within the client's own organization," explained Meiland. "Our fixed-fee is comfort to our clients. The second reason relates to the generally higher pay scale of Americans. If we were a percentage-based search consultant, and we recommended an American candidate above other equally qualified non-Americans, one might surmise we were simply trying to obtain the higher commission. With our fixed-fee approach, we won't make more money by recommending Americans. This practice is an effective demonstration that we will recommend the best candidate regardless of our own reward."

- No individual "selling" bonuses: "We always put our clients' interest first," states the EZI corporate brochure. Zehnder believed that EZI "must hire people who are true team players, people who get more pleasure from the group's success than their own advancement."[26] The manifestation for this ideology was Zehnder's decision that no EZI professional would be paid any kind of performance bonus—not a cent of it—for selling an engagement to a client. Instead, every professional would be paid a prorated slice of the firm's total profit. At first, this principle was followed for reasons of professionalism. Zehnder did not want his consultants to be motivated by the wrong incentive; he felt business developers too often "sinned" in their pursuit of a sale. The only emphasis, he felt, should be on organizing to solve the client's problem. "Most firms pay a bonus of 30 to 40 percent of the fee for a project that individuals generate," confirmed Meiland. "But we don't want people pursuing the wrong goals."

As time passed, it became clear that this model was also reinforcement for the firm's collaboration culture. A culture of individual rainmakers, EZI believes, builds internal competitiveness—and eventually a kind of psychological fire wall—among peers. This is a detriment to a firm's overall business health, and dampens the deep trust and collegiality that EZI seeks from its professionals. When the technique of awarding individual selling bonuses is not an option for *anyone*, however, people tend to share information more willingly. They can work together in a more team-oriented way. The potential for geographic or practice area business development vagaries is negated.

- *No hiring from competitors:* EZI's "no-selling-bonus" ethos is unheard of in its sector and in the professional service arena generally. Historically, many professional service firms, in their efforts to foster a rainmaker business model, built well-defined schemes for awarding monetary bonuses to the professionals (typically, but not always, these are equity partners) who sell the firm's engagements. Even today a majority of professional service enterprises maintain this practice. EZI finds that its global executive search competitors employ this "individual selling bonus" approach. Once search professionals have been exposed to this method, however, EZI believes, they are unlikely to be truly comfortable in EZI's uniquely egalitarian culture. The firm is so certain of this notion that it will not hire any consultant from other executive search firms who has participated in a commission- or percentage-based compensation model of selling.

There are still more examples. Zehnder, even though he is the firm's founder, made a deliberate choice from the beginning to pay some of his managers more money than he paid himself. Moreover, EZI has chosen to remain a privately held firm; it has also avoided a practice that until recently was pervasive throughout the executive search sector: giddy-up, instant-growth acquisitions.

Collaboration: Trouble Free? One wonders, "How can these people be so harmonious, so generous? Doesn't human nature drive us all to try to advance over others?" Indeed, EZI leaders acknowledge, a commitment to collaboration requires a strong will—and even a big wallet. There were times in the past when EZI partners had to finance the salaries of their global peers whose regional or country-specific economies had stumbled, making their ability to add to the firm's profits impossible. "Yes, we have had to remind ourselves about our values," acknowledged Meiland.

The Results. For the executive search sector, the last decade of the twentieth century saw unprecedented revenue gains. EZI, like others, grew steadily. It has been consistently ranked among the largest global retained executive search firms in the world.[27]

But the beginning of the new millennium did not smile with favor upon the executive search arena (especially in the United States). "After ten consecutive years of uninterrupted growth, the retained executive search industry in the U.S. posted one of its worst years ever as combined revenues for the 25 largest U.S. firms declined 30 percent or more than half a billion dollars ($523.5 million) in 2001." And for the top six global firms, "combined worldwide revenues for this entire group were approximately $1.8 billion, representing a decline of 23.7 percent or $600 million from the previous year's total of $2.4 billion."[28]

Egon Zehnder International was among those firms experiencing a revenue downturn. But, in a surprise to everyone but EZI professionals, its 2001 annual worldwide revenues were down only seven percent. This kind of financial performance demonstrates EZI's global strength and its ability to maintain a balanced revenue stream even in the midst of dizzying sector growth rates or precipitous sector downturns. But EZI's results demonstrate more than financial prowess. In the executive search industry, the average turnover rate among partners is 30 percent. EZI's attrition rate is dramatically lower, averaging only 2 to 5 percent annually.[29]

EZI's worldwide stature is the envy of many professional service firms, regardless of field. Its consultants are published in leading publications like the *Harvard Business Review*. Industry observers talk about EZI's competitive resilience with admiration.[30] Its research is respected worldwide. Its consultants are sought out by leading academics and governments for their insights and new methodologies. And its global clients return again and again.

USING ACCOUNT PLANNING AND RELATIONSHIP MANAGEMENT PROGRAMS

L.E.K. Consulting

The sixth case in the digging deeper building block reminds us of the power of *sheer will* to establish a competency in order to achieve a competitive edge.

Scene A: The largest revenue-generating client of a top-tier professional firm bolts for one of its strongest competitors. The client relationship had been shepherded by one of the firm's most successful practice leaders. Members of the executive committee are stunned at the defection. No one knew the client was vulnerable to being "picked off."

Scene B: A newly hired marketing director asks for a list of the firm's top 100 clients. She is astounded to learn that such a list does not exist, even though the firm brings in hundreds of millions of dollars in revenue each year. It takes her six frustrating weeks of explaining and even pleading with separate profit centers and far-flung practice leaders to build the list.

Each of these tableaux is real. Each, and others like it, illustrates a reality that exists in too many professional service firms today: an insidious gate-keeping culture in which "selling business" is built on a fragmented and hierarchical model of seniority and tenure, access to clients and client information is guarded, and firm-wide account planning is only given lip service.

L.E.K. Consulting's story is remarkable because of its early recognition of the competitive advantages that could be derived from the adoption of systematic relationship management processes, with strategic account planning as an end and a rigorous business development process as the means to achieve a competitive advantage. In the early 1990s, L.E.K.'s commitment was a bold step in a direction that few other professional firms had demonstrably embraced. By the late 1990s, the concept of client relationship management (with a multitude of accompanying software packages that offered technological support) had been well accepted in the professional service world. By then, L.E.K. already had made noticeable strides in its sector.

L.E.K.'s case is also extraordinary because it had the courage to embrace what would be a significant shift in the cultural fabric of the firm and it was refreshingly unabashed in its commitment. Through their words and their behaviors, L.E.K.'s partners communicated their conviction that the program would work.

But L.E.K.'s leaders gave their commitment much more than lip service. They did the heavy lifting that is required to succeed at a significant competitive mission. They made the program work by setting up the structure for it to become imbued throughout the firm. They reported on its accomplishments. They kept at it.

There is a final reason why L.E.K.'s approach to account planning and relationship management is so competitively savvy: it created a market-focused infrastructure that is built upon processes that are so unique to the firm that they are exceedingly difficult for rivals to copy. This market-driven infrastructure also gives L.E.K. the distinct advantage of having an early-alert system about shifts in the clients' needs and a framework for the firm's response.

The L.E.K. Consulting Story: Context and Background. L.E.K. Consulting is a global business-consulting firm that specializes in growth strategy, mergers and acquisitions, and shareholder value management. Founded in London in 1983 by three partners, it has grown to become a US$125 million firm with 450 professionals, including 70 vice presidents–owners, in 16 offices in Europe, North America, and Asia Pacific.[31] Since its beginning, the firm has advised more than 20 percent of the Fortune 500 companies in the United States, the Europtop 300 (akin to the Fortune 500), and the largest Australasia firms, as well as a rising number of start-ups, private equity firms, and government organizations.[32] In 1993 it merged with the Alcar Group as a way to increase its leadership in the value-based management arena. Since 1997, it has published an annual Shareholder Scoreboard with the *Wall Street Journal* of how 1,000 major companies returned value to their shareholders the year before.[33]

An "Uh-Oh!" Moment. L.E.K. makes it look easy, right? But professional service firms like L.E.K. don't get to the top tier of their sector without working to overcome some significant marketplace challenges. In 1994, the firm began training its vice presidents and senior managers in new approaches to selling and client retention. After an analysis of the life cycle and sources of the firm's revenues, L.E.K. management arrived at a sobering insight. More than half the firm's U.S. revenues were generated from its London or Australia clients. Moreover, for the firm's top ten U.S. revenue-generating clients in any year, there was a half-life of the total revenues. That is, revenues for the top ten revenue-generating clients for any given year dropped by 50 percent in each subsequent year thereafter.

Leon Schor, the firm's business development and quality vice president, realized that L.E.K. was facing the same pitfalls as its other management consulting brethren: the episodic nature of the sales cycle of a professional service firm. "It's part of the landscape of being a consulting firm," said Schor. "You can't count on having the same amount of work from clients every year. It's not just for one reason, but many: clients need time to digest our work; maybe the CEO position changes hands. Whatever. But that meant we had to replace half of each year's revenues just to stay even in the next year. We had to do something to retain client relationships while broadening our base." At about the same time as this moment of truth, the firm's U.S. management, including vice presidents Scott Shlecter, Francis Hawkings, Marc Kozin, Dan Schechter, and Stuart Jackson, had two critical epiphanies:

1. *Relying on the traditional professional services "rainmaker" selling model was an unacceptable competitive choice.* They believed this model in fact limited the firm's potential to compete effectively; it could only grow as much as those few rainmaking individuals could make it grow. Moreover, by 1993, L.E.K.'s U.S. founding vice president had moved on. L.E.K.'s vice presidents saw an opportunity to change the model—to turn *everyone* into a selling contributor, and to have the firm's revenue base become less dependent on any one individual.

2. *Competing by staging an extensive, monolithic branding campaign was an unacceptable competitive choice.* There was too much ground to cover vis-à-vis its competitors and there were too many young entrepreneurial unknowns at L.E.K. However, the vice presidents believed that L.E.K. could effectively compete by harnessing its proactive energy towards a new kind of competitive excellence: systematically following a defined program of relationship-oriented business development.

And so, L.E.K. began to vigorously—and meticulously—enact a distinctive set of relationship management processes. A U.S.-wide business development function was introduced to directly support and, in some ways, even manage the professionals who are selling. The central theme is *process*—to repeatedly, systematically, and strategically implement business development processes with potential clients and to emphasize referrals in highly "networked" industries. The mantra is to follow relationships.

"Our business development processes are founded on the principle that existing relationships are the most important driver of revenue," declared Kozin, now the president of L.E.K. North America. "We decided it was as important to build relationships with individuals, as with companies. We will stay close to an individual from job to job, company to company. And that takes a systematic planning and follow-up approach." But the real kernel is not that L.E.K simply tracks people as they shift from job to job, but that it discerns a pattern about the services they need, their recognition of their need to be helped, and their willingness to be helped.

Woody Allen the Sage. Woody Allen said, "Eighty percent of success is showing up." This "get-it-done" attitude is at the heart of L.E.K.'s relationship management approach. Everyone is expected to "show up" with positive energy and enthusiasm about selling business and managing accounts. Here's what it looks like:

- *Central coordination:* Along with heightening its expectations for professionals, L.E.K. built a framework of extraordinarily coordinated, centralized, and proactive internal support that enables professionals to plan, manage, and grow their relationships. It resembles a hive of activity on two levels. First is selling support. Business development managers follow up on all new U.S. contacts. Ten percent of these contacts are cold calls initiated by the business development team. They arrange meetings, request pre-meeting research, and obtain directions. They send electronic reminders to professionals about short-term follow-up action items.

They work to fill in business development days to optimize the vice presidents' travel time and expenses. They review proposals prior to their delivery to a prospective client. They coordinate selling activities with L.E.K.'s many marketing initiatives, so that each time a client is made aware of L.E.K., it can be recorded and tracked. Second is strategic account management and planning guidance. L.E.K.'s approach to business development morphs the traditional notion of account planning. "At L.E.K., account plans aren't the drivers of business development initiatives; they are the result of them," said Schor. As part of its strategic focus on all its relationships, L.E.K. business development managers notify the vice presidents of the timetable for reinitiating longer-term opportunities. They maintain and monitor a centralized contact management and calendar database, enabling them to work side-by-side with the vice presidents to manage both current and potential client opportunities. Twice a year, they lead detailed account reviews and forecasting sessions with each office.

- *Collaboration:* None of this bustle of activity could succeed without a deep commitment to collaborate internally. Each of L.E.K.'s vice presidents, their administrators, business development professionals, and marketing professionals agrees to perform a set of matrixed tasks in order for the others to work effectively. A set of norms has been adopted that everyone follows. For example, two vice presidents are expected to attend each sales appointment. Another example is that vice presidents are expected to proactively build their database of contacts and to plan the frequency of contact with them.

- *No secrets:* Collaboration could not occur if L.E.K. had a closed-door culture. All contacts are deemed the property of the firm, not of the individual professional who made the contact. (When L.E.K. instituted this practice in 1993, it was quite unusual for a professional service firm.) All contacts are expected to be recorded. Access to and use of the contact and activities database, although varying by role, is clearly explained in firm-wide documents and orientation sessions.

- *Measurement:* With its no-secrets ideology, L.E.K.'s commitment to measurement works well. On a monthly basis, the business development group measures the number of all sales appointments and referrals. It also tracks proposals (lost and won) and makes reminders about follow-up action items. In the United States, it also maps the number of contacts made at marketing-oriented, client-facing activities.

- *Training:* L.E.K.'s training programs set the tone for its cultural norms on developing relationships. They also teach the professionals about the firm's unique process and its eventual measurement. Every vice president worldwide participates in the firm's sales training. And, by their third year, consultants will have participated in L.E.K.'s systematic business development training program. A ten-step training document is also given to managers and newer vice presidents on how to build a book of business the L.E.K. way. But training isn't just a once-a-year event. In its refresher primers, internal written communications, and daily interactions, L.E.K. management makes it explicit precisely how it expects its professionals to sell new business.

- *Quality:* Business development professionals conduct a quality review on at least a quarter of all completed assignments. A few weeks or a month after work has been completed (with a special focus on new client projects), a business development manager contacts the L.E.K. vice president who headed the assignment to initiate a quality review. The business development manager asks if the project leader would like to have a quality review conducted on the project; the answer is usually "yes." Then the business development manager conducts a 20–30-minute, online-aided telephone interview with the project's client decision maker. They review a set of questions, some closed-ended and others open-ended. The questions are designed to obtain feedback and commentary about clients' impressions of the quality of L.E.K.'s work, perceptions about L.E.K.'s interactions with them, and, most important, how they are integrating L.E.K.'s work into their business. Business development managers offer clients a neutral agent to whom they can candidly offer their perceptions about the firm's performance and value, strengths, weaknesses, and areas for improvement and willingness to recommend L.E.K. to others. This process is as much about assessing client satisfaction as it is about paying attention to evolving client needs and marketplace shifts.

- *Standardization:* The glue for all the other elements is standardization. For each North American L.E.K. office, this includes: real-time calendars for all vice presidents; pre-meeting preparation and information for all vice presidents; introduction to L.E.K. and sector experience slides; client development packs; proposal templates; conference presentations; marketing event follow-up; mailing campaigns; and a formal inbound lead and information request process.

It's a Numbers Game. Imagine a virtual funnel into which prospects are drawn because of their attraction to a firm's valuable services and highly expert professionals. L.E.K.'s proactive account management program is based this model. It works to manage its connection with every individual who can either directly purchase its services or indirectly influence their purchase. The goal, of course, is to move the firm and its clients through this virtual funnel, providing extraordinary value with each step, toward a mutually beneficial end.

"We believe in the concept of six degrees of separation," stated Stuart Jackson, head of L.E.K.'s Chicago office. "Our business happens because we cultivate relationships intentionally with private equity investors, our alumni, and value-added resellers. We also include board members, venture capitalists, lawyers, our business school alumni, and of course our friends and social contacts." These numbers not only translate into revenues for the firm; they mean revenues for the individual professionals too. In multiple ways, from the earliest training exercise onward, L.E.K. management emphasizes that "working the network" and account planning are critical parts of each professional's compensation and reward. The goal is to increase their proficiency in understanding their buyers' decision making and in successfully meeting their needs with value-added services.

An important element of L.E.K.'s compensation and reward system is each professional's self-assessment regarding his or her effectiveness in client relationship management, account planning, and contribution to revenue growth. Yearly, each professional is asked to complete a hard-copy self-assessment tool to measure his or her progress in selling. As part of their review, vice presidents also receive feedback from Schor and from each other in peer reviews.

Clearing Out the Sand from the Wheels of Progress. L.E.K.'s makeover into a relationship management powerhouse wasn't seamless. It took the overt participation of L.E.K. leaders to ensure the successful early steps of the firm-wide shift to a formal program. "For example, from the program's first day, even through to today, we required professionals to submit account activity reports," recalled Schor. "Scott Shlecter, then the president of L.E.K. U.S., was the first one to get in all his reports. He demonstrated his belief in the importance of this approach." Others followed suit. The results spoke for themselves, as these and other L.E.K vice presidents began to noticeably—even dramatically, in some cases—improve their client retention and acquisition rates. Soon, from witnessing the demonstrations of their peers, it became clear to other L.E.K. vice presidents that they could increase their effectiveness by participating in a systematic program. "They began to 'get it' that a system could help them," said Schor.

Some of the hurdles were external. In the early days of the program, and even today, as business development managers continue to work to arrange appointments with prospective clients, they encounter unspoken skepticism: "This guy is not a management consulting professional. How could he *really* understand my business enough to help me solve my problem?" But each member of L.E.K.'s four-person business development group is cut from the same cloth: mature sales professionals, seasoned in business and deeply focused on increasing L.E.K.'s marketplace leadership. Their consistent and articulate manifestation of business acumen usually overcomes this skepticism, often to L.E.K.'s eventual competitive advantage. "It's more than just setting a certain number of appointments per month," reported Schor. "It's about understanding our business environment enough to tell a vice president, 'Here are three companies we should be working with. Let's write them a compelling letter and then call them.' We then work with the vice president to write the letter."

The biggest internal challenge is the learning curve. Vice presidents are still beginning to learn how the systematic L.E.K. program is supposed to work. A few others welcome the coaching they are offered by the business development group. Still others, perhaps those coming into L.E.K. with a book of clients from another environment, have had to adjust to L.E.K.'s unique process. In the main, however, this adjustment has unfolded smoothly.

The Results. L.E.K.'s client relationship development methods have achieved solid results. From 1997 to 2003, the firm achieved a 12 percent annual growth rate.[34] The firm's success in growing its revenues is backed up by a second important competitive achievement: Ninety percent of revenues are derived from referrals and past clients. By working to build its clients' loyalty and keep bringing them unsurpassed value, L.E.K. protects itself against competitive inroads while simultaneously growing the firm. In addition, L.E.K. has established a worldwide marketing committee whose focus is coordinating activities internationally and identifying and implementing business development and marketing processes worldwide. Moreover, account planning has become an accepted practice in most of the firm's international offices.

Another competitive accomplishment is the way L.E.K. reduced its dependence on a short list of rainmakers and simultaneously deepened its professionals' ability to understand and meet the needs of their clients. "Our top three sellers still only sell less than a quarter of the total of our revenues," noted Schor. "This also combats the perennial professional services challenge of balancing the 'selling the work' with the 'doing the work.' We are more balanced than we were before, and that helps us serve the clients more effectively."

USING MEASUREMENT TO INCREASE
STRATEGIC FOCUS AND COMPETITIVE
ADVANTAGE

ACNielsen

ACNielsen is a powerful example of a firm that understands the dramatic competitive advantages that can result from building a process-driven marketing infrastructure. Watch for two particularly notable achievements in this case. First, the level of effort, formality, and consistency with which ACNielsen's management communicated the importance of the many measurement initiatives it established, and the results those measurement efforts brought about. This is a firm that learned that measurement is not a bad word, and that it can be harnessed to help an organization move toward a strategic goal to lead its industry. Second was the way ACNielsen utilized its own core capabilities to best its competition. This approach is reminiscent of the firms I talked about earlier that intentionally use their cultural strengths to improve their ability to attract and retain clients. While not every firm can use this approach in the manner that ACNielsen has done, it's gratifying to see a real example of how it can be done well.

The ACNielsen Story: Context and Background. The ACNielsen case starts out with a familiar theme: the "cobbler's children have no shoes." This is no joke, and it's an all-too-familiar theme among many high-profile professional service firms. There are too many advertising and marketing communications agencies that have no Chief Marketing Officer and do not formally market their firms. There are too many architecture firms that work out of their own poorly designed spaces and too many management consulting firms that do not practice the very management principles that they offer to clients as gospel.

ACNielsen, one of the most respected names in the business of market research, information and analysis to the consumer products and services industries, was itself one of those cobbler's children. Yet, starting in the mid 1990s, it figured out how to utilize its own core competencies *on itself* in order to recapture a competitive edge. Globally, with more than nine thousand clients in one hundred countries, ACNielsen is one of the crown jewels for its parent, Dutch business information company VNU, itself one of the leading market research and business information publishers in the world. Since its founding in 1923, ACNielsen has built a solid reputation for its work in measuring competitive marketplace dynamics and consumer attitudes and behavior. It accomplishes this goal by compiling and analyzing retail store data and audits and tracking consumer household data, attitudes, and behavior.[35]

ACNielsen's service mission and portfolio of offerings features a simple value proposition: Help its clients develop advanced analytical insights that generate increased sales and profits.[36]

Yet with all its experience and well-deserved favorable reputation, ACNielsen had significant troubles in its largest market, the United States. In the mid 1990s, then owned by Dun & Bradstreet, it was struggling from the effects of frequent leadership turnover, low employee morale, and significant losses in revenue and operating income.[37] Even by late 1996, when ACNielsen went back to being an independent company trading on the New York Stock Exchange, the challenges continued: late product deliveries, poor customer satisfaction, continued low employee morale, and profits in a downward spiral.[38]

ACNielsen's return to a robust competitive position was led by ACNielsen CEO Steve Schmidt, in his former role as president of the U.S. business, along with the U.S. senior management team. Once an ACNielsen client, Schmidt, who joined ACNielsen in late 1995, collaborated with the corporate senior management team members throughout ACNielsen at the time, including Nick Trivisonno, Chairman and CEO; Bob Lievense, President and COO of ACNielsen; Mauricio Pagés, President–Americas region; John Lewis, Executive Vice President, Marketing; and Michael Brooks, Senior Vice President–Finance, to help move the firm toward a deeply integral position with its clients. Schmidt and his senior management team wanted to move the firm from being perceived as merely a "data company" to being globally respected as an insights and knowledge company that helps clients take action to be more profitable. "Our business must be embedded in our client's business—their internal objectives and their strategies. We have to develop solutions to help our clients make smarter business decisions," said Schmidt. "I don't want to be a variable expense in [our clients'] marketing research budget. I want to be a strategic asset in the marketing budget. ACNielsen's capabilities must be viewed as integral to the marketing story of these companies."

Driving the firm's shift toward a more robust integration with clients, though, required ACNielsen to drive its own shift internally. Schmidt described how he and his team realized a key principle: "Once you say, 'Okay, I want to be an insights and knowledge company,' that required [us to commit to capture] more insights [ourselves]." Beginning in 1995, for the first time in its history, and continuing through to today, ACNielsen began a series of initiatives to use measurement techniques to help the firm increase its strategic focus and competitive advantage.

ACNielsen used five critical measurement processes to drive its competitive advances.

1. *Measuring associate (employee) satisfaction* to increase shareholder value.
2. *Measuring client satisfaction* as part of a world-class client management program.
3. *Adopting a time-tracking approach* for the firm's client service organizations in order to better understand the client's profit and losses.
4. *Developing a set of quality measures* in order to better guide client use of ACNielsen's data.
5. *Creating and using a set of twenty-five internal productivity metrics* to help ACNielsen improve the way it manages itself for the benefit of the firm's clients.

Measuring Associate (Employee) Satisfaction. This initiative is the foundation for ACNielsen's overall approach to measurement. It is based on ACNielsen's wholehearted embrace of the concept of the Service Profit Chain as a basis for regaining competitive advantage.[39] Said Schmidt: "As a professional service organization, nothing is more important to ACNielsen than the service profit chain: improved employee satisfaction leading to satisfied customers, resulting in superior corporate performance and superior long-term shareholder value."[40]

Beginning in 1996, the company started administering a global study, the Business Effectiveness Survey (BES), to determine associate satisfaction. Where it finds gaps or shortfalls in the "index" established for each unit (and there always are gaps or shortfalls), the company initiates a series of review meetings firm wide to allow for associate feedback. From these meetings, associates and managers create functional action plans to work on throughout the coming year. ACNielsen's senior management team is then held accountable for the results those plans generate. During the year, associates receive quarterly progress reports about how the action plans are performing in helping ACNielsen achieve its business objectives. Said Schmidt in an interview:

> One unique aspect that we did do was we tied everyone's incentive target (25 percent) to associate satisfaction. That was significant. We let people know just how important this concept was by our actions: we set annual objectives and targets that we then communicated to all associates along with our performance against those objectives/targets. And every one of those business objectives was directly linked to the feedback from the annual associate satisfaction survey.[41]

Annually, Schmidt reports to his colleagues about how the firm scored on its associate-satisfaction levels. In his November 2002 communiqué to all VNU colleagues about the BES survey results, Schmidt wrote,

> Before I talk about the results, I wanted to reinforce to every associate how seriously we take these results. We are committed to making all VNU businesses the best place to work. The service profit chain of "Associate Satisfaction" leads to "Client Satisfaction" that leads to "Shareholder Satisfaction" is the foundation of this commitment, and is as true today as it was seven years ago when ACNielsen started this process. . . . Every business will have follow up meetings to discuss the results and then publish to all associates "action plans" that will be taken. Like I said, we take this survey process, its results, and action plans, very seriously.[42]

Measuring Client Satisfaction. In 1999, ACNielsen added another aspect to its repertoire of measurement initiatives: the Client Management Process (CMP). Key components of CMP include client briefing, needs assessment survey, objective setting, and demonstrated client ROI. Developed in the United States and eventually rolled out globally, the process is based on the notion that the firm has five customers in each of its clients: (a) the CEO, (b) the CMO, (c) the chief strategy officer, (d) the chief information officer (CIO), and (e) the Head of Market Research. Besides the obvious general objective (measuring and managing overall ACNielsen U.S. client satisfaction in order to increase patronage of its products and services), there are multiple specific objectives to determine:

- Customer perceptions of ACNielsen's performance vs. its main competitors
- The importance of factors which influence customer perceptions of ACNielsen
- ACNielsen's strength and weaknesses vs. its main competitors
- Priority areas for improvements to enhance the customer relationship
- A strategic tool for developing action plans to effectively grow and strengthen ACNielsen's market position

By identifying and documenting these clients' key business issues, needs, and objectives and then evaluating ACNielsen's performance against these parameters, Schmidt believes ACNielsen can significantly improve its viability to clients. From interviews with these key stakeholders, ACNielsen develops specific objectives and benchmarks for achieving improved client satisfaction. The diagnostic data is then used to develop specific action plans that address all identified areas of weaknesses as well as to drive overall levels of satisfaction. From there, it publicizes these objectives, benchmarks, and plans to other key stakeholders. As each quarter progresses, it measures its ROI on the outcome of its efforts. These ROI measures include revenue growth, shareholder value, and profitability. Annually, it repeats the process.

Time Tracking for Client Service Organizations. Time tracking was implemented broadly across the organization to help ACNielsen quantify the specific variable costs associated with each client's P&L. Sixty percent of ACNielsen costs are people, and each client has a unique service model. These insights allowed ACNielsen to target ten of their least profitable accounts. Subsequently, they launched a successful contract optimization initiative with these clients to improve profitability. Today, all major ACNielsen clients are profitable.

Quality Measures on How Clients Use ACNielsen's Data. ACNielsen began measuring two key elements that contribute most to client satisfaction: on-time delivery and initial database quality (i.e., how many data requests needed to be redone). Bonuses were then tied to these measures across the company's operations and senior management groups. These measures and the company's performance against them were also prominently featured in all new business presentations to allow ACNielsen to differentiate itself on the critical data quality platform.

Metrics for Internal Productivity. Beginning in 2000, the ACNielsen senior management team instituted a formal measurement program to improve its performance for clients and to improve its own bottom-line profitability. This comprehensive initiative encompasses twenty-five areas, from measuring cost- and resource-saving opportunities to measuring the success rate of the company's new service development efforts. In a key area, ACNielsen has measured the ways to achieve greater leverage on its technology software and systems. By measuring its costs and service delivery approaches, it decided to convert much of its decision support tools to the Internet rather than maintaining a proprietary capability in-house. Similar decisions were made to help the company improve its management of data processing, data collection, and coding work. From these assessments, the firm decided to concentrate all its data capabilities into one Web portal (called "ACNielsen Answers"), which also helps it conduct data mining. Schmidt said, "Every aspect of 'the factory' has been evaluated. We have productivity goals every year. These goals are continuously tracked." But ACNielsen's measurement goes beyond simply analyzing the most effective way to streamline costs and effort. In 2001, it also began measurement of the success rate of its own new service development process. "We still have a long way to go here," said Schmidt, but his optimism is palpable.

The Results. By enthusiastically committing to an intentional process of measuring its own performance in market-driven areas, ACNielsen has helped pay itself huge competitive dividends. Since 1995, when the first of ACNielsen's new measurement initiatives began, and despite the U.S. economy's rollercoaster performance, the firm grew its revenue and income dramatically. Since 1996, ACNielsen's global operating income has more than tripled and net income has nearly quintupled. Return on equity and return on assets have more than tripled as well.[43] By 2001, ACNielsen was an attractive enough acquisition candidate to become a member of VNU, the world's largest marketing and media information company.

These numbers certainly speak for themselves, but the results behind these numbers illustrate the real foundation of this success story. Associate satisfaction scores have risen 30 percent from the inception of the annual Business Effectiveness Survey process. And since 1996, ACNielsen has increased its share of the "Marketing Information" business arena by 10 percent over its next closest rival, Information Resources Inc., so that it now owns 54 percent of this marketplace worldwide.

Case Studies: Embedding Innovation

The embedding-innovation chapter includes four case examples that represent the competencies of building an R&D process (the process of innovation), using technology to build new services, and using incentives and rewards to stimulate innovation.

BUILDING AN R&D PROCESS

RSM McGladrey

Our first embedding innovation case features two firms that have taken different approaches to institutionalizing R&D. RSM McGladrey is included here for three reasons. First, this is a professional service firm that recognized the power of actively managing its service portfolio. This firm has a market-driven R&D mentality. Certainly, RSM McGladrey is not the only firm that can claim an R&D mindset. Some professional service firms have created formal R&D departments that feature teams working on client solutions that are ultimately shaped into formal offerings sold in the open marketplace. Teams then get rewarded for successful results. This model is adapted from one we've seen work very effectively in the world of consumer and business-to-business products. But, importantly, RSM McGladrey morphed the traditional products-oriented R&D concept in a completely new way, and built it into a potent differentiator in and of itself. This is innovation in spades.

Second, RSM McGladrey "worked the process." Once the idea of an experiential learning event was hatched, it took a discrete process *of building* to achieve the effect and the results that the concept's originators had imagined. RSM McGladrey created a valuable—and competitively advantaged—infrastructure for this kind of R&D to happen. This infrastructure included multiple, complementary processes: a communications process (all those brochures, meetings, e-mails!); a technology process (the creation of the on-line talent profiles that were available to all participants); an events process (to stage an event that was supported by a myriad of tangible visual tools and techniques); and a financial analytical tool and diagnostic process called ValueInsight™ to identify drivers of business value. It's an infrastructure that, once built, chugs along more easily time and time again, becoming literally embedded into the firm's culture, organizational structure, and strategic approaches. This is the business version of "poetry in action."

Third, this firm gleaned the significance of adding client "experience" to its services. Defined by Jim Gilmore and Joe Pine in their 1999 book, *The Experience Economy*, experiences are memorable, purposely staged events delivered to customers.[1] By grasping the attractiveness of "an experience" to its clients and its own professionals, RSM McGladrey has become one of the first professional service firms I've seen to effectively step into the new "experience economy." And it did it while not only delivering that experience to its clients (arguably a one-way street), but to itself simultaneously.

The RSM McGladrey Story: Context and Background. This case begins at an unlikely spot—the arena of continuing professional education for certified public accountants. In order to maintain their licenses, CPAs in the United States are required to complete a specific number of credits, typically biennially or every three years. Just any old educational program won't do, either. It has to be a formal program of learning or other means which contributes directly to the professional competence of a licensee in public practice.[2] Candidates for license renewal must submit formal documentation to demonstrate their completion of approved educational requirements. Understandably, the infrastructure that supports this obligation, and fosters its recognition across geographies, is itself quite official. In the United States, the continuing education committees at state CPA societies spend much of their time and resources in the business of educating their CPA members. Similar professional educational requirements exist in other countries.

Accounting is not the only profession that emphasizes ongoing learning. Despite a lack of formal licensure requirements, the management consulting industry increasingly fosters the notion of continuing professional education. Many management consulting firms encourage professional development as a must-do path for advancement; some offer it as part of their rewards packages.

As laudable and necessary as professional education is, however, the very fact that it is required (or even heavily encouraged) can make continuous learning seem tedious. And, as much as we might hate to admit it, the traditional alternatives available for learning do begin to seem repetitive, especially for senior-level accountants who have spent years complying with this requirement for licensure, or deeply experienced consultants who lead important, time-sensitive client engagements. It's no surprise, then, to see accountants or consultants nodding off in a here-we-go-again lecture on topics they mostly grasp anyway.

How refreshing, then, to see how RSM McGladrey, a Minnesota-based accounting and consulting firm, turned a forced learning activity into a platform for dynamic innovation. And how competitively very savvy of this firm to build what is essentially a new R&D capability. Our story describes how RSM McGladrey created an exciting, highly experiential learning laboratory to help itself build an R&D platform to move beyond its traditional accounting and consulting services and toward totally new and effectively integrated services.

In mid-1999, H&R Block bought the nonattest assets and business of McGladrey & Pullen LLP, then the seventh largest accounting firm in the United States, for $240 million, and integrated it into other firms to create RSM McGladrey, Inc.[3] As part of RSM International, RSM McGladrey, Inc., is one of the United States' leading tax, accounting, and consulting organizations serving mid-sized businesses. According to a survey released in the January 23, 2003, edition of *International Accounting Bulletin*, RSM McGladrey and McGladrey & Pullen, when considered together, represent the fifth largest accounting firm in the United States.[4]

Today, RSM McGladrey, Inc., and McGladrey & Pullen LLP are affiliated through an alternative practice structure (an arrangement approved by the U.S. Securities and Exchange Commission and the National Association of State Boards of Accountancy). Though separate companies, a professional services agreement between the two firms enables them to work together to serve clients' business advice needs.[5] Focused almost exclusively on mid-market (US$5–$150 million annual revenues) privately held clients, RSM McGladrey has built itself into a US$588 million business. Its more than 4,200 employees in more than one hundred U.S. offices deliver a mix of accounting and tax work, as well as strategy, operations, human resources, financial, and IT consulting. The firm also provides wealth management and retirement resource services.

Once the H&R Block acquisition activities were officially complete, RSM McGladrey leaders began to focus on ways to help the firm grow its integrated services. Some of their efforts, of course, were to cross-sell the McGladrey & Pullen accounting services into broader RSM McGladrey consulting engagements. In a November 2002 interview with *Consulting Magazine,* Jim Blayney, senior vice president of RSM McGladrey Business Services, said, "We're after a total relationship that will get us in at a level that will help clients achieve their objectives. One-audit-and-get-out would not be our cup of tea."[6]

Even as recently as 2000, however, the notion that innovation and continuing education could be effectively linked was nowhere on the radar screen. So, on a separate front, RSM McGladrey managers worked to advance their approaches to continuing education. Carol Thornton, director of continuing professional education (CPE) and management development for consulting services, described the situation. "We had had an annual consulting large-group educational event for some years. Our consultants were tired of it. It was a same-old, same-old CPE internal event. It wasn't innovative. We recognized that we needed to take it to another level, shape it up. As well, we wanted to focus our learning events on where the business was going in general—to grow consulting services more rapidly than traditional accounting services."

In response, a number of RSM McGladrey consultants formed a committee representing multiple practices from around the United States, to brainstorm ways to improve and liven up the firm's consulting services professional education initiatives, particularly its annual conference. Over the course of several months in 2000 they held several Web conferences to shape a new approach to learning. With the assistance of an outside consultant, the idea of a learning laboratory took shape.

Not Just Any Old Learning Laboratory. For me, this is where the story gets exciting. Committee members challenged themselves to stretch beyond tradition. "What if," they said, "we brought clients into a *live* learning forum—an open, improvisational learning environment where we can work *with* clients to discover more potent ways to accelerate their own—and our—growth?" The idea of an experiential consulting /client learning laboratory was born. Suddenly, the old model of continuing professional education was transformed into what would become a powerful competitive platform.

The firm's first experiential learning laboratory, a 48-hour event held in November 2001 in Kansas City, was called BiFF (Bigger, Farther, Faster). It was comprised of a mix of presentations, workshops, conversations, and work sessions, all designed to help clients and consultants develop real-time innovative approaches to complex business issues. Six client teams (with up to eight people on each team) were invited to participate, along with more than 250 RSM McGladrey participants including consultants and business advisors as well as firm executives. The goal was to create innovative business solutions on four key questions:

1. How will we find, inspire, and keep talented people in the next few years?
2. How will we determine and deliver on our critical business strategies?
3. How will we use technology to remain competitive?
4. How will we remain productive and profitable over time?

The BiFF invitation promised clients "access to RSM McGladrey's best and brightest consultants and a firsthand opportunity to experience an innovative business growth model."[7] It promised the following to its participants:

- Help people unlearn the old and jumpstart the new.
- Energize people and strengthen relationships.
- Support collaboration and partnering.
- Give everyone easy access to adaptable products and services.
- Capture great ideas and accelerate innovation.
- Understand and focus on strategy and customers.

The event itself used a unique mixture of elements to comprise the "work." With more than 250 individuals working together in one large space, the client teams combined the many tools and talents available to identify issues, discover opportunities, and develop integrated solutions to achieve those opportunities. Throughout the entire experience, the participants were surrounded by talent from RSM McGladrey, the client teams, and the external experts. These experts led guided presentations and interactive conversations to stimulate new and exciting ideas and thoughts.

The learning during the working sessions was accelerated when the participants took the experience and examples provided by the external experts and applied those ideas to help them think bigger, go farther, and move faster. The BiFF concept was dynamic, engaging, and innovative and the participants came away invigorated and ready to try this new technique with their clients. The BiFF experience was a living manifestation of RSM McGladrey's core values and was designed to put the firm's unique strategic position into practice in an innovative way, with real clients in real time. Most important, the entire learning experience created the conditions for all participants to act in unison in a very open way.

With the success of a "live" learning event behind them, the firm determined to hold another similar experience in November 2002—this time called "The Consulting Experience"—in Chicago. To provide more direction for conference participants and allow them to focus on their specific area of expertise, the planning committee for the 2002 conference made several changes to the format of the event, including reducing the number of client teams and attendees.

This time, the work began with an analysis of several value drivers using a new tool developed by a team of consultants with financial management expertise from around the firm. This tool and the redefined conference process allowed client teams to better recognize issues and opportunities available to the clients. Once the analysis had been done, the client teams were able to break into smaller, functionally focused groups to develop specific action plans in several areas. The results of these discussions became integrated into an overall action plan for each of the clients to take back at the end of the 48 hours. BiFF provided the inspiration and "The Consulting Experience" provided the tools.

The revitalization of learning continues beyond 2002 with RSM McGladrey's expanded use of distance learning for technical education and expanded conferences for professional development. The firm is no longer content with the same old routine. In August 2003 McGladrey's consultants joined other accounting and tax professionals for a dynamic experience focused on the McGladrey client service delivery model and developing industry expertise. This Industry and Consulting Conference brought together more than six hundred consulting generalists as well as financial services; manufacturing, wholesale, and distribution; and construction industry experts from a wide range of functional areas and locations. And in June 2004, the learning community will expand to more than 1200 as additional tax, governmental and nonprofit practitioners join the Industry and Consulting Conference.

Challenging the "Old Ways" to Embrace a New Competitive Advantage. The firm's early learning laboratory organizers did not set out intentionally to build a new set of services or a marketplace advantage. The activity was deemed an internal initiative from the very beginning. "It was simply to help us redirect our learning model," recalled Thornton. "Also, it was a convenient way to bring our geographically dispersed consultants closer to each other, and to bring the accounting side closer to the consulting side."

But as brainstorming and planning progressed on the new approach to learning and continuing education, committee leaders and other RSM McGladrey senior managers began to recognize that they were in the midst of leading the firm toward a deeply strategic competitive accomplishment. The firm determined to set aggressive goals for BiFF—to make it a continuing learning experience, to model a fast-moving, high-performance business environment, to have the event itself become a "net force" for achieving strategic goals, and to help the firm's consultants and clients "act their way" into thinking differently. The learning laboratory team was convinced that this new model of learning would inspire innovative behavior, that it was a great idea, and that clients would love it.

But getting there meant changing not only the old ways of learning, but also the traditional ways of relating to clients. "Some of our folks felt that we could be vulnerable if we didn't bring in the 'best' clients, or if we didn't perform our best in front of them," said Thornton. "But the more we talked about it, the less scary it seemed." Tom Dobosenski, managing director in the firm's upper Midwest region, concurred: "Our positive orientation never wavered. There was really never a crisis of confidence, but we realized we were taking our consultants out of their traditional mode of thinking, and making them think more broadly. We wanted to deliver a true team approach—to do what most other firms say they do, but don't actually do." Moreover, the team wanted to attract client participants that would provide the greatest mutual learning opportunity. That meant RSM McGladrey would have to carefully select the firms it would invite. The real challenges to creating a successful collaborative learning opportunity were in convincing potential attendees, both RSM McGladrey consultants and the firm's clients, of the value of the event.

The consultants didn't rush automatically to sign up, and it took a lot of work to get the desired clients. With BiFF scheduled in November 2001, the committee began communicating in February and March 2001. "There were lots of brochures and flyers, lots of internal e-mail messages, lots of personal contact and phone calls, followed up by committee members talking with the contributors," Thornton remembered. "We realized we were reinventing the professional education experience. We had to let them know the value." Once BiFF was under their belt, the consultants were primed and ready to participate in November 2002's "The Consulting Experience" event. By this time, communication activities were less intense and more focused. Describing the new and improved workflow of the event was the main topic for much of the communication.

The Results. RSM McGladrey's most basic accomplishment was that it delivered on its own promise to its professionals and its clients: to give them a great new learning experience. Another outstanding achievement was the fact that the firm saw a noticeable uptick in client revenues from the clients that attended the events. However, this firm actually achieved deeper, more potent results: for its own professionals, for clients, and in the marketplace.

First, RSM McGladrey leaders wanted to demonstrate, to their accounting brethren and consulting colleagues, the value of integrating the firm's core competencies to meet client needs. They also wanted to demonstrate that those integrated services could be delivered in a dramatically new way: unhesitatingly, collaboratively, face-to-face, differently, and in stimulating, congenial, and more visual ways than had ever been done before. "Our people see this as an investment in their careers," Dobosenski noted. "Our professionals feel a real sense of appreciation for their new knowledge—and new connections."

Second, clients that attended BiFF and The Consulting Experience received real-time business solutions that were invented, shaped, and delivered within a 48-hour duration. They participated in a seamless learning experience that produced instant answers to their complex challenges. They got to codevelop new services that benefited themselves as well as their mentors, tutors, and business advisors. Going forward, these clients will enjoy their own marketplace advantage as they implement the inventive and competitively advantaged solutions that they cocreated with RSM McGladrey. Now *that's* thinking bigger, farther, and faster.

Third, and equally important, were results in the marketplace. BiFF and its next generation, The Consulting Experience, became bold, value-added platforms for RSM McGladrey. By developing a process to evolve its service portfolio in a powerful way, it mounted to a new strategic level: cocreating, with clients, a new standard of services. This demonstration of marketplace leadership takes an enormous amount of focus, effort—and fortitude. It is marketplace mastery in action.

Rockwell Group

Rockwell Group, a New York–based architecture, planning, and design firm, is a second case demonstrating the process of researching and developing new services. There were two reasons why Rockwell Group's story intrigued me. One—the more obvious—is the firm's shrewd decision to move beyond its well-documented accomplishments in the fields of architecture, design, and planning. The other is related to a subject that gets short shrift in many professional service organizations: succession planning.

For a long time, Rockwell Group felt the constraints of the classic professional service conundrum: that clients can only perceive their need for a service that is available *today*. It is up to the professional to figure out how to anticipate what clients might need *tomorrow*, even if they cannot articulate it at all. By all accounts, Rockwell Group was performing excellently at delivering on its clients' current needs. Indeed, this firm could have simply ridden the tide of its own fame, built on the public's embrace of the creative genius of founder David Rockwell. Yet it embraced a firm-wide research and development mindset, and it created a formal infrastructure for its R&D efforts to succeed. Also, it was particularly savvy to set up and direct the R&D framework to explore both external and internal innovation opportunities, rather than to depend on one innovation avenue only.

The second reason I included the Rockwell case is an ancillary—though also critical—benefit of Rockwell's approach to innovation: a process so strong that it is likely to last even after its founder has left the stage. Succession planning is always a challenge in professional service enterprises, especially when the founders or powerful partners are still very much a part of the firm's current success and growth. The firm's R&D avenue—Rockwell Group Ventures—offers a platform for its survival past David Rockwell; it does so in a way that supports professionals to pursue genuine innovation rather than feign doing so while actually just competing for favor. It levels the internal playing field while simultaneously keeping the firm at the cutting edge.

Rockwell Group comprehends that there is more to the professional service value proposition than simply getting a piece of today's client's money—a point that too many professional service firms still do not grasp. Rockwell Group professionals could have held an ongoing pity party, whining that "Our clients could pay us more, but they won't." Instead, however, they decided to improve their own value proposition, becoming even more attractive to clients. They realized that real professional dominance requires leading at the front edge of an industry's evolution, building intellectual capital, and being able to shape the birth of new solutions to clients' problems. Money comes *after* leadership, not the other way around.

Indeed, Rockwell Group's mindful commitment to be at the forefront of its sector, with a desire to maximize its clients'—and its own—value, represents a clarity of purpose to be *good* at being in business, and all that that implies. Increasingly, clients will want to work with firms that have this kind of commitment.

The Rockwell Group Story: Context and Background. Staying ahead of the commoditization dragon is a significant challenge in many professions. Engineering, law, and accounting are good examples because they have to adhere to steep (yet appropriate) academic and licensure requirements. Architecture, a field whose foundations are creativity and "newness," also battles this commoditization dragon. Some architectural firms have addressed the challenge of fatigued services by focusing deeply on particular building types, like hospitals and health care, educational facilities, sports venues, or even aquariums. Others have "gone deep" by specializing in particular areas like historic preservation or landscape architecture.

Sometimes firms overcome commoditization by pushing themselves beyond the traditional boundaries of their profession: for example, real estate brokerage firms that offer construction services, construction firms that offer facilities management, or executive search firms that offer management appraisals. In each of these cases, and others like them, the firm retains its traditional professional service portfolio and focus, but "snaps on" a set of services that may blend into the services of other, also largely traditional, professions. The rationale is, "We're meeting our clients' needs for a broader set of solutions!" It's a kind of one-stop professional service shopping trip. Typically, this is not a capricious decision. In all likelihood, professional firms that decide to add on services conduct some kind of research in their marketplace (the "R" in R&D), and then bring in some new-to-our-firm-but-still-traditional service offerings (the "D"). Pitfalls abound, however; all too many snap-on services suffer a kind of stepchild existence, never achieving the respect, attention, or nurturing that the firm's core services do.

A more integrated process of R&D is underway at the Rockwell Group. Rockwell Group is celebrated for pushing beyond the traditional boundaries of its field. It has won numerous awards for its "spectacular, unexpected, piquant" work on restaurants, hotels, casinos, theatres, and sports and entertainment venues.[8] Pundits hail the way founder David Rockwell and his fellow collaborators have produced "friendly and stylish . . . playful fantasies" that are "outlandish and practical at the same time."[9]

One might argue that R&D, creativity, and innovation should be a natural strength for architects. ("They're designers, after all!") At the Rockwell Group, innovation is as much the result of a disciplined process as is the creative spark that fuels it. This firm's approach to formal R&D—the process of creating totally new services—has meant the creation of a dedicated infrastructure where innovation can occur, a dispassionate view of the changing marketplace, and a tolerance for business risk.

The Wonderland of Business. The ninety employees of the Rockwell Group, founded in 1984, are having a wonderful time. They have created venues—actually, three-dimensional emotional experiences— like Los Angeles' breathtaking Kodak Theatre (where the Academy

Awards are held), Connecticut's spectacular Mohegan Sun Casino, and Philadelphia's celebrated Pod restaurant. But this firm doesn't limit itself to designing buildings. It created the sets for the hit Broadway musical *Hairspray*, and interior designs for Planet Hollywood restaurants worldwide and New York's Rocky Horror Show theater. It's even created new products: a self-illuminated beaded chair and a hanging rear-projection gel clock for the World Studio Foundation, custommade dishware for New York's Payard restaurant, and even a Rockwell Group umbrella. The firm has been prolifically busy; Rockwell himself has been involved in more than 120 built projects since beginning his career.[8]

It's obvious that the theme of wonder runs deep at the Rockwell Group, starting with its founder. Rockwell believes that "acts of commerce should have a strong dose of wonder." The same is true for the theme of innovation. In a 2002 *Time* magazine interview, he said, "What drives us is invention. We are specifically looking for something new."[10] On the surface, Rockwell's quote refers to his firm's architecture, planning, and design services. Over the years, however, as he watched the way clients "consumed" Rockwell Group's services, he became convinced that he had to pursue this very same objective for increasing the value of his own business.

In the early days of the firm, Rockwell and his staffers served as traditional professional service providers: give the client your expertise, and the client pays you for your work; when the project is done, you go away. Under this time-tested scenario, clients respect their professionals' expertise, admire their skills, even delight at their powerful results. But at their core, they consider professionals to be vendors who have been tapped to provide a transactional service: architecture, design, or planning. Some professional services, like accounting or law, are well-suited to long-term transactional relationships. Many, though, like architecture, have a finiteness to them. Projects have a fixed beginning and a finite end. Once the project is done, the value exchange between client and professional service practitioner is complete.

Even though his firm's work was lauded widely, Rockwell began to observe early hints of this commoditization mentality. He grew increasingly concerned with what he saw as a (mostly) one-way value exchange. He wondered, "Could it be that Rockwell Group's clients are receiving *much more* than architecture, planning, and design services?" He believed the balance of mutual advantage between client and professional should be more evenly weighted, with all sides benefiting handsomely for results that literally delighted all.

"We knew we could bring clients even more substantial value than they were asking us to," concurred Marc Hacker, who joined Rockwell Group in 2000 as director of strategy and development. "We knew we had to move beyond being in a reactive mode with our clients. We decided not to wait for our clients to tell us what they want." Thus, in 2000, Rockwell and Hacker embarked on a formal journey to a new kind of business wonderland: actively, they began to look for ways to take the intellectual properties of Rockwell Group's service business and use them as a foundation to build a new business. They wanted to create a service model to more fully benefit the firm's clients—and the firm itself.

Three-Dimensional Branding. Rockwell's decision to build a formal R&D capability was fueled by his realization that his services lead clients into exciting but unknown turf. "We use architecture, planning and design to help clients dramatically re-define their businesses and their brands," declared Rockwell. "We help them develop an experiential, three-dimensional form of their brand, and in doing so, we help them transform their businesses to another level entirely." He is not kidding—Rockwell Group's work with the W Hotel helped build it into a highly valued brand and the billion-dollar Mohegan Sun Casino became one of the largest and most profitable in the world.

Moreover, Rockwell and Hacker knew, the Rockwell Group works in an arena where none have created a footprint before. By creating physical spaces and things to deliver specific emotional experiences, the Rockwell Group is bending the concept of branding into a new, almost theatrical, form entirely. Hacker's charge was to ask big strategic questions ("Where are we going with this?" "How can we stay ahead of inevitable commoditization?") and then to harness the Rockwell Group's evolved service mix into a pipeline of profitable new opportunities. In 2001, he created a proposal to build a formal Research and Development function at the Rockwell Group. Its mission was threefold:

- *Explore:* Leverage Rockwell Group's access to some of the most creative, dynamic, and successful business people in the United States and worldwide.
- *Develop:* Proactively create business opportunities both internally and in conjunction with clients and partners. Direct and focus those partnerships to actively package unique approaches to traditional formats of activity and experience.
- *Profit:* Actively participate in the equity structure or royalty payments of new concepts, projects, products, and events as the principal and in partnership with other companies and investors.

Simply put, the R&D function would seek to generate projects that would increase the firm's and its clients' value. It was built on two pillars. The first pillar was external opportunities. Early on, Rockwell and Hacker believed that "value" was directly tied to the structure of the working relationships and agreements between clients and professionals. They already knew that the Rockwell Group was perceived as a key source of fresh new ideas. Now, they wanted to extend the scope of their traditional client-consultant role by pursuing external projects that would be structured to share equity opportunities. "Professional service firms in our field and other sectors have grappled with the issue of 'mutual value' in their work with clients," said Rockwell. "One of the methods they've tried is to obtain some sort of equity position in their projects. There are circumstances when this makes sense for all of the collaborators in a project."

Hacker created a formal screening process, through which Rockwell Group collaborators would (1) generate ideas and concepts for new applications of three-dimensional branding, (2) research and analyze the feasibility and financial impact of each idea, (3) hone down the requirements and resources to bring the idea to fruition, and (4) develop the project, with outside financing if available.

By definition, this external R&D pillar is subject to the vagaries of the economy. When clients face economic uncertainty, they lower their risk profile and watch their purse strings. Investors become more conservative. It's an understandable response to the possibility of loss. In order to proactively access greater value, Rockwell Group decided to add an internal R&D pillar.

The second pillar was internal opportunities. This element of Rockwell Group's R&D model was structured to help the firm pursue internal business creation—transforming in-house concepts into viable businesses. The formal screening process (outlined above) applied to these internal opportunities as well. A key area of focus was to develop projects that put Rockwell Group at the nexus of "experiential" industries where people are in contact with each other and with brands. Increasingly, these industries represent an overlap of retail, dining out, sports and fitness, new media, entertainment, and leisure.

The Results. In late 2002, Rockwell Group formally put its R&D principles into action. This initiative encouraged Rockwell Group professionals to develop business in a different way and to formulate fewer but deeper relationships. "We've moved our business development initiatives and our client service relationships from reactive to proactive," said Hacker. "Of course, we'll always respond to our clients, but we won't have to rely on their requests alone anymore."

Rockwell Group's R&D framework proved its value nearly right away, when Meijer Inc. came calling. Meijer is a midwestern family-owned chain of nearly 160 combination grocery and general merchan-

dise stores. Competitors include Wal-Mart, Target, and Kroger. Besides
food, its huge stores stock about 120,000 items in hardware, apparel,
toys, and electronics. Some of its stores also sell gasoline, offer banking
services, and have multiple in-store cafes.[11] Meijer also has its own line
of private label products. In fall 2002, Meijer executives, having heard
about Rockwell Group's stellar reputation for design, asked the firm to
generate a proposal to create some of its private-label products. In the
past, Rockwell Group would have only been able to respond—with a
"yes" or a "no, thanks"—to Meijer's well-defined request. Instead, with
the Rockwell Group's new R&D principles backing it up, the firm was
able to respond in a way that brought more value to Meijer—and served
the Rockwell Group's desire to innovate beyond the limits of its own
traditional field. "We told Meijer 'Yes, we could develop your products,
but we'd like to do something different to help your business compete
more effectively,'" recalled Hacker. "We told them we thought they
needed a better platform to sell *all* their products, that they needed
better brand support mechanisms." Meijer's response was enthusiastic.
It asked Rockwell Group to create entirely new definitions of its corporate brand and related brand elements.

In December 2002, Meijer formally engaged Rockwell Group to design anything and everything that relates to a Meijer shopper's experience: from shopping accoutrements like product shelves and shopping
bags to marketing communications like brochures, flyers, and ad campaigns and building features like floors, ceilings, walls, and lighting. In
short, Meijer engaged Rockwell Group to do exactly what Meijer most
wanted to receive and what Rockwell Group most wanted to deliver: a
three-dimensional brand experience. This project signals the success of
Rockwell Group's R&D capability. And it's only the beginning.

USING TECHNOLOGY TO BUILD NEW SERVICES

DDB Worldwide

DDB Worldwide's story serves as an excellent embedding-innovation
illustration. At first glance, this case might seem to be about a repositioning strategy, which is critical to the story. But more important is how
DDB's finely tuned market-driven infrastructure effectively supported
the creation of a technology-enabled new service—one that was extremely well timed to take advantage of clients' increasing interest in
accountability and results. DDB's timing was not merely serendipitous;
it flowed from an orientation to anticipate continuously the market's
unmet needs.

Many professional service firms, when faced with commoditization,
consider enlivening their portfolio by adding a technology component

to their offerings. In some cases, they simply remove the "people" from the offering and substitute software and keystrokes instead. If their service is that routine, and if they intend to retire it eventually from their portfolio, this approach makes a great deal of sense. DDB Worldwide, on the other hand, chose to create a totally new value-added professional service unit, DDB Matrix, featuring econometricians whose intellectual capital is applied on a case-by-case basis and whose work is enabled by technology. DDB's move represents the way technology can be harnessed to enhance a professional service portfolio, not simply shore it up. Moreover, DDB's econometrics model is not proprietary; it is open at all times to inspection. Combined with the fact that it is not standardized (no cookie-cutters here!) or even trademarked, this makes the model extremely difficult for competitors to copy.

DDB Worldwide's new service launch strategy was smart. By integrating econometrics with its current services, it allowed clients to build gradual but unshakably favorable perceptions about the value of econometrics. Moreover, instead of a massive splash that would spark intense competitor scrutiny—and attempts at imitation—DDB Worldwide introduced its service incrementally, in a way that further solidified its loyal client base.

The DDB Worldwide Story: Context and Background. In 1998, colleagues Jim Crimmins and Bob Scarpelli sat in DDB Worldwide's Chicago office talking about how to improve the company's articulation of its value and service benefits to the marketplace. Crimmins, the company's worldwide brand planning director, and Scarpelli, U.S. chief creative officer, discussed the many significant shifts they had seen occur over the last decade in the professional service fields of advertising, market research, public relations, and marketing communications. Both agreed DDB Worldwide needed to deliberately separate itself from its competitors (both traditional and emerging) by moving toward a more advantageously positioned spot on the global map of professional service fields.

Making a move like this certainly would not go unnoticed. DDB Worldwide, Inc., an advertising agency network, is part of the Omnicom Group, one of the three largest advertising organizations in the world. DDB Worldwide's 15,000 employees operate from 206 offices in ninety-nine countries.[12] Moreover, even at the time this story begins in 1998, DDB Worldwide was far from holding an unfavorable marketplace position. It was known as a creative powerhouse, winning multiple Cannes Creative Awards (advertising's version of the U.S. movie industry's Oscars). Moreover, effectiveness was one of its historical strengths.

For Crimmins and Scarpelli, though, external recognition was highly desirable but simply not enough; they wanted to fortify the link between creativity and effective results. Their philosophy was based on a key principle articulated by one of the firm's founders, Bill Bernbach, back in the 1950s: "Properly practiced creativity can make one ad do the work of ten."

And so in 1998 they hatched DDB Worldwide's repositioning strategy, articulated in a new battle cry: BetterIdeasBetterResults. The tag line, Scarpelli's brainchild, has no spaces between the words; this technique dramatizes the fact that results and creativity are parts of a continual process. Each one flows into the other. DDB Worldwide Chairman Keith Reinhard issued his endorsement: "These four words succinctly state our purpose everywhere: To be more creative than our competitors in order to give our clients an edge over theirs" (see Figure 7.1).

Bringing a Positioning Strategy to Life. DDB Worldwide's repositioning is a critical element in this embedding innovation story because it occurred in parallel with the launch of a new technology-based service that brought the strategy to life. The service is called DDB Matrix, a consulting unit that uses econometric methods (statistical analyses of economic relationships) to forecast the effects of any number of marketing campaign variables over time. For example, with DDB Matrix services, the firm can advise a toothpaste manufacturer on how the sales of its toothpaste would be influenced by its price relative to competition, by the stores in which the toothpaste is sold, whether there is a coupon for it, whether it is put on display, and the like. DDB Matrix professionals can also forecast whether marketing communication vehicles (like advertisements) would have an impact on sales (for example, by weekly levels of exposure, by markets, by medium, by types of promotions, by displays or feature ads, by how many stores carry the product, and the like). DDB Matrix professionals provide the programming and choose the most appropriate statistical models; then a software application parses out the variables. From there, professionals produce simulations and forecasts that illustrate exactly which of a variety of causes could drive certain results.

DDB Matrix was born in two separate locations—Chicago and London—on slightly different timetables. In 1989, Doug Hughes, now a senior vice president and the U.S. director of DDB Matrix, joined DDB Worldwide's Chicago office as a strategic planner and researcher. His role was to bring consumer research to bear on shaping high-impact advertising campaigns. "We would provide statistical data analysis of consumer surveys," Hughes recalled. "These were the surveys that told clients how people think about 'x.'"

Hughes remembered the way the use of econometrics began in DDB's Chicago office. "Starting in about the late 1980s, clients began asking us

Figure 7.1 BetterIdeasBetterResults Logo

for more measurement of our recommended advertising campaigns. They asked, 'How can we be sure that this additional $20 million ad budget is going to work?'" Hughes recalled.

> Traditionally, ad agencies would say, "Trust us." But this claim was ripe for misunderstanding, because it wasn't just the work of these ad agencies that could derail the effective spending of that $20 million. Competitors could introduce a new product, or distribution could be cut. There are so many things that influence a product's success or failure. So even when we were right, it was hard to quantify the results. We didn't have great data to measure ourselves against. We didn't have the computing tools to analyze the data. And we didn't have the methodological tools to find a more directional indication.

During this same time period (the late 1980s into the late 1990s), Hughes noted a few phenomena occurring.

1. *Capabilities with data:* The great leaps made in computing power and the ability to transfer large amounts of data over the Internet made it possible to solve analytical problems that had previously required mainframe computers.

2. *Access to data:* DDB's clients were beginning to have greater access to data about the marketplace's consumption of their products. In the "old days," manufacturers would ship a batch of products to a warehouse. The warehouse would then ship the products to retailers for sale. Customers would buy, and the products would reach their destination. Information about these transactions, however, could be incomplete, flawed, or at least delayed. With the advent of the personal computer (PC) and scanners, data collection and analysis capabilities increased dramatically. Today, at a moment's notice, companies can obtain information about a host of marketing and selling transactions.

3. *Expectations about data:* Clients wanted more than just data; they wanted information. They began turning to market research firms for the implementation of consumer surveys and accompanying data analysis. Hughes saw an opportunity to provide them something they weren't able to get from market research firms: answers about how various aspects of the marketing mix—and their related budget allocations—can impact sales.

In 1997, DDB Worldwide's Chicago office began hiring econometricians. Hughes and his new econometrics colleague began offering time-series analysis on a project-by-project basis. Clients' adoption of this service was slow at first. To do so, Hughes and his colleagues had to educate clients about what the technique was, how it could be helpful, and why clients should pay for it on their campaign. It looked like it would be a slow road ahead.

That same year, Hughes traveled to the United Kingdom because he had learned that DDB's London office had a dedicated Econometrics Unit. It had been functioning for years. "We had been using econometrics for some time, for a variety of historical and geographic reasons that don't exist in the U.S.," said Les Binet, now the director of DDB Matrix in Europe.

First, we're in a smaller country; collecting data on sales and other transactions is a little easier to do. Second, we have the London School of Economics, which is a center for econometrics. Third, econometrics is more accepted in a U.K.-based advertising agency setting. There is not a significant professional demarcation between academicians and practitioners. In the U.K., it is not at all unusual to see economists working in advertising agencies. In the U.S., there aren't many economists working in an advertising agency setting.

Hughes learned that Binet and his U.K. colleagues were routinely winning IPA (the U.K.'s Institute of Practitioners in Advertising) effectiveness awards because of their econometrics approach. In fact, they had won more IPA awards than any of their U.K. competitors. This was just what Hughes needed to see: that the success of a client's media campaign could be directly tied to the econometrically derived recommendations of the advertising agency. Econometrics gave DDB Worldwide the ability to isolate the impact of various communication efforts from each other. Binet and his colleagues could demonstrate unequivocally the exact contribution of each specific element of the marketing mix and the magnitude of each element's contribution.

Hughes and Binet began a plan to bring the econometrics service under one roof and to raise its profile and distinguish it as a service to clients. Upon his return from his London trip, Hughes made a beeline to Crimmins's office. Crimmins was delighted. The service was a perfect fit with the DDB Worldwide repositioning strategy that was in formulation. The firm investigated whether competitors were offering a similar service. Indeed, some of the bigger agencies, including Omnicom cousin BBDO, were offering analytical services. None, however, appeared to be using econometrics specifically. Hughes also did an analysis of potential client demand, and he forecasted the number of professionals that would be needed, stateside and in Europe, to fully staff the unit.

And so, in 1999, DDB Matrix was formally launched externally with a press campaign. Its launch featured internal memos, an extensive introduction through a network-wide series of seminars delivered through its DDB University curriculum, and a series of Hughes-led presentations about the DDB Matrix to key professionals throughout the United States. Since its 1999 launch, DDB Matrix has continued to be introduced to DDB colleagues internally and in its selling initiatives. Currently, DDB Matrix's services are included in nearly every new client proposal.

Challenging Traditions. Hughes, Binet, and their DDB Matrix colleagues were prepared to overcome some marketplace hurdles after the new unit was announced formally. In the early days after its launch, they faced three main challenges, all related to the need to educate their marketplace:

- *Educating clients about what econometrics is and how it can help them.* Hughes discovered that merely *telling* clients about the capabilities of the DDB Matrix unit was not enough. "Clients are marketers, not mathematicians. They want results, not statistics," remarked Hughes. "And econometrics is still a poorly understood science." In response, Hughes and his U.S. colleagues began to demonstrate one of their econometrics capabilities: forecasts of future sales.

"For our early clients, we provided their first forecast with a money-back guarantee," continued Hughes. Once clients could "see" the results that DDB Matrix could deliver, that its results were useful, easy to understand, and highly accurate, they became much more enthusiastic. Hughes concluded, "We have never once had to give their money back."

- *Educating clients about DDB Worldwide's measurement credibility.* Some clients saw what they thought was a conflict of interest: that a firm that develops creative messages should not also measure its own work. They feared that DDB's measurement might even appear to inflate the contributions of the agency. Their skepticism is natural, but disappeared once they saw a demonstration of the capabilities of DDB's econometricians and the objectivity of the results. For example, clients could see where the impact of their advertising spending had been maximized and where it had not.
- *Educating clients to be patient.* Econometrics is a robust tool. Its very sophistication, however, requires time and people. DDB Matrix analysis can take up to six to eight weeks. It is labor intensive. This requires an explanation for clients who think software packages can work by themselves, and that they can do so instantly. Once again, DDB Worldwide's physical demonstration of its capabilities wins instant client converts.

DDB Worldwide has developed a number of mini–case studies that communicate the power of its DDB Matrix capabilities. A few examples follow.

- For a nationwide automotive retail chain:
  - Issue: What is the best mix of cable and broadcast media to support promotional and brand messages?
  - Solution: Linear optimization of sales based on historical responsiveness to advertising.
  - Results: Client could increase sales 6 percent with no additional expenditure by improving the mix of media and messages.
- For a chain of theme parks:
  - Issue: Which are the best northern markets in which to advertise client's Florida theme parks?
  - Solution: Market Allocation Planning System integrates historical market responsiveness with current media costs to identify markets with positive return on ad investment.
  - Result: Client able to concentrate media spending on most efficient markets, increasing attendance by as much as 22 percent.
- For a clothing retailer
  - Issue: How many phones need to be staffed after an ad appears?

- Solution: Predictive call model forecasts daily call volume based on advertising weight and other factors.
- Result: Easy-to-use software application allows call center management to reduce costs of overflow calls and ensure proper phone coverage by precise prediction of call volume.

DDB's focused commitment to introduce its new service effectively required a steady-as-she-goes mindset and a willingness to go the extra mile to educate its clients. DDB Worldwide understood that a successful challenge of client traditions takes time and patience. By demonstrating the openness of its DDB Matrix approach, the rigor of its capabilities and the actionability of its solutions, DDB Worldwide effectively demonstrated how to change the old ways of thinking.

The Results. DDB Worldwide is already well known for contributing to the successful growth of its clients. Budweiser, Dell, JC Penney, State Farm, and Volkswagen are stellar examples of companies that have achieved significant marketplace advances since beginning to work with DDB Worldwide. Its track record with DDB Matrix follows this pattern of success.

The firm's results with its technologically based econometrics service can be grouped into three areas. First, DDB Worldwide's econometrics service has demonstrated clear results for its clients: efficiencies in media spending; improved timing of campaigns and other promotion to get the most out of marketing communications; optimized media support for maximum return. With each new project, DDB garners more proof of the value of its new service.

Second, in the United States alone, Hughes and his colleagues have provided services to dozens of some of the world's largest advertisers; already, 50 percent have become repeat clients. Currently, DDB Worldwide uses DDB Matrix as a relationship-retention tool. The DDB Matrix unit itself is not a tremendous revenue generator. Instead, "DDB Matrix is a way that we can separate ourselves from other agencies, provide a valuable service, and help make our clients smarter," said Hughes. Third, the new service is a powerful demonstration of the firm's repositioning strategy and is an excellent fit with the company's cultural orientation of creativity backed up by accountability.

USING INCENTIVES AND REWARDS TO STIMULATE INNOVATION

Mitretek Systems, Inc.

Our last case about fostering innovation provides a wonderful capstone to the embedding-innovation building block. Watch for details about two features of Mitretek Systems's compelling incentives and rewards infrastructure: its employee-nominated Incentive Compensation Program and its company-sponsored research framework.

Which comes first, the chicken or the egg—the predilection to be innovative or innovation itself? It would be easy to dismiss Mitretek Systems's potent organizational support for innovation as simply a result of its industry (scientific research and engineering – *of course* these guys love to innovate!), its outgrowth from its parent's innovation-oriented culture, or even its nonprofit status. Indeed, these basics had a positive impact on Mitretek's early forays into innovation. Yet its ongoing success at innovation has nothing to do with these factors or with its technology-based service mix either. Instead, we must look at the following critical choices, ideological bases, and ongoing approaches that fed Mitretek's effective innovation. As you read through this case, take particular note of the following points:

- *Mitretek's commitment to a set of processes that encourage innovation to occur:* These processes are at the core of Mitretek's innovation infrastructure. They are distinct, managerially supported, and internally promoted. By signaling its enthusiasm to hold together a framework for innovation to happen, Mitretek communicates its belief that innovation is not solely the result of serendipity and those occasional sparks of a savant's creative genius. Rather, that innovation can be fostered in *everyone*.

- *Its orientation to innovate in the public interest:* What a fantastic mission! Mitretek's external focus, perhaps born from its nonprofit status, provides a powerful and clear reason for *any* organization to be in business. Mitretek has effectively demonstrated the benefits that can be had from having a market-driven mindset. This is more than many for-profit firms have allowed themselves to contemplate for their own "clients." Slowly, however, more for-profit professional service firms are realizing the fundamental soundness of a straightforward goal like Mitretek's. "Work for your client's benefit!" It's that simple.

- *Its predisposition to think proactively—not reactively—about achieving breakthroughs:* Too many for-profit professional firms wait until their clients demand innovation or their competitors force them to do so. Too many wait until they are sure they can make some money before taking bold steps to innovate. But the marketplace favors proactivity and business longevity requires it.

- *Its development of programs that build employee relationships and foster the attraction and retention of deep talent:* There is nothing like bonding through the achievement of a sought-after goal. This is where personal satisfaction starts.

- *Its ability to be clear-eyed about the organizational effects of its individually focused incentive and rewards programs:* Mitretek has demonstrated a commendable level of organizational sensitivity regarding the inevitable employee competitiveness that crops up. It balances this sensitivity with a strong conviction about the soundness of its programs and a commitment to help employees build a truly collegial environment, where personal anxieties and disappointments are replaced by confidence, camaraderie, and professional contentment.

The Mitretex Systems Story: Context and Background. When it comes to stimulating innovation, professional service firms face significant hurdles on a number of fronts. These can include ethical or practice standards that limit the adaptation of professional practices, trying to maximize the repeated delivery of a regular set of services in order to achieve an acceptable profit margin, appropriately segregating funds for innovation purposes ("How much is the right amount? How will we protect it when times are lean?"), deciding how to assign talented people to work on the development of services for which there is an uncertain future, or assigning them to work on innovation projects while they are underutilized, only to have to pull them back once a client project comes in.

These are significant hurdles indeed. And yet innovation is an imperative. As clients' needs evolve, so, too, must the services that their professionals offer them. It is incumbent upon professional service firms to be ahead of the marketplace, to be ready with services that meet their clients' needs even before the clients know what these needs are. This challenge brings us to one of the most delicate balancing acts regarding innovation: motivating people to be innovative, and doing so without simultaneously stimulating a negative form of internal competition. This case examines the use of incentives and rewards to stimulate innovation—something that Mitretek Systems, Inc., a unique scientific research and systems engineering company that is based in Falls Church, Virginia, does very effectively.

A nonprofit organization that spun off from MITRE Corporation in 1996, Mitretek was formed to provide a public benefit by conducting research and undertaking system engineering analyses to create scientific knowledge and technological solutions that strengthen the nation in key areas of public interest. Mitretek calls itself "the nation's technology company" with good reason: its approximately seven hundred people are systems engineers, physical and life scientists, computer scientists, and other technology experts working to solve problems related to criminal justice, delivering government services, e-commerce and e-government, environment, health care, meteorology, national and homeland security, and transportation.[13] As of 2002, Mitretek's annual revenues were more than $115 million. Of this amount, more than $1 million was spent on internal research and development.[14]

Mitretek's way of encouraging and rewarding innovation is notable for its emphasis on the *individual* and his or her interaction with peers. This approach is rooted in Mitretek's spinoff from its parent and in its nonprofit status, which provide the underpinnings for the way it culturally encourages innovation, the way it monetarily rewards individuals who pursue it, and the way it organizationally supports innovation initiatives.

Cultural Encouragement. Mitretek's predilection for the pursuit of intellectual advancement was born from its days as a part of MITRE, which fostered a well-honed and broad-based innovation program. The employees who joined Mitretek were already familiar with their employer expecting them to strive for new breakthroughs. In the mid-1990s, as the restructuring got underway, MITRE's innovation orientation was slanted largely towards customer-required research. Mitretek's mission, however, is to focus on solving daunting public issues that have broad societal implications. At the time of the spinoff, Mitretek's leaders realized they had to motivate their people somewhat differently—to encourage them to pursue innovation even when there was no customer directly asking for it, in areas where the challenges were deeply complex and ultimately crucial to the welfare of humankind. Nevertheless, when the spinoff occurred, new Mitretek leaders decided that there were many aspects of what they had encountered at MITRE that would fit culturally well in the new entity: a pursuit of thought leadership, a peer-to-peer acknowledgement of effort, and senior leadership's widely visible kudos for intellectual accomplishment.

They set out to build an organizational infrastructure that would emulate this model, but with a stronger focus on individual effort and collegial encouragement—innovation that would be as much as possible self-perpetuated by the Mitretek employees themselves. Their innovation programs would be based on nominations, collegial assessments of achievement, and capped with managerial recognition of accomplishment.

Monetary Rewards. "There was a fair amount of organizational anxiety from the spin-off and restructuring," remembered Pam Walker, vice president for Mitretek's Center for Science and Technology. "In the early days, we struggled with how to differentiate ourselves in the marketplace." Walker and her colleagues had reason to be anxious; Mitretek was formed right in the middle of the dot-com heyday. They knew innovation was a critical aspect of the fulfillment of their corporate mission. As a nonprofit company, though, Mitretek could not offer stock options or profit-sharing bonuses that for-profit companies used to encourage breakthrough thinking. How, they wondered, will we attract and retain the kind of talent we need in order to fulfill this mission? The answer was in incentives and rewards.

Outside advisors pointed out that as long at Mitretek's employee compensation was not directly tied to the size of its projects or the amount of its earnings, the company could motivate and reward its employees in any way it chose. Walker and her colleagues were delighted. "We began building an Incentive Compensation Program that would encourage our people to engage in certain behaviors," she recounted.

They chose to reward employees for demonstrating thirteen behaviors. Many of the behaviors have a direct link to the achievement of innovation—some more overtly than others. They are:

1. Benefit to corporation
2. Initiative
3. Marketability/capability expansion
4. Public interest
5. Team support
6. Customer satisfaction/recognition
7. Inventiveness
8. Mentoring
9. Resource/cost savings
10. Heroism
11. Leadership
12. Perseverance
13. Responsiveness

In keeping with their commitment to enmesh innovation deeply into the fabric of the company, Mitretek's managers decided to build the company's Incentive Compensation Program from an internal nomination base. At first, Walker designated a team of Mitretek employees in the Center for Science and Technology (one of the four units within Mitretek at the time) to help her start the Center's program. She looked for thoughtful people who had independent judgment and high standards and could probe a bit below the surface of a nomination to determine its true merit. Working together, Walker and the Incentive Compensation Program committee developed their charge, their guidelines and their process. Today, although the committee continues to report to Walker, the nomination program is fully and independently functioning. Nominations come from all levels and functions within Mitretek, even management. The nomination form, now available on

Mitretek's intranet, provides clear instructions about how an employee can nominate another person. The instructions follow.

Mitretek's Guidelines for Submitting Effective ICP (Incentive Compensation Program) Nominations:

- *Review all of the categories and criteria listed on the last page of this form before selecting the category that best reflects the performance you wish to nominate.* While you may select more than one category, you are encouraged to limit your selection to one category—this will help you focus your nomination. Focused nominations are usually more persuasive and compelling than general laudatory nominations.
- *Make sure your write-up matches the category you have selected.* Extraordinary employees have many outstanding characteristics. Stick to the category you have selected and resist the temptation to write about every exemplary aspect the employee possesses.
- *Provide supporting evidence of the behavior or activity.* The committee must have a credible "paper trail" to support its recommendations in the event of an external audit. If your nomination is based on casual observation of a productive, successful employee, do not hesitate to contact others who may be able to give specific examples to support your nomination.
- *Focus on results as well as process.* The review committee finds it helpful to have nominations that detail both the individual's contributions *and* the results of those contributions. In addition, any innovative, repeatable, and/or translatable processes used to achieve an especially high degree of effectiveness should be described. Provide specific examples of processes and results.
- *Corroborating nominations are encouraged.* Multiple nominations—submitted on separate forms or as a single cooperative nomination—tend to give greater weight to the individual's accomplishments.
- *Multiple individuals may be nominated on the same form.* However, all individuals nominated must have made significant and substantive contributions of essentially equal value to the effectiveness of the overall effort with respect to the chosen criterion or criteria. An individual should not be included in the nomination simply because he or she was a member of the group carrying out the effort. Clearly identify individual involvement in various aspects of the effort. This will help the committee understand how each nominee contributed to the effort's success. Be sure to provide specific examples of individual activities that support the chosen criterion or criteria. If the contribution of those nominated is not of essentially equal value, individual nominations should be submitted.

These guidelines make it clear that a person can be nominated solely for his or her innovation work, and then be compensated directly for it. The Incentive Compensation Program committee not only collects all the nominations, but is responsible for vetting them too. "The program had to be viewed as legitimate and not just another 'Manager's Pet' program," declared Walker. "At the same time, it had to reflect our values and our intention to motivate individual achievement. We make it well-known that everyone can qualify to be nominated in this program."

Awardees receive a one-time check that is drawn from segregated pools of money that are held by the three current Mitretek organizational units. This pool equals approximately 1.25 percent of the entire Mitretek population's salary base. For each successful nominee in her center, the ICP committee recommends to Walker the relative value of the reward, which can range from never lower than $500 to as much as $10,000. The number of nominees varies from year to year; nominations are given subjective weight, irrespective of the individual's salary. In addition, there is a separate set-aside of money within the Incentive Compensation Program that is strictly earmarked for scientific and technological innovation, and that is awarded each year among those staff demonstrating innovation documented by a published paper.

The ICP awards are very public. At a free quarterly luncheon, Walker describes the nominations, the initiative the person undertook to receive a nomination, and her commentary of the initiative's impact. She then unveils a plaque and the envelope containing a check. Back at the awardee's office, s/he finds balloons attached to the doorway that are visible to all. After the luncheon, Walker's office broadcasts a company-wide e-mail with the names and photos of all awardees and a group photo is included in the next version of the company's electronic news-paper, *Mitretek Times*. Mitretek's ICP awards process isn't the only avenue to recognize and reward staff for innovation. The company also supports a number of named awards that recognize both individuals and teams for unique advances in science and technology or for significant scientific or technological problems solved in the public interest.

Organizational Support for Internal Research. Mitretek also motivates its people to innovate by providing annual funding for an internal research program, called Mitretek Sponsored Research (MSR). Directed by Mitretek's chief technology officer Gil Miller, Mitretek's research is designed to be an integrated attack on a scientific or technological problem or on the advancement of a specific body of knowledge. The MSR program is funded through a variety of sources typically beginning with the company's own internal funding. These funds vary according to Mitretek's business results; since the company's founding they have averaged a little over 1 percent of revenue. In each of the last three fiscal years, they have ranged from $650,000 to $1 million. It is not uncommon for Mitretek internal funding for a research project to be followed by client funding and grants (for example, from the National Science Foundation). In any case, though, Mitretek employees are not constrained by external customer demands for the conduct of this or that research project. Instead, Mitretek itself is the "customer."

Mitretek's officers define a few research topics that they feel are important to the company. (Besides Miller, this management team is comprised of Mitretek's president Lydia Thomas, chief operating officer Rich Granato, chief financial officer Mark Simione, vice president for corporate initiatives Bob Clerman, and technical center vice presidents Pam Walker and Craig Janus.) The research interest areas are derived from the officers' perspectives on the emerging needs of Mitretek's clients, their vision of how the company could evolve to meet these needs, and their expectations about the evolution of a variety of technologies. Research areas have in the past focused on telecommunications and networking, biometrics, toxicology, public key infrastructure security, and transportation systems, to name a few. "We think quite carefully about these issues, and then we publish our list of suggested MSR priorities," reported Walker. "When we communicate this 'wishlist' to the organization, we suggest that if an employee or team applies to work on one of these projects, it might be considered a bit more favorably than if a different project was pursued." Nevertheless, any employee can propose to undertake any kind of research initiative, and many do so successfully.

At designated times in the fiscal year, Miller posts management's prioritized research areas on an internal electronic forum (which is always open for posting and discussion). With this specific "call," Miller makes clear Mitretek's current and future strategic research goals. Immediately afterwards Miller seeks out individuals to encourage their contributions of ideas and plant seeds of specific research projects. He also coaches them on how to improve the science and technology in their proposals. The proposal, often a one- or two-page letter, must articulate the project's expected outcome and how this outcome will help Mitretek fulfill its business mission. After a month or two of posting and discussion in the electronic forum, Miller prioritizes the proposals down to two-thirds of the original total. He then convenes a multi-day workshop for experts in a given technology area and the prioritized proposals' originators. After this workshop, approximately one-third of the originally received proposals are deemed viable to remain.

The process, designed to stimulate broad participation in innovation, is itself a kind of reward. "Mitretek officers understand that they do not have an exclusive hold on all possible ideas," declared Miller. "As we pursue innovation, we are attempting to develop a culture of influence and contribution, where those who propose ideas, provide constructive criticism, or volunteer as principal investigators get to participate in the decision making about proposals that ultimately are selected for funding. Literally, then, if you contribute to the proposed ideas, you get to influence Mitretek's science and technology directions."

Based on the workshop results, Miller takes about a quarter of the original number of proposals to the company's officers for final funding decisions. Ultimately, Mitretek's officers select the projects that help the organization to innovate most effectively in the public interest and that best fit the funding available, strategic corporate needs, and interest of the clients. In recent years, the company has selected an average of eight projects per year, averaging 10 months in duration. Funding on these projects has ranged from $20,000 to $1 million, with an average of $150,000.

There are no rigid guidelines as to when and under what circumstances an employee could submit a proposal. "The key is the qualifications of the proposed individual or individuals," said Miller. "We encourage broad cross-functional involvement, where anyone from the newest staff to join the organization to a senior level technical staff or manager can work together to develop proposals, in the same way that they already work together to affect the company's ongoing client commitments."

Recognizing "The Team" versus "The Individual": A Balancing Act. Sometimes Mitretek's multiple awards and nominations opportunities can cause their own challenges. "This is not a horrible problem; we are really quite a strongly collegial organization," Walker explained. "But there have been some instances when Person A gets wind of Person B being nominated for something that was done while they both served on the same team. Person A may say, 'I was on that project. How come I didn't get an award?' To us, this kind of a question signals that Person A needs to hear more about the objective of these programs." In cases like this, a Mitretek committee member or manager will sit down with Person A to discuss his discomfort. Often, it simply requires a reminder that the goal of the program is precisely to acknowledge individual accomplishments, a review of the role that each person played on the project, and a reminder that no two roles are identical on a team.

The Results. Mitretek's peer-to-peer incentive compensation program, originated in one of its two current technology units (the Center for Science and Technology), is now used throughout more than three-quarters of the company.

There are four other ways in which Mitretek's incentive and rewards programs have benefitted the organization internally and externally:

- *Attracting and retaining top-notch talent.* Mitretek has helped create an atmosphere that is indeed different from most other professional environments. Employees are energetic, curious, hopeful, and forward-thinking. Mitretek is an exciting place to be. As evidence, Walker told a story about a returning employee who had been gone from Mitretek for four years. Soon after his return, she met with him in her office and asked him how things were going. He replied, "Not much is new, but I frequently find myself sitting at my computer smiling about how glad I am to be back at Mitretek—this is a great place to work." Clearly, his sentiments are held by many others; Mitretek has won multiple "great employer" designations, including AARP's list of the fifteen best employers for workers aged fifty and older.[15]
- *Advancing individual careers.* Participation in an R&D project or getting nominated for an incentive compensation reward does not mean an employee automatically gets promoted, explained Walker. Nevertheless, these events do give the employee the opportunity to get in front of colleagues internally, thus building innovation opportunities even further.
- *Fulfilling its mission.* Mitretek management took seriously its mission statement. By creating an internally visible organizational framework for "innovative technology in the public interest," the organization has literally hatched new technologies or services. These include three notable examples. First, a new mathematical approach to estimating performance (e.g., time to download material from the Web) of Internet-based traffic. Mitretek experts found that this new technique significantly reduced performance estimate errors. Second, Mitretek security experts developed a strategy that allows interoperability in the new security area known as public key infrastructure. Their developed strategy and resultant software are essential to the security of business transactions conducted in cyberspace. Third, Mitretek demonstrated the feasibility of an Internet-based system to manage the cumbersome process of effectively and quickly responding to alerts issued to hospitals by manufacturers of products used in the delivery of health care. This innovation will contribute to impressive improvements in patient safety.
- *Becoming more visible for its work.* Mitretek's innovation work is *meant* to be made public. Indeed, the more external collaboration that Mitretek employees can foster, the better. Innovative solutions are more likely to be effective if they are developed with an end-

user's participation. A number of Mitretek's R&D projects are conceived of with clients; often, the resulting innovative technology is piloted with them as well. In other cases, Mitretek employees present their innovation ideas at conferences of potential clients and other professional peers.

The preceding fifteen portraits are compelling because they show us professional service firms that addressed their marketplace challenges in a process-driven way—building the competencies of a market-driven infrastructure with a mixture of patience and enthusiasm, deliberation and passion. These firms are on their way to becoming Marketplace Masters. After reading these cases the inevitable question crops up. How can my firm take steps to become a Marketplace Master? What do we have to do to develop the competencies of looking out, digging deeper and embedding innovation?

Part III

Becoming a Marketplace Master

They always say time changes things, but you actually have to change them yourself.
                                                    —Andy Warhol

Small changes, great gains. Andy Warhol's words remind us that the work of becoming a marketplace master will have to come *from within*, steered by the very same people who will ultimately benefit from the changes that result. But professional service firm leaders will need to give their colleagues solid reasons why they should do the heavy lifting to develop the competencies of a market-driven infrastructure. In the final two chapters, I present a diagnostic framework and a presentation structure that marketplace mastery champions can use to guide their professional service firm to look out, dig deeper, and embed innovation.

8

Assess Your Firm's Readiness to Build a Market-Driven Infrastructure

FRUSTRATION TABLEAU 1

Sanjay was among several of his firm's practice leaders who had been asked by Mark, a senior executive, to attend a two-day internal strategy session to help the firm respond to perceived market shifts. The senior executive wanted the team to brainstorm about new initiatives that could meet clients' emerging needs. Sanjay eyed his watch as he sat through day two of the session. He was tired of stifling his frustration. At the break, he approached the facilitator to urge the inclusion of a new element to the agenda. "Don't you see? It doesn't matter how good our service offerings are if we don't have a compelling brand message! Why aren't we dealing with *that* issue? Why doesn't Mark get it?"

FRUSTRATION TABLEAU 2

Kelly, a senior vice president at an elite, midsized professional service firm, had asked an external marketing consultant to join an emergency strategic planning meeting for her firm's newest practice. This new unit, recently launched with much fanfare and hope, had run into considerable road blocks within the firm. In fact, it was in jeopardy of imploding. There were significant questions about how the new practice's positioning "fit" with the positioning of the parent organization; consultants had begun raising objections about how to introduce this new practice to their clients without jeopardizing their current service offerings and long-standing relationships. Prior to the meeting, Kelly earnestly confided to the marketing consultant her concerns about the lack of marketing "enlightenment" of some of the other members of the strategic planning committee. "In particular, I'm not sure Bruce 'gets it,' and he's a prominent member of the group," she said. "He keeps trying to move us ahead from *the old paradigm*—tweaking the way we *used* to go to market. He doesn't see that we need to *throw out* his old marketing approach and start with a clean slate that's relevant for today's marketplace!" Her frustration was real, and she was right. Bruce did not "get it."

Sanjay and Kelly may be the exceptions to the rule. In fact, it isn't easy for service industry professionals—even those with marketing responsibilities—to "get" the fundamentals of strategic marketing. Why? Relatively speaking, strategic marketing is a new discipline for many professional service firms; as a result, their managers are still ramping up the learning curve. Consider the following:

- In all likelihood, most professionals never learned about marketing (save for an introductory-level, products-focused course during their academic or professional preparation for their field).
- Firm-supported professional development opportunities are generally more focused on the tactical implementation of the firm's services or business development initiatives than they are on teaching professionals about the newest trends in strategic marketing and competition.
- Most likely, their firm's profit structure simply does not yet support the pursuit of enlightenment about issues about competition ("I'd like to take a sabbatical to learn about the emerging strategic issues of our marketplace."). Moreover, most firms don't directly reward their professionals for the kind of big-picture thinking that strategic marketing requires.
- Many professional service firms still isolate their marketing departments from their professionals. Whether physically ("Oh, marketing is on the seventh floor; I have never met most of them") or functionally ("Our marketing director doesn't report to our practice, only to Corporate"), too many firms simply don't effectively integrate their staff marketers into the fabric of their organization. Marketing is viewed as a removed entity that only emerges except to make professionals do extra (unnecessary) work.

If not carefully managed, frustrated people like Sanjay and Kelly could end up as sour cynics, undermining, *sotto voce*, every market-driven baby step their firm takes.

Do you want your professional service firm to become a Marketplace Master? It *can* be achieved, with the development of a market-driven infrastructure—those linked, integrated processes and methods to look out, dig deeper, and embed innovation. But, like all significant initiatives, it doesn't happen overnight. Professionals like Kelly and Sanjay need to become champions for their firms to create this infrastructure. If you are like Sanjay or Kelly, you'll have to become a champion, *guiding* your firm to "get it" the way you do. It is a three-step process. First, you'll need to make a diagnosis of your firm's readiness to undertake the creation of a market-driven infrastructure. Second, you'll need to be able to state your case that it can do so; third, you'll have to make the pitch that it must.

Assessing a firm's readiness to rethink and rebuild its infrastructure is a tall order; it also relies heavily on reporting skills and your ability to gather, organize, and analyze information. This chapter is devoted to that task. The second and third steps are of a different nature; they will rely more on your ability to craft an argument explicitly for the intended audience. Those steps are more personal, involving issues of framing, delivery, persuasion, and personality; I talk about them in the final chapter of the book, which follows this one.

Assessing readiness begins with a dispassionate view of your firm. Think of yourself as a sleuth or a reporter, looking for positive and negative things (and as much as you can) without judgment. Ask yourself a series of 30,000-foot questions that will give you an overview of your firm's current state of marketplace mastery (or lack thereof). In this Step One, take yourself through the following two-part assessment to determine your firm's readiness to develop one or a few of the competencies that are part of a market-driven infrastructure.

Before you start, create the framework for your work. Will it be extensively detailed, with a full-blown case study of your firm that includes original research, background articles, quotes from people you have interviewed, or snippets from past business plans, or will it be very brief, maybe consisting of an outline or just a series of headlines? Next, envision the ultimate form for this information: A set of slides for a presentation you plan to make, a memo that you intend to circulate to your colleagues, a three-ring binder full of separate sections, or a bunch of folders on your desktop? The ultimate form really doesn't matter as long as your work results in a package that allows you and your colleagues to determine your firm's readiness to build an infrastructure that will help it pursue marketplace mastery.

PART A: EVIDENCE OF FUNDAMENTAL READINESS

Your goal here is to discern to what extent your firm possesses the most fundamental basics of readiness to build a market-driven infrastructure in order to compete more effectively. In this exercise you will be cataloguing concrete examples that it possesses these fundamentals (yes, every firm possesses *some*).

In the order below, catalog evidence about the following:

1. *Evidence of past success at implementing processes:* Is there some recent evidence that your firm has successfully developed and implemented *any* kind of internal processes? Which ones were they? Do you think these processes could serve as models for your firm to develop the market-driven methods and tools that are critical for marketplace mastery? Your goal, as you review the evidence for this area, is to determine how prepared your firm might be to build a market-driven infrastructure. You might be concerned that your review will turn up evidence of a total lack of past success at implementing processes. You might wonder, "If we've never succeeded here before, it will be difficult to succeed at doing so in the future!" Fear not. The vast majority of professional service firms, in the practice of their craft, have indeed had to learn how to implement *some* sorts of processes—at least including the delivery of their methodologies, as well as other critical processes like billing and timekeeping. So *you will* find evidence of past success at implementing processes. Your firm can do it again, and with increasing effectiveness, especially if you can find what we are looking for next: evidence of strategic (market-focused) thinking.

2. *Evidence of market-focused thinking:* Does your firm undertake some form of strategic planning that features an "external" focus? (Including definable market-focused goals; succinct differentiation, positioning, and branding platforms; well-targeted clients; a defined portfolio of service offerings; distinct methods for service delivery; and integrated pricing strategies?) Or is the culture totally at odds with externally focused strategic thinking? Finding evidence of market-focused thinking may be harder than finding evidence of success at process implementation. It may appear in practice- or firm-wide planning documents, internal slides from executive management presentations, inneroffice memos, or on the firm's intranet. It may also appear in the form of positioning tag lines, advertising slogans or the title to speeches given by the firm's senior leaders. Wherever you find it, try to discern if your firm has any intended external goals or a discernible marketplace direction in which it is trying to go. The more evidence you can find of strategic thinking that has some linkage to your firm's external environment (its marketplace), the better. After this exercise, you may believe that there is *no evidence of market-focused*

thinking at your organization. However, even if it is not recent, your firm *has embraced market-focused thinking* at least once in its past—when it was founded. This is when the firm's founders had to make decisions about the services they would offer, to which potential clients, where their office would be located, which professionals would do what, and what they would charge for their services. Market-focused thinking happened when they made a decision about what to name the new firm. They also had to be at least somewhat aware of the services that other professionals were offering (that might impact their own offerings)—this is also evidence of an external focus. As you proceed through this exploration, and later try to build a case for your firm to embrace one or more of the eleven market-driven methods, it will be important to point to evidence of even this level of external thinking at your firm. It was done at least once, and it can be done again, even more effectively.

3. *Evidence of a desire to win:* This is the most important element to have in the adoption of a market-driven infrastructure. Does your firm's leadership demonstrate a spark of desire to have the firm become a competitive leader? In their words and behavior, do the firm's executive managers, practice leaders, and internal "influencers" collectively display their hunger for your firm to be the most powerful cat in the jungle? If you cannot find any evidence of a *firm-wide* desire for marketplace success, look for it within practices or even individual professionals. Try to find evidence of a determination to surmount an obstacle in order to do something important in the firm's market. Perhaps it was the retention of an almost-lost client, the publication of a book that resulted in someone's elevation to partner, or the launch of a content-rich seminar series. Look for significant initiatives; if you can't find them, look for smaller, yet still successful, examples of a marketplace-related desire that was fulfilled (e.g., the revamping of a brochure or the completion of an internal training session on working with the press—anything where someone took responsibility for an externally focused effort that had to be mounted, and then saw it through to its completion). When it comes time to making the pitch for your firm to build a market-driven infrastructure, show your firm's leaders that your organization *already has* the most critical element to succeed: the desire to win in the marketplace.

The evidence you gather will help you visualize your firm's grasp of the building blocks of marketplace mastery. This evidence will also help you estimate how big a step your organization might need to take to create a market-driven infrastructure; it will also inform your choice of focus areas in Part B of your assessment. Even if the evidence points to a bleak picture ("I see no evidence of a competitive desire, market-focused thinking, or past success in implementing processes!"), remember two things. First, refocus back on your passion for helping your firm achieve a greater level of marketplace effectiveness and success. Recall your conviction that your firm must take the steps it can to compete more strategically. Second, remember that all you need to do is start where you are. You can lead from there.

PART B: THE BUILDING BLOCKS OF A MARKET-DRIVEN INFRASTRUCTURE

Now, with the evidence in mind, examine each of the three building blocks of a market-driven infrastructure: looking out, digging deeper, and embedding innovation. Does your firm naturally tend towards a good "fit" with one or another? Your goal here is to conduct an assessment that will allow you to home in on the competencies most suited for your firm, and then craft a plan that is both practical and actionable.

Use the following outline and suggested set of questions to help you get a picture of your organization's approaches to each building block. Under each building block heading, you will first find a general set of questions designed to help you get your arms around the pertinent issues. After that, you will find a series of questions that are keyed to the main competencies of each building block as I described them in Chapters 2, 3, and 4. These questions fall into four areas about each competency: your firm's past track record about the particular competency; its knowledge about the competency; its attitudes about it; and queries that might help determine if there are the potential champions and influencers for that competency. Keep in mind that you know the intricacies of your own firm better than I do; add or edit the list of questions as needed for your own situation.

A "LOOKING OUT" ASSESSMENT

This line of inquiry is designed to help you determine how comfortable you are that your firm can use *information* to build solid, market-focused strategies.

- Does your firm have a formal, dedicated budget for ongoing research? If so, has this budget been protected over time, or has it been sacrificed when revenues are challenged?
- Is client research conducted regularly, or not? Has it ever been?

- When it is done, who does it?
- How robust is the research?
- How widely are the research findings shared throughout the firm?
- What happens after the research findings are disseminated? (Nothing? Initiatives that dissipate quickly? Fairly defined initiatives that have resulted from the research findings?)
- How familiar is your firm's management with the host of qualitative and quantitative research methods that could be applied to the firm's marketing strategies? There are many more qualitative methods being employed than, say, one-on-one interviews or focus groups. There are many more quantitative techniques being used than multiple-choice questionnaires. Do your firm's leaders give you a blank stare when you mention research terms such as conjoint analysis, clustering, or dynamic price-sensitivity modeling?
- What are your firm's policies and practices regarding research? ("You ninny, we only conduct research for *corporate* initiatives, not for individual units!")
- Is there a culture of skepticism about research ("Y'know, you can make statistics say *anything!*") or stonewalling ("You'll have to get my permission to talk to my clients!")?
- Does your firm have one or more internal advocates for looking out (people who have the personal stature or tenure to make a credible pitch to undertake a more potent effort in this area)?
- How much internal political stock do these people have with their colleagues? ("Nadia really pulled out all the stops last year to get us to do the XXX project; I think people are tired of hearing from her!")
- What is the nature of their roles within the organization (peripheral and honorary or central and deeply accountable)?
- Beyond these champions, is there another layer of potential advocates, perhaps those who might benefit the most from the adoption of a looking-out practice?

Competency: Studying a Firm's Clients Using Qualitative and Quantitative Research

Past track record on qualitative and quantitative research
- What kinds of research have been undertaken (client satisfaction research only or deeper explorations of marketplace opportunities)?
- Did your firm set meaningful goals for its research? Was the most deeply critical information gathered that could be gathered? For example, can your firm now more effectively understand the psychological motivation behind its clients' purchase behaviors or their attraction to certain service attributes or service providers?

- Has your firm been able to *use* the research findings it captured? If so, to what end? If not, this may be evidence of three things: ineffective research instruments, research objectives that were too simplistic or narrowly focused, and/or research findings that were not effectively integrated into other initiatives of the firm, for example, the firm's contacts database or practice management systems.
- Did your firm try to conduct client satisfaction research at the same time it conducted "marketplace opportunity" research, thus possibly compromising both?
- To which targets was your research directed? If research was only conducted on current clients, there may be less of a chance to build market share with prospective clients.

Knowledge about qualitative and quantitative research
- Does your firm use qualitative and quantitative research initiatives appropriately? Is qualitative research used for exploring and revealing information such as attitudes, perceptions, and difficult-to-articulate client needs? Is quantitative research used to verify and validate? Are these types of research ever used to complement and enhance each other?

Attitude about qualitative and quantitative research
- Is there evidence of certain preferences about research? Does it appear that your firm favors quantitative over qualitative methods, or vice versa? For instance, does the firm heartily endorse focus groups or eschew multiple-choice surveys, and why?
- How integrated have been your firm's qualitative and quantitative research efforts? Are they ever used to complement each other, or are they usually conducted separately?
- How longitudinal (watching for changes over time) or latitudinal (exploring new things for each research effort) is your firm's research?

Research champions and influencers
- Does your firm have a dedicated research team or staff? Where within your organization are these people housed? ("Our researcher is our corporate librarian, located in our firm's midwestern headquarters.") If your firm does not have a dedicated research staff, is there any other identified research "team" at your firm (for instance, within the "quality" or "client services" unit, or the marketing department)?
- Who are your firm's main professional users of research? Is it typically the purview of the executive management team, or does

it appear that research is generated ad hoc throughout the organization? Who has the power to call for research?
- Within your organization, which individuals or practices could benefit the most from a one-time qualitative or quantitative research project? Which ones could benefit from repeatable or ongoing research?

Competency: Researching the Market Using Economic Forecasts and Trend Analyses

Past track record on forecasts and trend analyses
- Has your firm ever undertaken a formal forecasting initiative to answer questions in marketing such as "Will this new service be successful?" or "What might our market share be next year under so-and-so conditions?" Other uses could include finance ("How much is our consulting division worth?") or talent ("How can we find the best new associates?").[1]
- Has your firm ever undertaken trend analyses? Simple examples could include reading and trying to incorporate overall market perspective from sources like *Megatrends 2000* or *Dictionary of the Future*.[2] Examples could also include assimilating the insights from industry-specific "annual outlook" reports that are published by many trade publications.
- Does your firm typically conduct trend analyses and economic forecasts in-house (as YaYa Media did when it wanted to catalogue the intersection of market shifts in several distinct areas), or does your firm purchase these as outsourced reports (implying that the reports are more general and perhaps less strategically targeted)?
- How did the firm use trends analysis and forecasts? For specific practice initiatives or as part of a corporate strategic planning effort? Do you see evidence of these analyses and forecasts in your firm's corporate or practice plans or marketing strategy documents?

Knowledge about forecasts and trend analyses
- How up-to-date is your firm on trends analysis techniques? These techniques include content and interrelationships analyses from information captured from a myriad of databases of practices, tools, case studies, and the like; trade and press reports; statistical data from surveys; interviews with experts; and more.
- How comfortable are your firm's leaders with some of the techniques of forecasting (for example, judgmental forecasting, the Delphi technique, intentions studies, or time series analysis)? Have they ever utilized conjoint analysis or statistical models of any kind?

- Does your firm know how trends analysis and forecasting is used to aide decision-making in business? (An example of how this is done is offered in one of our case studies, that of DDB Worldwide, which developed a new service that is built on forecasting techniques.)

Attitude about forecasts and trend analyses

- Do your firm leaders reject forecasting and trends analyses as a waste of time because they contain information that inevitably features some level of unreliability and uncertainty? On the other hand, are there at least some small examples of trends analyses and forecasting underway at your firm? For example, does your firm develop annual budgets or estimates on next year's hiring for entry-level professionals? If so, it is practicing at least a *small* rendition of forecasting and predictions of trends.
- Does the firm internally communicate the data from trend reports and forecasts? Does your firm's leadership communicate how the trends and forecasting information it has gathered will be built into its strategies?

Forecasts and trend analyses' champions and influencers

- Is there a "go-to" trends-and-forecast professional or team? Perhaps there is a member of a firm-focused market research team or a corporate librarian who is accountable for conducting or obtaining these tools and assisting in their advantageous use.
- Which firm leader has voiced his or her concerns about the future shifts in the marketplace? These concerns are especially noticeable when the economy takes a downturn; for example, "How much will our clients cut their budgets and therefore how should we adjust our staff capacity?" These concerns are also especially noticeable when an industry has been strongly affected by a new trend or regulation—for example, design-build in the architecture-engineering-construction arena, multidisciplinary practices (MDPs) in law, and the U.S. 2002 Sarbanes-Oxley Act, affecting the global accounting and business consulting arena (with even wider ripple effects for businesses globally). Which leaders would have most appreciated a forecast about how to address these marketplace hurdles, or would stand to benefit the most from a forecasting or trends analysis exercise?

Competency: Researching the Competitors by Gathering Competitive Intelligence

Past track record on competitive intelligence

- Has your firm ever conducted a competitive intelligence exercise? If so, was this exercise conducted on behalf of the entire firm, or for a solo practice or group of practices? Is it a regularly funded effort or done only when the firm is in a crisis?

- If it has been done before, what was the level of prominence of the competitive intelligence effort? For example, was it plainly called "competitive intelligence," or was it buried within a larger market research initiative?
- Who paid for competitive intelligence at your firm? For example, did your practice leader have to scheme to sneak away funds to conduct a competitive intelligence project, or, like at Towers Perrin, was it funded from a corporate initiative?

Knowledge about competitive intelligence
- Do your firm's leaders truly understand what competitive intelligence is—and is not? In the professional service sector, with its historical reticence about "aggressive" marketing, many misconceptions still exist about competitive intelligence. (It is *not* a simple compilation of innumerable Web-site pages, detailed charts and lengthy reports.) Many questions still exist about the role of competitive intelligence for an organization.

Attitude about competitive intelligence
- Is competitive intelligence a dirty word, viewed as an almost unethical activity? Is it conducted secretively, or openly as a firm-wide, endorsed project?
- How well is your firm organized to take advantage of the competitive intelligence it gains? Competitive intelligence that languishes in the managing partner's office is of little use to the firm as a whole.
- What expectations might your firm have about what it can "get" from a competitive intelligence effort? (Good competitive intelligence allows a firm to critically perceive marketplace opportunities and threats from which to make clear business decisions.)
- Does your firm's leadership communicate openly and formally about its competitors and their activities? Moreover, is competitor information available in a coordinated fashion, or for example, buried piecemeal deep inside the firm's intranet?

Competitive intelligence champions and influencers
- Does it appear that the only people calling for competitive intelligence are your marketing or business development team members? How long and how stridently have they been calling for competitive intelligence to be conducted? If they have other battles to wage for the firm to undertake other initiatives that they have been long awaiting, how high up on their wish list is competitive

intelligence in comparison? What is their perception of its value to their—and the firm's—future growth?

- What is the personal political stock of the likely champions of competitive intelligence? Are they viewed as credible team players, or peripheral whiners? Has any of them endorsed a "controversial" project that previously failed?

A "DIGGING DEEPER" ASSESSMENT

This area is entirely about organizational implementation. Each one of the digging-deeper initiatives requires a firm-wide focus, commitment, verve and a "let's do this for the firm" mindset. The following line of inquiry is designed to help you determine how comfortable you are that your firm has the *organizational focus* and *implementation muscle* it needs to achieve a competitive edge.

- Is there past evidence of your firm's success at implementing its chosen initiatives? Which areas appear to be working the most smoothly? Has your firm been stuck in start-up mode for new processes that never get fully inculcated into the firm's way of doing business?
- From which sources do you see new methods, processes, or tools being introduced? From the firm's executive management team ("Today we're introducing a new incentive compensation program") or from specific functional areas such as human resources, accounting, quality and client satisfaction, or marketing and business development?
- Does your firm provide enough administrative and technological support in order to ensure that processes and programs run smoothly? Conversely, are professionals not well supported by administrative staff or technological tools?
- What is the level of understanding and agreement about each of the digging-deeper practices? For example, relationship management is sometimes considered simply a software program rather than a strategic approach to developing business. How much of a learning curve would there be for your organization to arrive at a common understanding of one or more of the digging-deeper practices?
- How good is your firm at implementing processes? Do people appear to welcome the announcement of new procedures as a symbol of increased effectiveness? Conversely, do your colleagues appear to be overprocessed? ("Argghh! I can't get my client work done because I'm too busy entering my business development notes into the central database! And now they want *more* details!")

- How effective is your firm at communicating to its people to help them understand the importance of their implementing the firm's avowed policies and methods, and reporting to them about the results of their efforts? Do people appear to be successfully focusing their behavior on practices that help the firm achieve its strategic goals, or do they appear unable to do the "heavy lifting" that market-focused practices require?

- Will it be difficult to find a ready-made champion for the digging-deeper practices? If so, can you discern which person or group might have a level of affinity for one of the digging-deeper practices? For example, a star business developer could become a champion for your firm's creation of account planning and relationship management programs. How about dual champions— one with a human resource "hat" and one with a marketing "hat" to help spearhead a pitch to align the firm's marketing strategies with its culture?

Competency: Embracing Competitive Differentiation

Past track record on differentiation
- Has your firm ever undertaken any kind of differentiation initiative? What was the outcome? (All too often it's a blandly broad *statement*, residing in a pretty report or perhaps on a firm's Web site, that expresses how your firm is different.)

Knowledge about differentiation
- How well do your firm's leaders understand differentiation? That it means your firm is the only firm to be, to do, or to have something that no other firm is, does, or has? Many professionals (and marketers too) have varying definitions of the terms "differentiation," "positioning," and "branding." Often, they treat these strategies as if they are the same (they are not), or at least interchangeable (again, not at all). What does each platform mean separately, and in relation to the other?

- How keenly do your firm's leaders perceive the crucial role of differentiation in a professional service firm's corporate strategy? Is it viewed as a critical firm-wide strategy, as it should be? Is it viewed as a marketing communication initiative, rather than an organizational platform that is supposed to be *implemented*? Instead, do you see evidence of a lightweight approach to differentiation? (It is lightweight if you see that your firm has not set up any processes or tools to operationally support its differentiation strategies.)

- How much do your firm's leaders understand about the numerous possible foundations of differentiation—that a differentiation strategy can be built on a firm's geographical focus, service offerings, client needs addressed, "point of entry" (e.g., only when the client is in a crisis, or only in leadership transitions), staff, service delivery, value delivered, image, clients' emotional "experience," targets, and more?

- Do your firm's leaders understand how to assess the criteria for determining the most robust possible differentiation platform for your firm (value for clients, credibility, attractiveness, sustainability, narrow focus, and protection against copycats)?

Attitude about differentiation

- Do many of your firm's professionals scoff at the notion of real differentiation, that it cannot be achieved? If so, this is a signal that they may not understand the elements or foundation of differentiation strategies.
- Are your firm's leaders convinced that the firm *is* different, when, in fact, this is nowhere near the case (and everyone else knows it)?

Differentiation champions and influencers

- Does your firm have a professional-side partner or director whose voice on marketing has earned his or her colleagues' respect? This would be a person who is not viewed as terribly avant-garde, someone who has demonstrated successful leadership on previous firm initiatives. If so, how "tired" or "skeptical" is the organization of seeing this person step up to the plate to push the firm toward a new initiative? ("There goes Jean-Phillippe again—he has such a strong voice that people have begun to tune him out.")
- Does your firm have a staff-side chief marketing officer or marketing director? If so, is this person mainly responsible for marketing communications activities (anything related to building visibility and not the development of marketing strategy)? What is the level of "power" of this person in your firm? For example, is she or he an influential lynchpin on your firm's executive management team or someone viewed mostly as a support staff person who is only supposed to respond to partners' promotional needs?

Competency: Mining Client Data

Past track record on data mining

- Does your firm have an automated contacts database? When did this database get adopted, and how deeply integrated is it within the firm? Is this the firm's first, second, third (or more) adoption of a database? ("We used to use the XXX software platform but it was a disaster; now we use YYY and it's been much better received.")

- How integrated is your firm's contacts management platform with its practice management and accounting systems? Do they "communicate"? How easy is it for someone to connect information about a client's project team with the firm's delivery of work on that project? For example, recall Numerica's ability to examine the many aspects of its client relationships, from the levels of decision-making of its client contacts to the relative profitability of this client for Numerica. These pieces of mined data are found in separate databases that are nevertheless deeply integrated within Numerica. A firm with disconnected systems would have a more difficult time discerning connected patterns of this nature.
- How uniform is the firm's use of its contacts database or practice management systems? For example, do some geographical areas use them extensively, while other geographies do not? Are there some offices that are not using the firm's database or practice management platforms yet? ("We just merged with ABC & Associates; the full integration of our firms' incompatible systems will take *three years!*")
- How thoroughly has your firm trained its personnel to use the database? For example, are the administrative people well versed in its use, while the professionals have not yet been trained? Are there certain practices or partners whose record is spotty for inputting information into the database?
- Does your firm have an identified protocol for getting information into the database? ("We've set up a system whereby our partners meet with their administrative assistants once a day to share information that needs to go into our contacts management or our practice management system.")
- Has your firm ever conducted a formal data-mining project before—even a simple one? If so, who led the project, who used the information generated, with what results? Many firms already *do* undertake data mining yet have never labeled it as such. For example, in its hope to discern patterns about its selling effectiveness, has your firm ever implemented a database query to explore its proposal success rate within certain client sectors? This is data mining.

Knowledge about data mining
- How sophisticated is the data housed in your firm's contacts management or practice management systems? Does the contacts database mostly include basic information on clients' names, addresses, phone numbers, industry sectors, and the like, and not include information like growth outlook, legislative issues affecting the clients, or their service satisfaction scores? Does the prac-

tice management system information mostly include hours billed and project expenses and the like, but not features that can help conduct a skills inventory, analyze client service demand, and optimize the firm's staffing resource allocations?

Attitude about data mining
- How much of a cultural fire wall exists between your firm's marketing and IT departments? Are there turf issues between these two camps? For example, do marketing leaders roll their eyes when someone suggests that "we should bring IT into this discussion" or vice versa? Conversely, have there been times when technology staffers have worked well in tandem with marketing staff?
- What is the firm's cultural attitude about sharing and reporting information? For example, do partners hold the details of their client and prospect interactions fairly closely, or is most client information openly shared across the firm?

Data mining champions and influencers
- Which people appear to be credible data mining leaders from marketing and IT? Is there anyone in either area that has a statistics background or familiarity?
- Regardless of interest or background in technology, marketing, or statistics, is there a leader in your firm who demonstrates a high level of curiosity, loves to solve puzzles, and leans toward researching things?
- How esteemed are your firm's marketing and IT staffers? For example, do the partners speak glowingly of times when IT team members have solved critical problems or when marketing professionals were particularly effective in leading a certain project?

Competency: Aligning Marketing Strategies with Culture

Past track record on aligning marketing strategies with culture
- Has your firm ever undertaken a formal assessment of its culture? If so, when? Were any of the elements of this initiative intentionally incorporated into your firm's annual marketing or firm-wide strategic plans? As evidence, have you seen reference to the results of this assessment in the firm's published strategic or marketing plan documents?
- Have the firm's past "culture" initiatives been pursued with a mind to enhance the firm's external distinctions within the marketplace? Instead, have culture initiatives been pursued more as a means to coalesce its people around the firm's common values, regardless of their marketplace distinctiveness?

Knowledge about aligning marketing strategies with culture

- In order to effectively align marketing strategies with culture, a firm must commit to operationalizing the marketable aspects of its culture (as Egon Zehnder International did in the way it built collaboration into its day-to-day activities so that collaboration effectively "showed" in the marketplace; or as Marakon Associates did when it built "challenge with empathy" into its client interactions). The practice of "aligning marketing strategies with culture" requires more than simply communicating all aspects of the firm's culture. We've all probably seen a declaration of culture and values on professional service firm Web sites, on wall plaques in lobbies, or on the back of business cards. ("We are honest, dedicated to excellence and hardworking.") Does your firm understand the dig-deeper aspects to this practice—that its marketing strategies must tap culture whenever possible and that the more differentiated aspects of culture that are aligned with the firm's marketing strategies, the better? In fact, there may be multiple elements of a firm's culture, but only one or two elements that are differentiated or demonstrable enough to be integrated into the firm's marketing strategies.

Attitude about aligning marketing strategies with culture

- Many professional service firms are still at the level of trying to be all things to all clients. As such, they strive to achieve the lowest common denominators of culture—those that are the safest and the most acceptable to their marketplace. Yet there are indeed nuances of every firm's culture that are unique to each. Some of these nuances may have to do with a firm's founder or founding partners ("Sven certainly was a stickler for details, and that is undoubtedly reflected today in our firm's pursuit of accuracy!"). Some nuances may be the result of past marketplace moves that ended up shaping the firm's culture ("Smith & Smith became so adept at developing visionary solutions for its life sciences clients that it soon became known as the firm whose cultural norm is to 'push the boundaries' for *all* its clients!"). How open are your firm's leaders to dig below its cultural surface, to parse out the competitively advantaged cultural elements to incorporate into the firm's marketing strategies?

Champions and influencers for aligning marketing strategies with culture

- Which of your firm's leaders has the vision to discern aspects of your firm's culture that are competitively advantaged and that could be marketed?
- Can you identify someone whose firm-wide profile, charisma, and drive could help the rest of his or her colleagues to agree on

highlighting one or a few pillars of the firm's culture, while reassuring them that other equally valuable cultural pillars will not be internally negated?

Competency: Using Account Planning and Relationship Management Programs

Past track record on account planning and relationship management
- Has your firm ever engaged in any kind of formal examination of its client projects, from a macro perspective, where it assesses the value (to the firm) of its client work? For example, have you been asked to catalogue your "best" clients, or attend meetings to expand your services to one or more clients? If so, what happened with these initiatives?
- Is there a protocol that must be followed when one wants to interact with a client? ("Stop! You have to ask Sergio to call the client before you can contact her.")
- Has your firm ever published a list of its "Top 10" clients (or Top 25, 50, or whatever)? Did you then receive follow-up communiqués from your marketing or business development leaders about the firm's progress in building these client relationships?
- Has your firm ever published a list of relationship teams, with some of your colleagues assigned to shepherd and increase the relationship (that is, grow the size of the firms' revenues from this client)?
- Has your firm undertaken deliberate steps to "cross-sell" its services between practices, where one practice introduces its services to a current client, in the hopes of expanding the number of services that the client could buy from your firm?
- Has your firm begun to use terms like client relationship management (CRM), or strategic account management (SAM), or "our share of our client's wallet"? What programmatic initiatives have accompanied your firm's use of these terms?

Knowledge about account planning and relationship management
- How much does your firm know about the latest techniques regarding account planning and/or relationship management? These concepts are receiving increasing attention within the professional service arena, and yet there is little solid agreement on exactly what they are. Are they simply software programs? Where does one concept start and the other stop? Can one engage in account planning without managing client relationships, and vice versa? Does your firm have a solid grasp of its own definition of these concepts? Many firms might consider "targeting" to be ac-

count planning. It is not. Moreover, a firm might consider account planning to be simply listing its clients by the size of revenues they represent for the firm. This would be one step in the early stages of account planning, but certainly wouldn't be the only step. Account planning is a process where firms might ask, "How hard do we have to work, and how much do we have to spend (in time and expenses) to sell our services to this client?" They might also ask, "Once we have gained this client assignment, how efficiently are we able to provide services to this client?" Has your firm asked these and other analytical questions to determine which of its clients are strategic priorities—and which clients might not be? Relationship management is a process that goes well beyond a simple assignment of an account steward. It requires a thoughtful mapping of the decision-making capabilities and/or influence posture of the individuals within a client's organization, accompanied by clearly designated relationship counterparts within the professional service firm. As the example in the L.E.K. Consulting case showed, robust relationship management also requires the ability to track and "follow" individuals as they progress through their careers, regardless of where they work. In addition, a true relationship management program drives toward an outcome—a discernible flow, usually toward the client's purchase of services or referral of the professional service firm to another potential client.

Attitude about account planning and relationship management
- Account planning and relationship management require almost as much of an external organizational focus as an internal organizational focus. How much does your firm embrace the management of *its own* relationships? For example, do new hires receive a warm, thorough orientation to the firm, or are they pretty much expected to swim on their own right away after starting their jobs? As another example, does your firm have a mentoring program for its newer professionals? How successful is it?
- How resistant are your firm's managers to the idea of directing the flow of relationships with clients? Do they believe that it can be done, or do they believe that your firm must be more "flexible," responding to clients' requirements rather than directing clients toward your firm's desired outcome? Similarly, are your firm's leaders reluctant to pronounce their plans to grow a client account (mostly, you suspect, because they secretly fear that their personal stature will be reduced if they don't achieve the firm's hoped-for goals)? The essence of account planning and relationship management is grounded in "intention," with your firm either implicitly

or overtly saying, "This is what *we* want from our relationship with our clients." By taking steps to plan accounts or manage client relationships, professional service firms ultimately declare their willingness to work to win a client's assignments and their intention to dig deeper to expand these assignments toward greater and greater value for the firm. This attitude is a decided departure from the more passive approaches that were taken in the past by many professional service firms. Is your firm ready for this mindset shift?

Champions and influencers for account planning and relationship management
- Which of your firm's prominent individuals are great business developers? These role models are likely the people whose relationship talents are instinctive. Do you believe these people can help others to surface the more hidden aspects of planning an account or managing a relationship? Do you think they can help lead (and later mentor) their colleagues to develop a firm-wide, formal framework of how to plan for a strategic client account or manage a client relationship?
- Is there an individual or group whose tactical skills are legendary? This would be someone whose follow-up is unflagging, whose track record of reporting on the progress of a relationship is undisputed, and whose personal stake in his own prominence with a client is secondary to his desire to contribute to the firm's overall success with that client.
- Is there an individual whose personal charisma is such that he or she can credibly nudge his or her partners into making plans and then striving to execute them — in front of everyone?

Competency: Using Measurement to Increase Strategic Focus and Competitive Advantage

Past track record on measurement
- Does your firm utilize measurement tools (e.g., any kind of performance reviews) in its human resource programs?
- After the conclusion of any of your firm's marketing initiatives, has it ever conducted a follow-up evaluation (for example, after a seminar, checking to see how many of the invitees actually attended, or after a speech, checking to see how many business cards were collected out of the estimated number of people in the audience)?
- Has your firm ever undertaken a formal *internal* survey?
- If your firm has previously undertaken a marketing-program measurement activity, what was the outcome? Do you recall ever

seeing the results of that measurement, or any announced changes in the marketing program as a result?
- Has any measurement activity been abandoned after having been started? If so, why?

Knowledge about measurement
- Traditional measurement methods featured simple return-on-investment examinations at the conclusion of marketing initiatives or a particular period of time. Marketers would ask, "How many people came to our seminar?"; "How many visitors have we had to our Web site in the last week?"; or "How many proposals did we win last quarter?" Increasingly, sometimes with the help of a number of powerful software applications, marketing leaders are using sophisticated measurement methods: for example, comparing "before" and "after" buyer perceptions, choices, and behaviors; measuring response rates by client segments; assessing the costs of acquiring new clients; and much more. Going forward, professional service firm leaders will want the answer to questions like, "In what ways should we tweak our marketing campaign in order to increase our client's response rates to our upcoming seminar invitations?" or "How can we measure the ROI of our client satisfaction program?" Are your firm's leaders asking these kinds of questions, or not? Do they appear comfortable with such marketing measurement techniques as "predictive analytics"?[3] Do they understand terms like *performance indicators, brand equity,* or *conversion rates*"?[4] Do they know what to measure and how these measurements could help them lead your firm?

Attitude about measurement
- It has been said that professional marketers believe that *every* opportunity to reach out to clients also contains an opportunity to measure the effectiveness of a firm's interactions with them. Do your firm's leaders feel this way or do they think of measurement as a necessary evil that would probably get in the way of your firm's doing its work?
- Are your firm's professionals culturally comfortable with analytics, mathematics or statistics? For example, is your firm's core discipline based on or does it include a focus on analytics, statistics or mathematics? On the other hand, are your firm's professionals culturally averse to analysis?
- Measuring things typically supports a firm's making changes from one scenario to another. How good has your firm been at making changes—from starting up and moving ahead to definitely *finishing* an initiative?

Measurement champions and influencers

- The case of ACNielsen reminds us that a company's achievement of certain marketplace goals requires one or more of its leaders to envision a beneficial end-state or goal that the company needs to attain. Does your firm have leaders who can articulate an end-state or goal that they wish the firm could attain? Some of these goals could be quite broad, for instance, "We need to capture market share from our competitors," or "We need to increase the return-on-investment of our direct mail program."
- Is there a particular practice group or business unit that would welcome the opportunity to become a firm-wide showcase for measurement? It could be a practice group that has recently struggled but that has not yet lost the firm's favor or a unit that, with a definable goal against which progress could be measured, could become a marquee for the rest of the firm. An example is measuring the effectiveness of a new business development technique as a means to boost the practice's revenues.

AN "EMBEDDING INNOVATION" ASSESSMENT

This area is entirely about a firm's having the curiosity and enthusiasm for figuring out a client's unmet needs before they do, and about having the organizational discipline to build new capabilities in order to attract them. The following line of inquiry is designed to help you determine how comfortable you are that your firm has the *risk tolerance* and *organizational framework* it needs to achieve marketplace mastery through innovation.

- Who drives innovation at your firm? Does innovation bubble up periodically (on an ad hoc basis) from within practices, or does it appear to be driven from the firm's senior levels?
- How culturally supported does innovation appear to be at your firm? For example, have you witnessed a group or groups of professionals leaving the firm en masse in order to offer services that they felt they could not make "fit" within your firm's portfolio of services, or has the firm embraced the in-house development of new services and celebrated their introduction and successes?
- At your firm, does innovation take a cultural backseat to "responding" to clients' currently expressed needs, or does your firm have an "exceeding client expectations" mentality?
- Is professional development and learning a significant focus for your firm? Does the firm have an in-house "director of development"? Do employees receive formal recognition when they do new things?

- How often do you see individuals taking on new roles at your firm—for example, an administrative assistant who becomes a research associate? Can you think of other examples of your firm's flexibility and risk tolerance?
- How well does your firm "notice" it when clients' service fatigue begins to build? Is service fatigue setting in with *your* firm's clients? (Think back to the architectural firm that we met in Chapter 1, whose hospital client was about to signal its service fatigue with the firm's traditional architectural design services by building its own in-house design team. How might this firm's leaders figure out a way to tap into the hospital's still-unexpressed need for hospital-specific facility planning services? How might the architects devise a way to integrate their services with other disciplines such as strategic planning, hospital operations, patient flow modeling and the like?)
- Does your firm have procedures or processes that robustly—or weakly—support innovation? How are new ideas handled when they come up? For example, is there an ongoing innovation committee or R&D "department?" Are ad hoc task forces created to examine new initiatives? If so, how high a profile do these task forces or committees receive within your firm?
- Is the firm actively communicating about its exploration of new initiatives, new services, new *anything*?

Competency: Building an R&D Process

Past track record on building an R&D process

- Has your firm ever "retired" a service before or folded it back into a broader practice (as Towers Perrin did after its competitive intelligence project)? Has it ever built and launched a new service? How did the firm undertake these initiatives? If so, how long ago were these steps taken?
- If, in the past, your firm created an innovation committee or R&D department, what were the structures and terms of this group? Was participation in this group offered to people as an honorary "reward"? ("Of course we have an innovation committee—it is staffed by our soon-to-be retired partners.") Was participation voluntary and temporary? ("All the losers are on *that* committee!") Instead, was this group led by respected leaders who are in the prime of their tenure at your firm?
- Has your firm ever obtained venture capital in order to be started up, or in order to build its business? At this point, could this process (or elements of it) be replicated in order to stimulate internal innovation?

- If your firm does have an R&D committee or department, to whom does this group "report"? How strong a link does this group have to your firm's executive management?
- Is there staff support for R&D at your firm? For example, a dedicated or partially dedicated researcher or research team that is responsible for assisting the R&D group to explore new service opportunities?
- How well linked is R&D to your firm's market research efforts? Has anyone ever tried to link these initiatives before, and failed—or succeeded? If so, why?
- How much has R&D been included as an element of compensation within your firm? For example, does a stint in an R&D role translate into bonus opportunities for your firm's professionals?
- Does it appear that enthusiasm for R&D waxes and wanes according to who is the firm's managing partner or CEO?
- Has your firm ever conducted an analysis of the shelf-life of its services, or their level of commoditization in the marketplace? In a related manner, has your firm ever expressed concern about shrinking profit margins on any of its services and then attempted to tweak their pricing?
- If your firm does have an R&D framework, how well does it communicate about it? For example, does the R&D team have a recognized name throughout the firm? Are updates about its work regularly distributed around the firm?

Knowledge about building an R&D process
- What is your firm's real understanding of "new"? Does it mean a "totally-new-to-the-world, never-been-seen-before" service or does it mean simply acquiring a service that's been well known in another industry or sector?
- Has your firm studied the structure, responsibilities, performance and/or best practices of R&D or innovation functions in other professional service firms or the way R&D is managed in other industries or businesses? Has it tried to apply these "R&D lessons learned" in any way?

Attitude about building an R&D process
- Many professionals reject the idea that there could be a totally new service within the framework of a profession's performance standards. They point to strict rules of licensure and ethics as their evidence that indeed, their profession is not *allowed* to innovate. Is this attitude in evidence at your firm? If so, how pervasive is it? Does there appear to be an interest in meeting the needs of the shifting marketplace? An example is the way RSM McGladrey was

able to develop a new approach to serving a subset of its clients, while still staying within the ethics and performance standards of its industry.

Champions and influencers for building an R&D process
- Are there professionals who express interest in innovation, and whose performance of your firm's services appears to be creative, client-focused, passionate, even joyful?
- Is there a person or group that has successfully led the introduction of *anything* new at your firm? It could be a new benefits plan, the introduction of a new practice, or the acquisition of a smaller firm? In fact, it could be anything new that the firm has done as a result of the work of this group or person. Was the outcome of this effort deemed a positive one? At this time, how busy are these people on any other initiative? Can they be tapped for another tour of duty on doing something about innovation?
- Does your firm have a new managing partner or CEO? Is there someone who is looking for a platform upon which to develop his or her legacy or someone whose past track record indicates he or she could be a strong leader for innovation?

Competency: Using Technology to Build New Services

Past track record on using technology to build new services
- Has your firm ever turned any of its services into a software application, and then tried to sell the software program with in-person services wrapped around it? What happened to this effort? Was it successful, with the software application's revenues growing progressively and its related in-person services either growing concurrently or at least holding steady, or has it floundered or out-and-out failed? Why?
- If your firm used technology to build new services, did it do so in order to serve clients more effectively, or was it done because your firm was trying to shore up a service from which it had previously enjoyed robust revenues and now does not? In other words, did your firm use technology to develop new services to benefit the marketplace—or just to benefit *itself*?
- If your firm used technology to build a new service, did it do so as a result of a planning exercise or from a platform of research or because of a strategic marketplace decision? For example, did it first examine the new service's role within the firm's entire service portfolio? Did it project how a "technologized" version of its service would affect the rest of the portfolio, or did it just pull the trigger without these strategic underpinnings?

- Did your firm pilot the new technology-based service with clients and/or prospects before it went "live"?
- Did your firm make any investments in personnel to support the new technology-based service? What were their capabilities; were these capabilities effective in supporting the eventual success of the service?

Knowledge about using technology to build new services
- Many professionals assume that substituting computer keystrokes for the stepwise aspects of a commoditized service is a form of innovation. How much do your professionals truly understand the nature of technology and its potential for delivering value to users?
- Do your firm's leaders have a clear picture of the way your clients and prospects perceive their need for assistance (the way clients unconsciously assign value to a spectrum of offerings, from tangible products to productized services to intangible (intellect-based) services)? Can your firm's leaders imagine a technology-based service that would meet or exceed their clients' perceptions of value, while still keeping that service in the realm of an intangible, intellect-based offering? If they cannot, are they willing to seek the assistance of technology experts and/or development specialists?
- Are your firm's leaders familiar with the emergence of new or technology-supported methods that could be applied to a new service? DDB Worldwide's example with econometrics is a good one; with DDB Matrix, it developed a new intellect-based service that uses technology but is not technology itself.

Attitude about using technology to build new services
- Are your firm's leaders gun-shy about technology in general? Or are they overly enamored with it in an unrealistic way? Another way of examining this issue could be to review the tenure levels of the senior leadership of the firm. Are they mostly grey-haired old-timers or baby boomers? Is there a corps of younger leaders whose vision and understanding of technology could be tapped here? Be careful, though; do not assume that age is the most appropriate indicator of being able to be a technology visionary.
- How companionable—or fractious—is your firm's executive management team? Is there a vocal Luddite among the group? How hard would it be to get the group to have a shared epiphany about the future role of technology in your firm's innovation efforts? Will they need extensive guidance to build consensus about innovating through technology?
- How have your firm's past forays into using technology or innovation shaped the viewpoints of your executive team (the very folks whose budgetary purview can make or break a new initiative)?

Champions and influencers for using technology to build new services

- Has the firm recently hired a new executive director, technology-savvy practice leader, or chief technology officer? How has this person's early tenure been perceived (with unabashed kudos or with a growing swell of envy)? Could this person's spectrum of responsibilities include a stint on the development of a technology-based service?

- Who was the last person at your firm to lead the development of a new service of any kind—even if it was the firm's founder? How did this new service fare? Is the person willing to serve in at least an advisory capacity to a team charged with creating a new technology-based service?

- If your firm is global, are there leaders in other countries or regions who could be tapped to be champions of using technology to develop a new service?

- Is there a leader who is vocally concerned about your firm's decreasing profit margins? Someone who is not a cynic or a whiner, but someone whose track record features proactive work to solve client or firm-wide problems? Could this person be persuaded to put his or her concerns toward a potentially positive outcome—the development of a new service?

- Is there a member of your firm's executive committee who has in the past successfully argued for and won the firm's agreement to expend funds for a particular initiative (even unrelated to innovation or technology)? Is there someone whose persuasion about expending those funds resulted in a positive outcome?

Competencies: Using Incentives and Rewards to Stimulate Innovation

Past track record on using incentives and rewards to stimulate innovation

- Does your firm have an incentive and rewards program in general, or any kind of recognition program? If so, for what behaviors or for the performance of what tasks does it reward? Do any of these incentives, rewards, or recognition have anything to do with innovation, or is innovative performance or behavior buried within a long list of other desirable behaviors or tasks? Is the firm's bonus program only based on a percentage of the firm's achievement of annual revenues?

- If there are specific incentives or rewards for innovation, how meaningful or potent are they? Are they merely tepid gestures for the sake of lip service to innovation?

- How visible have your firm's communications been about its incentives and rewards for innovation? Is it like Mitretek Systems, where award winners are recognized publicly with fanfare and verve or is it more understated, perhaps a memo circulated to a select group of practitioners only? Do employees expect regular communication about innovation, or is it more periodic and unexpected?

- Has your firm embraced any kind of peer-review or 360-degree performance measurement process? Did the firm employ any kind of accompanying coaching and mentoring in order to steer the appropriate behavior? What other kinds of performance management processes were introduced, and could these be applied to stimulating innovation?
- Can you discern your firm's strategy for rewards and incentives? For example, regarding innovation, have your firm's leaders pursued a performance program that rewards innovation *after the fact* or a program that manages the opportunity *from the start*?[5] In your opinion, which would work the best for stimulating innovation at your firm?

Knowledge about incentives and rewards to stimulate innovation
- In general, are your firm's leaders up to speed on newer performance management approaches or personal long-term value creation for professional service firms, or have they kept your firm's incentives, rewards, and personal value-creation programs unchanged for a long time?
- Has your firm undertaken a looking-out initiative to learn about the incentives and rewards programs of other professional service firms? How much have these other firms worked to incorporate innovation deeply into their professionals' work, and with what results? Are there any of these lessons learned that your firm could apply to itself?

Attitude about incentives and rewards to stimulate innovation
- The attitude about rewarding innovation is integral to the attitude about innovation in general. Review your impressions about how your firm has or has not embraced innovation. If the firm has (or is developing) a positive attitude about innovation, how much further could it go toward overtly fostering it?
- How expansive is your firm's overall incentive and rewards program? Is your firm miserly in its rewards program? As another example, are bonuses or rewards only available to a particular subset of the firm, or are they available to all employees? Do these programs vary by functional level? ("Our entry-level associates and principals are not eligible for our firm's in-house innovation grants; you have to be a partner to participate.")

- Is innovation a muted "should" at your firm, rather than an overt and well-communicated strategy? For example, does your firm expect participation in innovation as a given, with recognition of this behavior occurring only at times of salary adjustment and promotion?
- Is there a discernible level of grumbling going on at your firm that its entire compensation program is out of whack, therefore leaving little hope that an added element about encouraging and rewarding innovation could actually happen in the near term?
- Are your firm's leaders skeptical about new programs in general? What kind of evidence do you think they would need in order to endorse and direct the creation of an incentive and rewards program for innovation?
- What other evidence of your firm's attitude about innovation can you discern? Is this evidence a positive sign—or a negative one— that innovation could be more overtly rewarded at your firm?

Champions and influencers for incentives and rewards to stimulate innovation
- How influential are your firm's human resources leaders? Do these people assertively take leadership on a variety of HR issues, or do they largely serve as the benefits department for your firm? Could they help lead a revamping of the firm's job descriptions to include a focus on innovation? What other building blocks have they used in other circumstances that could be applied to a new focus on stimulating innovation?
- Is there anyone who has the charisma and credibility to create a compelling argument for recognizing and rewarding innovation? What is this person's recent track record of success in leading change within your firm?
- Is there a recent new addition to your firm's senior staff whose participation in an innovation-oriented incentive, reward or recognition program could be used to help your firm embrace this idea?

I've said that professional service firms that achieve marketplace mastery have likely done so because they have built a market-driven infrastructure. You have just completed the first step of a process to help you firm do so, too. By finding evidence of your firm's building blocks to achieve marketplace mastery and by taking yourself through an assessment of one or a few of the eleven market-driven infrastructure pillars, you can now visualize your firm's readiness to compete more effectively.

Make the Case to Build a Market-Driven Infrastructure

By now, you have assessed your firm's most advantageous potential market-driven infrastructure competencies. You have gathered compelling evidence. You are impassioned and oh-so-ready for your firm to make a grand resolution to *do things in a new way.* Does this sound familiar? Do you remember the professional service firms in Chapter 1, rushing toward mountainous new initiatives without a clear comprehension of their actions or the real determination to stay the course once they'd begun? What about those enterprises that appeared to be on the other end of the spectrum—the ones that avoided the deeply organic work it takes to make systemic change? This time, though, with a maturing service marketplace, an evolving technological landscape, and new competitive approaches being adopted every day, your firm's collective conviction to do things differently is likely to be high.

Consider just one of the looking out building blocks: studying clients using qualitative and quantitative research. As more firms become acutely aware of the competitive environment in which they now conduct business and begin to see the benefits they could realize from a formal commitment to market research, an increasing number will consider market research to be a core activity that they will undertake regularly. They will plan and protect these market research expenses, with an objective to provide them with increasingly beneficial marketplace perspectives. They will undertake research that:

- Adds to the established foundation that they already bring to their client satisfaction research.
- Examines their unique position within their client's choice of potential service providers.
- Helps them understand their client's purchase criteria, attraction to a set of service attributes, or perceptions of potential new service offerings.
- Gives them a solid foundation on which to set future strategies to master their marketplace.

Now consider one of the digging-deeper building blocks: embracing competitive differentiation. A professional service firm may not be competitively differentiated *today*, but more and more firms will commit to pursuing a strategy that helps them *become* different over time. They will differentiate by:

- *Service offerings:* "We only specialize in such-and-such services"; or "We are the only firm to offer such-and-such services."
- *Client needs addressed:* "We only work with clients that are experiencing so-and-so challenges."
- *The point of entry to solving client problems:* "We address our clients' [XXX] challenges [like our competitors], but we are the only firm that always begins our assignments by starting with [for example,] an organizational assessment."
- *Staff:* "We are the only firm whose strategy is to be the most female-staffed firm of any of the major firms"; "We only hire professionals from the top three graduate schools in our sector"; or "We are the only firm that tests our candidates for their capabilities in problem-solving and curiosity."
- *Service delivery:* "We will only work at *your* site"; or "We are the only firm that uses a particular technology to maximize the [XXX] aspects of our work."
- *Level of client served:* "We only work with CEOs."
- *Size of client:* We only serve companies that are [larger/smaller] than [XXX]."
- *Targeted segment:* "We only serve manufacturing companies"; or "We only work for the public sector."
- *Geographic location:* "We only do work in North America"; or "Europe is our only specialty."
- *Value delivered:* "We are the only firm to offer cost-effective results" (very hard to prove).

- *Image:* "We are the only firm in our sector to be young, hip, and fast-paced"; or "We are the only blue-chip, upper-crust firm in our sector."
- *Client "experience":* "We are the only firm in [XXX] sector to make humor our client's experience."
- *Position (if first):* "We were the first to develop the so-and-so method; we are the only firm that owns the trademark."

The firms that pursue robust differentiation (and many are actively undertaking this strategy) will fully grasp the notion that they must be, have, or do something that makes them "the only." They will be comfortable with the fundamental differentiation requirement: saying "no" to some of their past services, clients, or regions. They will "get it" that differentiation is not simply a statement that should be communicated, but rather a set of operational decisions and processes.

Last, consider one of the embedding-innovation building blocks: using incentives and rewards to stimulate new things. As an increasing number of professional service firms begin to institutionalize their own unique set of innovation processes, so they will embrace the notion that each person is responsible for the success of those processes. In addition to rewarding innovation with good, old-fashioned merit awards ("Innovator of the Month") and cash bonuses, we will see innovation incentives that look like frequent-flyer programs, with people accumulating points toward a well-known set of rewards. We will see innovation contests, membership clubs, and certifications. We will see increasingly sophisticated incentive methods, including those that tap the sort of personal sources of motivation that go deeper than money: peer approval, professional stature, and personal camaraderie. Undoubtedly, we will see permutations of incentives and rewards that themselves are even more innovative than models we can conceive of today.

MOVING TOWARD MARKETPLACE MASTERY

It is time to begin the move toward marketplace mastery. Your charge is to guide your firm to move ahead in the best way it can: with an infrastructure of market-focused processes, tools, and methods that are built on its natural aptitudes and a genuine organizational dedication to move forward incrementally and continuously.

This chapter is about the personal side of making the case to build a market-driven infrastructure. It is where we are reminded about the wisdom of making continuous small changes that can ultimately drive great gains. My goal is to motivate you to balance passion with patience, as you guide your firm to take the necessary baby steps, which it may find unfamiliar and uncomfortable but so crucial to its ultimate competitive success.

Chapter 8 presented the first of three steps to help professional service firms contemplate the creation of a market-driven infrastructure. This chapter outlines the second and third steps in this process, in which you will present an argument for action and coalesce another group of influencers to iterate the message again and again and again. In Step Two, you will state your case that your firm can start building its own market-driven infrastructure. By Step Three, you will become a true champion for change.

STEP TWO: STATE YOUR CASE

This is the step that you must take in order to educate your firm's leaders that they can develop one or more of the competencies of a market-driven infrastructure. As you begin to form your talking points, remind yourself about the natural skepticism and reticence of professionals to an aggressive "hard sell." Professional service practitioners are notorious for needing evidence. Give it to them as succinctly and as compellingly as you can. Treat your internal colleagues as if they were prospects. They need to see and hear the evidence of the challenges they know they face but have not yet figured how to overcome. They need to be part of the eventual development of the solution.

From the prior readiness exercise, you have probably got more information than you need. Let's assume you picked digging deeper as the area in which you felt your firm could succeed and for which you have some personal passion. Within the digging-deeper framework, let's say you're specifically keen to see your firm develop a client data mining competency.

Figure 9.1 presents a suggested way to create a visualization of your readiness assessment. Develop this visual so that it can be presented in front of a group of people, while also being able to be clearly understood if it is read. Use the box at the bottom of Figure 9.1 to feature a few points from each area of your Part A investigation: the evidence of your firm's past success at implementing processes, its market-focused thinking, and its desire to win in the marketplace (see Figure 9.1).

Now, move to your work from Part B: your assessment of your firm's market-driven infrastructure competencies. For the section called "Today—An Assessment of Our Digging Deeper Competencies" (the left-hand box on the top of Figure 9.1), pick out two or three key points about your organization's past track record, knowledge, attitude, and

Step One

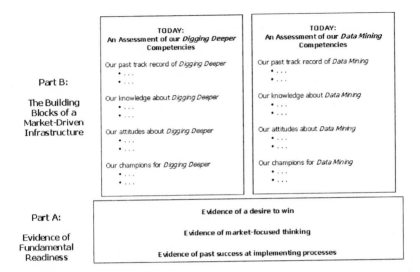

Figure 9.1 Assess Readiness

champions in digging deeper. Choose information that paints a realistic picture yet allows a perception of possibilities for improvement.

Next, move to the top right-hand box in Figure 9.1. It's called "Today—An Assessment of Our Data Mining Competencies." Following the same format, pick a few key points that specifically highlight your firm's data mining competencies. Once again, showcase the facts that provide a candid view of your firm's data-mining situation, while leaving room to begin contemplating the deeper potential of data mining.

The final box is shown in Figure 9.2. It's called "A Data Mining Snapshot." Your goal is to build momentum from the picture you have already painted from your readiness assessment. Here, you will provide an at-a-glance illustration of how data mining is being used to achieve competitive success in other business sectors and other professional service firms. Now, you'll need to feature a snapshot of stimulating information to help your firm's leaders see the potential marketplace gains that could be had from implementing this practice. What kind of information would be persuasive enough? Certainly, it would have to be from other firms in your sector; perhaps it may be from firms whose profile might be similar. In addition, from the materials in this book, you can to include some of the specific research findings about how professional service firms are using data mining. But you'll probably need to gather other quick facts as well. Search the Web for information

Step Two

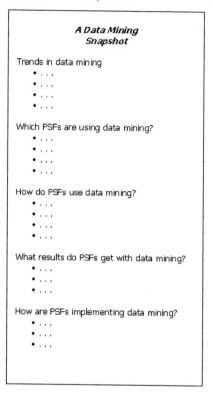

A Data Mining Snapshot

Trends in data mining
- · . . .
- · . . .
- · . . .
- · . . .

Which PSFs are using data mining?
- · . . .
- · . . .
- · . . .
- · . . .

How do PSFs use data mining?
- · . . .
- · . . .
- · . . .
- · . . .

What results do PSFs get with data mining?
- · . . .
- · . . .
- · . . .

How are PSFs implementing data mining?
- · . . .
- · . . .
- · . . .

Figure 9.2 State Your Case

about data mining, citing articles or quotes that help illuminate the way it is being used successfully. If you can, ask friends or your counterparts at other companies if they think their companies are using data mining effectively, and if so, how. You can also contact trade associations whose purview relates to the practice you're highlighting, to see if they have published research or white papers or have sponsored conferences on the topic.

Cull through all; the idea is to select the information that compellingly (but not offensively) makes the point that data mining is an effective competitive practice. Your selections might fall into the following five categories: trends about data mining (the way it is being used in other industries, for example); which professional service firms are using data mining; how they use it; the results that other professional firms report about their use of data mining; and how they are implementing it. Wherever possible, add anecdotes or examples about actual firms or prototype firms from the cases presented in this book or elsewhere.

MAKE THE PITCH

If you are at the partnership or management level at your firm, your leadership role should afford you the ability to command your colleagues' attention. But you do not have to be a senior-level executive or equity shareholder in order to initiate a discussion about your firm's development of market-driven competencies. In either case, you should proceed as if this were an internal marketing campaign. Find a potential champion. Share your findings with him or her. Incorporate your champion's perspectives into your document. Get him or her to refer you to another champion. The two of you should discuss your information with that third person. At each iteration, widen the circle until it encompasses a handful of key leaders who will help you take your case to the appropriate decision makers at your firm.

As you continue to gather champions and present your evidence and findings, at each stage you will be asked, sometimes pointedly, about the potential return on investment of your firm's developing this competency. Your colleagues may ask why they should establish such-and-such a process or adopt a particular method. Be prepared to answer questions like, "How will we know this initiative will result in increased revenues and profits for our firm?"

Once you reach this stage, you will know that passion alone is not enough. Be prepared to deliver the answers to these questions. Look to results that a market-driven infrastructure has produced in other industries if you have to. If you cannot find quantitative measures, find authoritative experts (even outside your firm if need be) to provide convincing corroboration that this or that competency indeed is as effective as your evidence illustrates that it is.

STAY ON THE CASE

The firms showcased in this book have demonstrated positive— sometimes extraordinary—results from having built one of the competencies of a market-driven infrastructure. Each had to make significant commitments to do so; each had to undergo a series of iterative internal organizational changes in order for these competencies to produce results. You are about to embark on such a change initiative. You and your ever-larger team of champions must to be prepared to stay on the case: to leap over the hurdles that will crop up as you move forward.

Do not lose hope in your convictions; building a market-driven infrastructure may be a challenge, but it does not mean it is a bad idea.

If you need guidance or encouragement to stay the course, become familiar with change management principles and techniques. John Kotter's 2002 book, *The Heart of Change*, offers a practical eight-step framework for successful large-scale change.[1] Another good source, Jeannie Duck's 2001 book, *The Change Monster*, is about the emotional and personal aspects of making significant organizational shifts. Duck tells us that "For a change initiative to succeed, the emotional and behavioral aspects must be addressed as thoroughly as the operational issues."[2] She also writes: "Change can be exhilarating and bring about the best work of a lifetime. . . . Executives are seldom so challenged, managers so fully engaged, and individual contributors so intensely connected to the essential work of the organization. For the company itself, a successful transformation brings increased success, heightened recognition, and confidence."[3]

Andy Warhol said it well: "They always say time changes things, but you actually have to change them yourself." For professional service firms, building a market-driven infrastructure will require courage, care, and optimism—an attitude clearly apparent in Warhol's words. People—the essence of professional service firms—will exhibit a new competitive vigor, selecting and coalescing around internally developed and culturally shaped competencies for the purpose of achieving a strategically focused goal: mastering the professional service marketplace.

Let's get started.

Notes

CHAPTER 1

1. Colin C. Haley, "ADL Files Ch. 11, Plans to Sell" (online article), cited 2 July 2003 from Jupitermedia Corporation, http://www.atnewyork.com/news/print.php.969001.

2. "Washington Group International Inc. Company Capsule" (Web page), cited 2 July 2003 from Hoovers.com (online database); http://www.hoovers.com/co/capsule/9/0,2163,11019,00.html.

3. Eric Walgren, "The Incredible Shrunken Headhunters" (online article), cited from *Business Week Online*, 11 March 2002, http://www.businessweek.com:/print/careers/content/mar2002/ca2002038_7665.htm?ca.

4. Scott B. Nelson, "Hill & Barlow Decision Shakes Hub's Legal World," *Boston Globe*, 10 December 2002, sec. C, p. 1.

5. Ann Grimes, "Brobeck Law Firm Could Dissolve as Merger Folds," *Wall Street Journal*, 31 January 2003, Sec. C, p. 2.

6. Elliot Spagat, Ken Brown, and Gary McWilliams, "For EDS, Some Gambles Turn Sour," *Wall Street Journal*, 1 October 2002, sec. A, p. 8.

7. Susan Hart and Gillian Hogg, "Relationship Marketing in Corporate Legal Services," *Service Industries Journal*, 18, no. 3 (1998): 56.

8. Suzanne C. Lowe, *Becoming More Market Driven: How Are Professional Service Firms Getting Closer to Their Clients?* (report) (Expertise Marketing LLC, January 2001), 108.

9. Lowe, *Becoming More Market Driven*, 112.

10. Expertise Marketing's research was conducted annually in 1997, 1998, 1999, 2000, and 2001. Separate studies were conducted in collaboration with more than a dozen North American associations and Internet sites that repre-

sented the professions of accounting; architecture; construction/general contracting; engineering; executive search; law; and consulting in the fields of environment and energy, health care, human resources, information technology, and management. Each study was guided by an advisory panel of chief marketing officers or managing partners of nearly two dozen North American professional service firms. These firms represented the professions examined in our research.

CHAPTER 2

1. Suzanne C. Lowe, *Becoming More Market Driven: How Are Professional Service Firms Getting Closer to Their Clients?* (report) (Expertise Marketing LLC, January 2001), 11.

2. Lowe, *Becoming More Market Driven*, 17.

3. Lowe, *Becoming More Market Driven*, 117.

4. Lowe, *Becoming More Market Driven*, 25.

5. Suzanne C. Lowe, *Measuring the Effectiveness of Your Promotional Vehicles* (report) (Expertise Marketing LLC, January 1998), 25.

6. Lowe, *Becoming More Market Driven*, 17.

7. Lowe, *Becoming More Market Driven*, 119.

8. Lowe, *Becoming More Market Driven*, 17.

9. Lowe, *Becoming More Market Driven*, 120.

10. Lowe, *Becoming More Market Driven*, 120.

11. Lowe, *Becoming More Market Driven*, 16.

12. Leonard Fuld, *The New Competitor Intelligence*. New York: John Wiley & Sons, 1995.

13. Leonard Fuld, "What Competitive Intelligence Is and Is Not!" (online article), cited 24 April 2003 from Fuld & Company, Inc., http://www.fuld.com/Company/CI.html.

14. Lowe, *Becoming More Market Driven*, 112.

15. Lowe, *Becoming More Market Driven*, 112.

CHAPTER 3

1. Suzanne C. Lowe, *Differentiation: How Are Professional Service Firms Using It to Compete?* (report) (Expertise Marketing LLC, January 2000), 14.

2. Lowe, *Differentiation*, 15.

3. Lowe, *Differentiation*, 20.

4. Lowe, *Differentiation*, 17.

5. Lowe, *Differentiation*, 17.

6. Lowe, *Differentiation*, 21.

7. Lowe, *Differentiation*, 26.

8. Lowe, *Differentiation*, 28.

9. Suzanne C. Lowe, *Technology and Marketing: A Comparison of Professional Service Firms and Industries* (report) (Expertise Marketing LLC, February 1999), 22.

10. Lowe, *Technology and Marketing*, 23.

11. Lowe, *Technology and Marketing*, 42.

12. Lowe, *Technology and Marketing*, 26.

13. Lowe, *Technology and Marketing*, 27.

14. Lowe, *Technology and Marketing*, 28.

15. Suzanne C. Lowe, *Becoming More Market Driven: How are Professional Service Firms Getting Closer to Their Clients?* (report) (Expertise Marketing LLC, January 2001), 26.

16. Lowe, *Becoming More Market Driven*, 27. Studied professional sectors included accounting, architecture, construction and general contracting, engineering, environmental and energy consulting, executive search, health care consulting, IT consulting, management consulting, and "other" (usually a combination of professions).

17. Lowe, *Becoming More Market Driven*, 29.

18. Lowe, *Becoming More Market Driven*, 28.

19. Lowe, *Becoming More Market Driven*, 26.

20. Lowe, *Becoming More Market Driven*, 20. The methods used by each group were not mutually exclusive. Firms in every cultural group used methods from other cultural groups. Indeed, these cultural groups were not important for what they *were*, but rather for the role they played in responding firms' effectiveness at getting closer to clients.

21. Lowe, *Becoming More Market Driven*, 21–22.

22. Lowe, *Becoming More Market Driven*, 23.

23. Lowe, *Differentiation*, 22.

24. Lowe, *Becoming More Market Driven*, 11.

25. Lowe, *Becoming More Market Driven*, 108.

26. Lowe, *Becoming More Market Driven*, 14.

27. Lowe, *Becoming More Market Driven*, 13.

28. Lowe, *Becoming More Market Driven*, 93.

29. Lowe, *Becoming More Market Driven*, 18.

30. Lowe, *Becoming More Market Driven*, 105.

31. Lowe, *Becoming More Market Driven*, 106.

32. Lowe, *Becoming More Market Driven*, 107.

33. Lowe, *Becoming More Market Driven*, 108.

34. Lowe, *Becoming More Market Driven*, 108.

35. Sallie Sherman, Joseph Sperry, and Samuel Reese, *The Seven Keys to Managing Strategic Accounts* (New York: McGraw-Hill, 2003), xv–xvi.

36. Suzanne C. Lowe, *Measuring the Effectiveness of Your Promotional Vehicles* (report) (Expertise Marketing LLC, January 1998), 12–14.

37. Lowe, *Measuring the Effectiveness of Your Promotional Vehicles*, 24

38. Lowe, *Measuring the Effectiveness of Your Promotional Vehicles*, 28.

39. Lowe, *Measuring the Effectiveness of Your Promotional Vehicles*, 26.

40. Lowe, *Measuring the Effectiveness of Your Promotional Vehicles*, 31.

41. Lowe, *Becoming More Market Driven*, 13.

42. Lowe, *Becoming More Market Driven*, 95.

43. Lowe, *Becoming More Market Driven*, 95.

CHAPTER 4

1. Claire Ansberry, "The Outlook: Manufacturing Confounds Economists," *Wall Street Journal*, 5 May 2003, sec. A, p. 2.

2. Suzanne C. Lowe, *Differentiation: How Are Professional Service Firms Using It to Compete?* (report) (Expertise Marketing LLC, January 2000), 21.

3. Suzanne C. Lowe, *Becoming More Market Driven: How Are Professional Service Firms Getting Closer to Their Clients?* (report) (Expertise Marketing LLC, January 2001), 15.

4. Lowe, *Becoming More Market Driven*, 100.

5. Lowe, *Differentiation*, 26.

6. Lowe, *Differentiation*, 21.

7. Lowe, *Becoming More Market Driven*, 100.

8. Lowe, *Becoming More Market Driven*, 102.

9. Lowe, *Becoming More Market Driven*, 102.

10. Lowe, *Becoming More Market Driven*, 100.

11. Lowe, *Becoming More Market Driven*, 11.

12. Lowe, *Differentiation*, 22.

13. Lowe, *Differentiation*, 23.

14. Michael Hammer and James A. Champy, *Reengineering the Corporation: A Manifesto for Business Revolution* (New York: HarperCollins, 1993).

15. Robert S. Kaplan and David P. Norton, *The Balanced Scorecard: Translating Strategy into Action* (Boston: Harvard Business School Press, 1996).

16. "About Stern Stewart—Overview" (Web page), cited 6 May 2003 from Stern Stewart & Company; http://www.sternstewart.com/ssabout/overview.php.

17. Lowe, *Becoming More Market Driven*, 15.

18. Lowe, *Becoming More Market Driven*, 101.

19. U2, *With or Without You* (Island Records, Inc.), compact disc 042284229821, March 1987.

20. We defined external technologies as technologies that are used to build a firm's visibility with its target audiences—those that are directed toward a firm's outside publics, including clients and prospects. Studied vehicles included online magazines or newsletters, broadcast faxes, Web pages, CD-ROMs, and video- or audiocassettes. We also reviewed others independently mentioned by respondents, including multimedia presentations, such as liquid crystal display (LCD) or computer projection of slides, with or without video import, broadcast e-mail, screensavers that feature information about a firm, online advertisements (banners that are featured on the Web pages of other firms), online seminars, and online articles and newspapers (those that are not available or distributed through a Web page).

21. Suzanne C. Lowe, *Technology and Marketing: A Comparison of Professional Service Firms and Industries* (report) (Expertise Marketing LLC, February 1999), 16.

22. Lowe, *Technology and Marketing*, 17.

23. Lowe, *Technology and Marketing*, 18–19.

24. Lowe, *Differentiation*, 21.

25. Lowe, *Becoming More Market Driven*, 86, 104–5.

26. Craig Terrill and Arthur Middlebrooks, *Market Leadership Strategies for Service Companies: Creating Growth, Profits and Customer Loyalty* (Chicago: NTC Business Books, 2000), 11.

27. U2, *I Still Haven't Found What I'm Looking For* (Island Records, Inc.), compact disc 042284229821, June 1987.

28. Bernard Jaworski, Eric Litwin, Wendy Miller, Kimberly White, and Randal White, *The Evolution of Ernie—the Online Business Consultant* (case study) (University of Southern California Marshall School of Business Electronic Commerce Program, 1997; revised 15 January 1998), 1.

29. Jaworski, Litwin, Miller, White, and Whittle, *The Evolution of Ernie*, 9.

30. Füsun Özatav and Murat Albayrakoglu, *ERNIE: An Online Consulting Service by Ernst & Young* (case study) (spring 2001), cited 26 March 2002 from Istanbul Bilgi University Web site, http://www.ibun.edu.tr/comp202/finex.doc.

31. Marci M. Krufka, "Chief Legal Officers Have Spoken . . . Are Law Firms Listening?" *Report to Legal Management* (newsletter) (Newtown Square, PA: Altman Weil Publications, Inc., 2003), 9, 12.

32. *Revolutionary Marketing: AAM Summit 2003* (invitational brochure) (Association for Accounting Marketing Annual Conference, June 2003), 9–10.

33. Lowe, *Becoming More Market Driven*, 13.

34. Lowe, *Becoming More Market Driven*, 94.

35. "Survey: Compensation Plans Favor Quantity over Quality," *Consultants News*, 32, no. 8 (2002): 1.

36. Jay W. Lorsch and Thomas J. Tierney, *Aligning the Stars: How to Succeed When Professionals Drive the Results* (Boston: Harvard Business School Press, 2002), 76.

37. Lorsch and Tierney, *Aligning the Stars*, 104.

38. William C. Taylor, "The Leader of the Future," *Fast Company Magazine*, no. 25 (1999): 130.

39. Taylor, "The Leader of the Future," 130.

40. Taylor, "The Leader of the Future," 130.

CHAPTER 5

1. "About Us" (Web page), cited 13 June 2003 from Winstead Sechrest & Minick Web site, http://www.winstead.com/aboutus/.

2. Ernest Dichter, *Motivating Human Behavior* (New York: McGraw-Hill, 1971); Kathleen Yeaton, "Are You Using All the Tools in Your Toolbox?" *Strategies: Journal of Legal Marketing*, 4, no. 4 (2002): 1.

3. "Homepage" (Web page), cited 13 June 2003 from Winstead Sechrest & Minick Web site, http://www.winstead.com.

4. Peter Zeughauser, *Lawyers Are from Mercury, Clients Are from Pluto* (Granite Beach, CA: ClientFocus Press, 1999), 4.

5. William D. Neal, "Satisfaction be Damned, Value Drives Loyalty" (online article), cited 13 June 2003 from SDR Consulting Web site, http://www.sdr-consulting.com/article4.html.

6. David Swaddling, "Why Customers Buy," *Customer Value* (newsletter), November/December 2002, cited 2003 from Insight MAS Web site, http://www.insightmas.com/pages/ref_matrl/2002/nov-dec.htm#why_customers_buy.

7. Charlie Nelson, *Simulated Choice Modeling for Pricing Decisions* (presentation), October 2000, slides 9–12, cited from foreseechange Web site, http://www.futuretoolkit.com.

8. Kathleen Yeaton, *Dynamic Price Sensitivity Model* (methodology) (Dallas: Marketing & Research Partners, 1987).

9. "PR & News" (Web page), cited 16 June 2003 from YaYa Media Inc. Web site, http://www.yaya.com/about/about_pr.html.

10. Jane Chen and Matthew Ringel (online article), *Can Advergaming Be the Future of Interactive Advertising?* (report) cited 29 January 2003 from kpe Web site, http://www.kpe.com/ourwork/pdf/advergaming.pdf.

11. Keith Ferrazzi, *The Value of Games* (report) (Los Angeles: YaYa Media Inc., 2002).

12. YaYa Media Inc., *Press Kit* (report), slide 9, cited 29 January 2003 from YaYa Media Inc. Web site, http://www.reports.yaya.com/presskit.pdf.

13. Keith Ferrazzi, "Manager's Journal: Advertising Shouldn't Be Hard Work," *Wall Street Journal*, 30 April 2002, sec. B, p. 4.

14. "Why Games?" (Web page), cited 31 January 2003 from YaYa Media Inc. Web site, http://www.yaya.com/why/index_why.html.

15. Ferrazzi, "Manager's Journal."

16. "Why Games?"

17. Mike Wendland, "Automakers' Ads Go for a Joy Ride on Video Games," *Detroit Free Press*, 7 September 2002, retrieved from the Detroit Free Press Web site, http://www.freep.com.

18. Ferrazzi, *The Value of Games.*

19. Ferrazzi, *The Value of Games.*

20 Dorothy Pomerantz, "You Play, They Win," *Forbes*, 14 October 2002, p. 201.

21. YaYa Media Inc. *Press Kit*, slide 3; "Technology" (Web page), cited 31 January 2003 from YaYa Media Inc., http://www.yaya.com/tech/index_tech.html.

22. YaYa Media Inc. *Press Kit*, slide 7.

23. "Who We Are" (Web page), cited 16 June 2003 from Towers Perrin Web site, http://www.towers.com/towers/about_firm/about_our_firm_tp.asp?target=default.htm.

24. G. Bennett Stewart III, "Eva Works—But Not If You Make These Common Mistakes," *Fortune*, 1 May 1995, retrieved from *Fortune* Web site, http://www.fortune.com/fortune/articles/0,15114,377931,00.html.

25. John Graham, "Taking Stock of Economic Value-Added: What EVA™ Is—And Isn't," *Consultants News*, 26, no. 11 (1996): 6.

26. Gary Hamel, "Debate: Duking It Out over EVA," *Fortune*, 4 August 1997, retrieved from *Fortune* Web site, http://www.fortune.com/fortune/articles/0,15114,375140,00.html.

CHAPTER 6

1. "About Us" (Web page), cited 30 December 2002 from Malcolm Pirnie, Inc., Web site, http://www.pirnie.com/aboutus_main.html; and "Malcolm Pirnie, Inc. Company Capsule" (Web page), cited 30 December 2002 from Hoovers.com (online database), http://www.hoovers.com/co/capsule/7/0,2163,44117,00.html.

2. Garrett P. Westerhoff, Diana Gale, Paul D. Reiter, Scott A. Haskins, Jerome B. Gilbert, and John B. Mannion, *The Changing Water Utility: Creative Approaches to Effectiveness and Efficiency*, ed. John B. Mannion (Denver, CO: American Water Works Association, 1998).

3. Garrett P. Westerhoff, Diana Gale, Jerome Gilbert, Scott Haskins, and Paul Reiter, *The Evolving Water Utility: Pathways to Higher Performance*, ed. Nancy Zeilig (Denver, CO: American Water Works Association, 2003).

4. "About Us" (Web page), cited 1 January 2001.

5. Garrett P. Westerhoff, "Executive Viewpoint: Independence—More Important Today Than Ever!" (online article), 22 June 2002, cited from Malcolm Pirnie, Inc., Web site, http://www.pirnie.com/aboutus_news_rs.cfm?NewsID=115.

6. "Entrepreneurs" (Web page), cited 17 February 2003 from Numerica Group plc. Web site, http://www.numerica.biz/entreprenurial.asp.

7. "History" (Web page), cited 5 March 2003 from Numerica Group plc Web site, http://www.numerica.biz/history.asp.

8. *Numerica Group Interim Report* (online document), 30 September 2002, slide 2, cited from Numerica Group plc Web site, http://www.numerica.biz/resources/InterimReport.pdf.

9. "About KT" (Web page), cited 25 June 2003 from Kepner-Tregoe, Inc., Web site, http://www.kepner-tregoe.com/aboutKT/AboutKT.cfm.

10. Harold Arlen and E. Y. Harburg, "If I Only Had the Nerve," sung by Bert Lahr, Ray Bolger, Jack Haley, and Judy Garland (Rhino Records), 1939.

11. "Top Executives Join New Advisory Board for Marakon" (press release), 18 November 2002, cited from Marakon Associates Web site, http://www.marakon.com/pre_re_021118_advisory_board.html.

12. "Differentiation Helps Marakon Grow While Others Struggle," *Consultants News*, 32, no. 12 (2002): 3.

13. "Offices" (Web page), cited 19 January 2003 from Marakon Associates Web site, http://www.marakon.com/offices.html.

14. "Our History" (Web page), cited 19 January 2003 from Marakon Associates Web site, http://www.marakon.com/diff_history.html; "What We Bring" (Web page), cited 19 January 2003 from Marakon Associates, Web site, http://www.marakon.com/diff_capabilities.html.

15. "At a Glance" (Web page), cited 19 January 2003 from Marakon Associates Web site, http://www.marakon.com/glance.html.

16. "Our Difference" (Web page), cited 19 January 2003 from Marakon Associates Web site, http://www.marakon.com/difference.html.

17. "Differentiation Helps Marakon Grow," 3.

18. Thomas A. Stewart, "Marakon Runners," *Fortune*, 28 September 1998, retrieved through Fortune.com, http://www.fortune.com/fortune/articles/0,15114,379008,00.html.

19. "Marakon Associates: The Scoop" (Web page), cited 21 January 2003 from Vault.com (online database), http://www.vault.com/companies/company_main.jsp?co_page=2&product_id=1159&ch_id=252&v=1&tabnum=2.

20. "Marakon Associates: The Scoop."

21. "Differentiation Helps Marakon Grow," 3.

22. David Fondiller, memo to employees of Marakon Associates, March 2003.

23. "Twenty Largest Retained Executive Search Practices in the World," *Executive Recruiter News*, 24, no. 3 (2002): 4.

24. *Unleashing the Power of Business Leadership* (corporate brochure) (Egon Zehnder International, 2001), 5–7.

25. Egon Zehnder, "First Person: A Simpler Way to Pay," *Harvard Business School Publishing Corporation*, Reprint R0104B. http://harvardbusinessonline.hbsp.harvard.edu/b02/en/common/item_detail.jhtml?id=R0104B.

26. Zehnder, "First Person."

27. "Twenty Largest Retained Executive Search Practices in the World," *Executive Recruiter News*, 24, no. 3 (2002): 4; "Twenty Largest Retained Executive Search Practices in the World," *Executive Recruiter News*, 23, no. 3 (2001): 4; "Twenty Largest Retained Executive Search Practices in the World," *Executive Recruiter News*, 22, no. 3 (2000): 4; "Twenty Largest Retained Executive Search Practices in the World," *Executive Recruiter News*, 20, no. 3 (1999): 4.

28. Brian P. Lee, "Executive Search 2002: State of the Industry Report" (report overview), 10 May 2002, cited from Hunt-Scanlon Corporation Web site, http://www.hunt-scanlon.com/research/esi_index.htm.

29. Zehnder, "First Person."

30. Diane E. Lewis, "Lean Times for Headhunters (as the Need for Executives Drops So Does the Business of Recruiters)," *Boston Globe*, 19 November 2002, retrieved through Boston Globe.com, http://www.boston.com/globe.

31. "Strategy Firms Don't Expect Recovery until Mid-2003," *Consultants News*, 32, no. 8 (2002): 8.

32. "Why L.E.K.?" (Web page), cited 22 June 2003 from L.E.K. Consulting Web site, http://www.lek.com/why/index.asp.

33. "News: L.E.K. and *The Wall Street Journal* present the Shareholder Score-board" (online article), 10 March 2003, cited from L.E.K. Consulting Web site, http://www.lek.com/ideas/newsDetail.asp?PageID=113.

34. L.E.K. Consulting, telephone conversation, February 2004.

35. "ACNielsen Company Capsule" (Web page), cited 2 December 2002 from Hoovers.com (online database), http://www.hoovers.com/co/capsule/9/0,2163,51029,00.html; "VNU N.V. Company Capsule" (Web page), cited 2 December 2002 from Hoovers.com, http://www.hoovers.com/co/capsule/3/0,2163,42393,00.html.

36. Andy Kaufman, "Service Profit Chain in Action: An interview with Steve Schmidt," *Horizon Time* (Institute for Leadership Excellence and Development [I-LEAD] newsletter), February 2002, 1.

37. "1997 Person of the Year: ACNielsen's Steve Schmidt," *Research Business Special Report* (newsletter), November 1997, 1.

38. Kaufman, "Service Profit Chain in Action."

39. Kaufman, "Service Profit Chain in Action."

40. "1997 Person of the Year."

41. Kaufman, "Service Profit Chain in Action."

42. Steve Schmidt, memo to employees of ACNielsen, November 1, 2002.

43. Kaufman, "Service Profit Chain in Action."

CHAPTER 7

1. James H. Gilmore and B. Joseph Pine II, *The Experience Economy* (Boston: Harvard Business School Press, 1999), 2.

2. "AICPA Membership Eligibility Requirements" (Web page), cited 10 December 2002 from the American Institute of Certified Public Accountants Web site, http://www.aicpa.org/about/qualif.htm.

3. Stacey Collett, "The New Kid on the Block," *Consulting Magazine, 4*, no. 8 (2002): 42.

4. "Focused on the Middle Market" (Web page), cited 2 July 2003 from McGladrey & Pullen Inc. Web site, http://www.mcgladrey.com/about.html.

5. "Firm Facts" (Web page), cited 22 June 2003 from RSM McGladrey, Inc. Web site, http://www.rsmmcgladrey.com/About_Us/firmfacts.html.

6. Collett, "The New Kid," 42.

7. *The BiFF Event* (brochure), RSM McGladrey Business Solutions Event, 11 November 2001, 1.

8. Belinda Luscombe, "Creating Spaces," *Time*, 16 September 2002, 66.

9. John H. Richardson, "The People's Architect," *Esquire, 137*, no. 3 (2002): 148.

10. Luscombe, "Creating Spaces."

11. "Meijer, Inc. Company Capsule" (Web page), cited 12 February 2003 from Hoovers.com (online database), http://www.hoovers.com/co/capsule/7/0,2163,40307,00.html.

12. "Work with Us" (Web page), cited 22 June 2003 from DDB Worldwide, Inc., Web site, http://www.ddb.com; "The World's Top 25—Special Agency Report," *Advertising Age*, 21 April 2003, 22.

13. "Overview: What We Do" (Web page), cited 19 February 2003 from Mitretek Systems, Inc. Web site, http://www.mitretek.org/home.nsf/AboutUs/Overview; "History" (Web page), cited 19 February 2003 from Mitretek Systems, Inc. Web site, http://www.mitretek.org/home.nsf/AboutUs/History.

14. "Financials: Statements of Activities," *2001 Mitretek Annual Report*, 30 September 2001, p. 23, cited from Mitretek Systems, Inc. Web site, http://www.mitretek.org/ar01/AR_2001_Financials.pdf.

15. "Mitretek Named to AARP's List of Best Companies for Over-50 Workers" (press release), 27 September 2002, cited from Mitretek Systems, Inc. Web site, http://www.mitretek.org/home.nsf/communications/aarp.

CHAPTER 8

1. J. Scott Armstrong, ed., *Principles of Forecasting: A Handbook for Researchers and Practitioners* (Norwell, MA: Kluwer Academic Publishers, 2001).

2. John Naisbitt and Patricia Aburdene, *MegaTrends 2000* (New York: Avon Books, 1990); Faith Popcorn and Adam Hanft, *Dictionary of the Future: The Words, Terms and Trends That Define the Way We'll Live, Work and Talk* (New York: Hyperion Books, 2001).

3. "Rapid ROI: How Top Marketers Are Leveraging the Power of Predictive Analytics" (seminar), 11 June 2003, description of seminar retrieved 2 June 2003 through the American Marketing Association Web site, http://webexevents.webex.com/webexevents/onstage/g.php?d=662025126.

4. "Redefining Marketing: The Three Ultimate Measures of Your Web Success" (seminar), 17 June 2003, description of seminar retrieved 2 June 2003 through the American Marketing Association Web site, http://onstage3.webex.com/onstage3/onstage/g.php?d=693783449.

5. Roger Brossy and Stuart H. Sadick, "Professional Service Firms: Building a Franchise, Supporting It with Talent" (online article), January 2003, cited from Semler Brossy Consulting Group LLC Web site, http://www.semlerbrossy.com/pdf/PSAFINAL.pdf.

CHAPTER 9

1. John P. Kotter, *The Heart of Change: Real-Life Stories of How People Change Their Organizations* (Boston, MA: Harvard Business School Press, 2002).

2. Jeanie Daniel Duck, *The Change Monster: The Human Forces That Fuel or Foil Corporate Transformation and Change* (Three Rivers, MI: Three Rivers Press, 2002), xii.

3. Duck, *The Change Monster*, xiii.

Index

Page numbers in **boldface** indicate citations in tables or figures.

About the Author

SUZANNE C. LOWE is President of Expertise Markting, LLC, in Concord, Massachusetts. An adviser, analyst, and writer on best practices and emerging strategies in professional services marketing, she has written or been quoted in more than 50 articles and several books in the field, and speaks regularly to leading trade associations, industry groups, and in-house firm audiences. Her work has also been presented internationally at such venues as the American Marketing Association's annual Frontiers in Services conference.